GETTING BI

GETTING BI
Voices of Bisexuals Around the World

Robyn Ochs, editor
Sarah E. Rowley, co-editor

Bisexual Resource Center
Boston, MA, USA

Bisexual Resource Center
P.O. Box 1026
Boston MA 02117-1026
United States of America

Printed in Canada.
15 14 13 12 11 10 09 08 07 06 05 9 8 7 6 5 4 3 2 1

ISBN 0-9653881-4-X

Library of Congress Cataloguing-in-Publication Data

Ochs, Robyn and Rowley, Sarah E., editors.
　　　Getting bi: Voices of bisexuals around the world / Robyn Ochs and
　　　Sarah E. Rowley
　　　ISBN 0-9653881-4-X
　　　1. Bisexuality 2. Gay and Lesbian Studies—bisexuality

Chapter 1 contains an excerpt from Kazumi Matsunagi, "A Bisexual Life" in *Queer Japan: Personal Stories of Japanese Lesbians, Gays, Bisexuals, and Transsexuals,* ed. Barbara Summerhawk et al., (New Victoria Press, 1998), excerpted and edited with permission of the author. Chapter 2 contains an excerpt from Elizabeth Andrew, *Swinging on the Garden Gate: A Spiritual Memoir* (Skinner House Books, 2001), reprinted with permission of the author. Nana Kwame's essay in Chapter 4 is excerpted from an article entitled "Ghana: Ready for Gay Rights?" published by the non-profit organization Behind the Mask, online at http://www.mask.org.za/SECTIONS/AfricaPerCountry/ABC/ghana/ghana_11.htm. It appears courtesy of the publisher. In Chapter 5, the poem "was ist bin" appears courtesy of copyright holder Ahimsa Timeteo Bodhran; and Erynn Rowan Laurie's poem "the land between," first published in *The Fence* (2002) is reprinted with permission of the author.

Ronald C. Fox's Nonfiction Bibliography appears courtesy of the author.

Mia Anderson's photo was taken by Anh Dao Kolbe for the Walk Don't Run Productions calendar, 2004. All other photos appear by permission of their subjects. All other illustrations are the property of their creators.

Cover and interior design by Evoke Design.

To the memory of
Kaelin Bowers and Musa,
contributors to this book
who passed away during the past year

and to all the contributors to this book,
who inspire us and give us hope for the future.

TABLE OF CONTENTS

List of Translated Essays

Carlos Iván García Suarez [*translated from the Spanish by José Falconi*]

Jiao Tian [*translated from the Mandarin by Mindy Zhang*]

Georgina Antillón [*translated from the Spanish by Joaquín Terrones*]

Lauris Ledi [*translated from the Flemish by Hilde Vossen*]

Musa [*translated from the Portuguese by Nadejda Marques.*]

Xiao Mei [*translated from the Mandarin by Mindy Zhang*]

Jiao Tian [*translated from the Mandarin by Shen Rui*]

Zhang Jing [*translated from the Mandarin by Shen Rui*]

Toño [*translated from the Spanish by Juan Pablo Rivera*]

Jorge Pérez Castiñeda [*translated from the Spanish by Iliana Pagán*]

Jorge Luis Puentes [*translated from the Spanish by José Falconi*]

Angélica Ramírez-Roa [*translated from the Spanish by José Falconi*]

Christian [*translated from the Spanish by José Falconi*]

Alexandra Martins Costa & Alexandre Toledo [*translated from the Portuguese by Megwen Loveless*]

Lin Mu [*translated from the Mandarin by Shen Rui*]

Introduction

What does it mean to identify as bisexual in today's world?

The landscape has changed substantially since the first significant book of personal writings by bisexual people (*Bi Any Other Name*) broke ground in the United States nearly a generation ago. A tremendous surge of visibility for gay and lesbian—and sometimes bisexual and transgender—people has transformed our worlds. Many more people are coming out and claiming a bisexual or related identity. Many are doing so at younger ages, while others continue to discover or come to new understandings of their sexual identities later in life. The internet and other new technologies have made information on bisexuality more readily available, and allowed some who might have struggled in isolation to find support. The increasingly interconnected world, linked by technology, economics, immigration and cultural exchange, has also made our communities more international. This global exchange of ideas, information and strategies enriches and complicates all of our activist movements. For those in regions and countries that lack organized support for sexual minorities, connections across national lines provide critical validation. Those in more supportive environments can also learn a great deal from crossing such borders.

Even as sexual minorities have become increasingly visible, a revolution in attitudes toward identity has had a particularly strong impact on bisexuals and bisexual community. As more and more people have come to recognize the limitations of rigid classifications, sexual orientation labels have become less fixed and permanent. People are becoming not only increasingly willing to embrace identities that cross lines, but also immensely creative and playful in their use of terms and labels. Some identify as queer, pansexual or omnisexual. Some publicly acknowledge attractions and/or relationships with people of more than one sex while simultaneously claiming the right to identify as heterosexual, lesbian or gay. Some deliberately use labels strategically, identifying differently in different social contexts. And some eschew labels altogether. In fact, as we debated possible titles, we considered subtitling this book "Voices of Bisexuals and Other Folks Along the Sexuality Spectrum," recognizing that the word bisexual cannot possibly encompass all whose identities challenge the binaries of gay and straight. Although brevity eventually won out in the title, we want this book to be a safe and nourishing haven not only for those who identify as bisexual, but for everyone.

Yet the process of creating safe space outside this book remains incomplete, and is taking place (when it does at all) across a wildly uneven background. Reading through the pieces collected in this book, perhaps most striking are the pressures that remain widespread. Bisexuals still confront shame, fear, homophobia, biphobia, invisibility, oppression of all types and—above all—isolation, even in the midst of the most accepting societies. Increased visibility has created a backlash that takes many shapes and forms. In some places, conditions for lesbian, gay, bisexual and transgender people have not improved, or have even gotten worse. The result is a bisexual world that reads like a patchwork map, where experiences of safety, acceptance, tolerance, repression, isolation and invisibility vary wildly with the terrain. Wide variations exist not only across national borders, but within them—and within the lives of individuals.

This unevenness of experience and the persistence of isolation have made it all the more important to bring together the diverse voices of bisexuals in one place. Although committed to an international anthology, we found that the early responses to our call for submissions came overwhelmingly from the United States. This far more international form of the final book resulted from concerted effort, and particularly the extraordinary efforts of Robyn Ochs, who made internationalizing this anthology a personal mission. Thanks in large part to her energy and indefatigable networking, we received over 300 submissions from writers in thirty-two countries. But this would never have happened had we not committed to actively recruiting voices from the rest of the world. (Yes, it's true; bisexuals do recruit!)

Although the internet and electronic mailing lists provided us with vital tools to find writers scattered across the globe, personal networks proved crucial for outreach outside of North America. As two women based in Boston, we often lacked the personal knowledge necessary to locate—and motivate—writers on our own. We owe an enormous debt of gratitude to those who served as bridges from their own activist networks and communities to this project. Conferences, often critical hubs for the bisexual community, were also vital. When all else failed, repetition and persistence sometimes paid off. We sent our call for essays to individuals and email lists around the world, sometimes receiving a response only after the third or fourth attempt. Long past the official submission deadline, we continued to recruit and accept essays that would increase the range of this anthology.

We brought the same commitment and tactics to recruiting contributors from diverse class, race, ability, age, gender identity and language backgrounds. We were particularly attuned to the importance of the latter, as the word and even concept of bisexuality have different meanings in different tongues and cultural contexts. We translated our call for submissions into Mandarin Chinese, Portuguese and Spanish, and accepted submissions in any language. Our loyal team of volunteer translators rendered Brazilian Portuguese, Mandarin Chinese, Flemish and several dialects of Spanish into English for publication. In several instances, we worked from oral transcripts and interviewed contributors to ensure that our versions accurately reflected their beliefs.

It was, of course, immensely difficult to find writers from countries that lack organized LGBT communities, writers who remain closeted, and writers for whom identity is an unimportant consideration (why, after all, would they respond?). But we actively pursued contributions from all these groups, as well as other underrepresented communities. Though gaps remain, we are proud of the diversity in this finished product.

We hope the book you hold in your hands shows the immense variety in bisexuality lived around the globe, and puts a face—in fact, many faces—to what remains too often an obscured identity. We hope too that bringing these voices together can help ease the isolation felt by many bisexuals. The details of our circumstances may differ, but in our stories are common threads. Wherever you may be, you are not alone. Finally, we hope to further strengthen the bisexual community and nourish a space for bisexual and other identities that defy binaries.

With these goals in mind, we have given pride of place to the personal writings that form this book's heart and soul. Grouped in nine chapters, these writings provide snapshots into bisexual people's lives, thoughts and emotional landscapes. The articles which follow further develop these themes, with a particular emphasis on our relationship with the larger world. Along with guidelines for integrating into lesbian, gay and transgender communities, we include helpful information on how to cope with external hostility and incomprehension to keep one's self safe both psychologically and through practicing safer sex. Finally, for those who find this book has only whetted their bisexual appetites, our resources section at the end includes fiction and non-fiction bibliographies for further reading and some valuable web resources.

By sharing their stories, the writers in this book are creating a community based not upon physical geography but upon the common threads of their diverse experiences. By telling the stories of our lives, we create a wider space of possibility for ourselves and for others. We hope this book will help you "get bi," or at least learn more about bisexuality.

—Robyn and Sarah

Acknowledgements

This book would not exist without the efforts of many, many people; it has been an exercise in community-building in more ways than one, put together entirely by volunteers from around the world.

We thank each and every one of our contributors for having the courage to put words to paper and sharing with us very private parts of their selves.

Special thanks to Alejandra Sarda, Ramki Ramakrishnan, and Shen Rui for actively and enthusiastically tapping their own networks to draw more contributors into our web. Their spectacular outreach efforts in India, South America and China, respectively, helped increase the book's scope and depth.

We owe a particular debt to the 8th International Conference on Bisexuality (Minneapolis, USA, 2004), the 2nd European Bisexual Conference (Dublin, Ireland, 2003) and the 2nd North American Conference on Bisexuality (San Diego, USA, 2002). Both the attendees who contributed their words, energy and enthusiasm to this book and the hard-working organizers who made the conferences happen have our gratitude.

Thank you to our team of stalwart translators: *Spanish*: José Falconi, Joaquín Terrones, Iliana Pagán, and Juan Pablo Rivera; *Flemish*: Hilde Vossen; *Portuguese*: Nadejda Marques and Megwen Loveless; *Mandarin*: Shen Rui and Mindy Zhang.

Enormous gratitude goes out to the Bisexual Resource Center in Boston and all its funders, who made this work possible. We are particularly indebted to Sheeri Kritzer, bisexual goddess and all-around wonderwoman, for her behind-the-scenes help with many of the practical details of this project. Matthew Boyd did an amazing job laying out the book and designing its cover, and Scott Lefton shared his formidable artistic skills, served as an invaluable technical counselor and provided moral support. Carla Imperial, Debbie Block-Schwenk and Julie Ebin helped proofread the manuscript. Arthur Cohen, our marketing maven and Publisher, drew on his deep professional knowledge to bring this book to the world. We also thank Cecilia Tan for sharing her publishing expertise and helping to locate a printer, and Asya Mikhailenko, Bridget Boyle and Stephanie Clarkson for their design suggestions.

From Sarah: A very special thank you to Peg Preble for welcoming me into her home over the past year (and then some).

From Robyn: Another thank you to Peg Preble, *my wife* (I love saying that!), for graciously welcoming this book project into our lives and, of course, for being her wonderful self. Thanks to Sonny Ochs, my mom, for her enthusiastic support of my activism; and to the many amazing students and community activists I have the extreme good fortune of encountering in my work.

VOICES

Chapter I:

What Is Bisexuality?

NATIONAL COMING OUT DAY

bi·sex·u·al

1 a : possessing characters of both sexes
  b : sexually oriented toward both sexes
2 : of, relating to, or involving both sexes

One of the challenges of talking about bisexuality is that the word has many different meanings, yet we rarely acknowledge their variety. The dictionary definition above provides three very distinct uses of the word, each preeminent in a different time, place and field of study. This book concerns bisexuality as a sexual orientation, and even within this narrower scope, bisexuality has many possible meanings.

What defines bisexuality? The answer varies, depending upon who is asking the question. An epidemiologist, for example, might use behavior (regardless of self-identity) as the main criterion, while a social scientist might focus on self-identity (regardless of behavior). Where does bisexuality begin and end? If we view sexuality as a spectrum, how much territory does the word bisexual cover? How much bisexual attraction and/or behavior does it take to make a person bisexual? Is the concept meaningful across cultures, and does it always have the same meaning? Some cultures may not use the word bisexual, and even in those that do, many people may be unfamiliar with or misunderstand it. Does bisexuality encompass people whose attractions change over time? If you are once bisexual are you always bisexual? Is there a statute of limitations? And for each of these questions, who gets to decide?

I find it useful to distinguish between behavior and identity. Someone who has had sexual experience or even just attractions to people of more than one sex can be described as bisexual, but may not identify that way. Likewise, one can identify as bisexual regardless of sexual experience. Furthermore, identities can change over time.

So can definitions. My own understanding of bisexuality has changed dramatically over the years. I used to define bisexuality as "the potential to be attracted to people regardless of gender." Then one day I was chatting with my friend Alberto, who, like me, identifies as bisexual. I blithely stated my definition and he looked at me incredulously.

"Regardless of gender? No, no, no! There's no 'regardless' about it for me. For me it's all about difference. I'm attracted to cheerleaders and football players. It's precisely the extremes of difference that attract me." He looked me up and down, smirked, and said, "Robyn, you would be way too butch for me!"

I threw a pillow at him, he threw it back and we laughed. But I learned from that conversation. Some of us who identify as bisexual are in fact "gender-blind."

For others—in fact for me—it's androgyny—the blending of genders—that compels. Still others, like Alberto, are attracted to the poles.

Then, to complicate things further, I learned a lot from my intersex, genderqueer and transgender friends. I came to realize that I had been confusing gender with biological sex and that the two are not synonymous. Though in reality the difference between sex and gender is far more complicated, I find useful the expression, "Sex is what's between your legs; gender is what's between your ears." In real people, sex and gender do not always correspond. I also learned that sex and gender each exist on a continuum; thus there are more than two sexes, and more than two genders. A male-bodied person can identify as a woman, or as a combination of male and female; so can a female-bodied person. And some people's bodies do not fit their cultures' standards of male or female.

What does all this mean for our understanding of bisexuality? Dictionary definitions of bisexuality that rely on an idea of "both sexes" are inadequate. As human beings, we live and love in a world that is far more complicated than these narrow ideas allow. Our attractions do not stay within tidy borders, and our understanding of bisexuality must rise to this level of complexity. People are attracted to both gender and sex, gender and sex do not necessarily coincide, and neither is a simple binary. Someone might be attracted, for example, to masculinity in women or femininity in men, or femininity in anyone, and on and on. And on.

Then I started to question the meaning of attraction itself. I now see attraction occupies a spectrum of its own. At what point, for example, does affection become attraction and attraction become sexual and/or romantic? Each of these complex emotions has many varieties, each as distinct as the interactions between individual human beings. Every one of us must make sense of our own experiences and assign them meaning.

Every new idea I grappled with changed my definition of bisexuality. I have a new working definition: **I call myself bisexual because I acknowledge in myself the potential to be attracted, romantically and/or sexually, to people of more than one sex, not necessarily at the same time, not necessarily in the same way, and not necessarily to the same degree.** I expect that this definition will change yet again, as I continue to learn.

Perhaps the most important way to learn is to listen to the voices of others as they grapple with their own understanding of sexual attraction, romance, relationships, love, desire. The following essays, from China, Colombia, Japan, Spain, Turkey and the United States, provide a small taste of this.

—Robyn

SHEN RUI
CHINA & USA

Conversation 1

June 14, 2004, Beijing
Shen Rui's mother is a retired housewife with no formal education who lives in Beijing, where she was born in 1935. During the Cultural Revolution (1966-76) she was forced to take a job in the bureau of housing administration in Beijing.

Shen Rui: Ma, what do you think of bisexuality?
Mother: What? What are you talking about?
Shen Rui: Bisexuality, or bisexuals. That means, a man loves a woman but perhaps he also loves a man. Or more specifically, he not only loves the woman and man, but he also makes love with them. It is the same for a woman.
Mother: What? I have never heard about that kind of thing.
Shen Rui: Really? Never?
Mother: Yes, never.
Shen Rui: Well, now you have heard about it. What do you think?
Mother: I have no idea. Why do I have to think about it?

Conversation 2

(July 7, 2004 Beijing/the USA, by telephone)
Wang Jiaxin is a poet and critic who was born in 1957 in Hubei Province. He is a professor at the Beijing Institute of Pedagogy, and Shen Rui's ex-husband.

Shen Rui: What do you think of bisexuality?
Wang Jiaxin: Why do you ask me? I have never had bisexual experience.
Shen Rui: I am not asking about your experience. I am asking your opinion. What do you think of homosexuality or bisexuality?
Wang Jiaxin: It is not my business. That is other people's problem. What can I tell you if I have never had that kind of experience?
Shen Rui: It is not your experience but your view. You are a professor of literature, a poet and an intellectual. How can you not have a view about it?
Wang Jiaxin: I don't have any view about it. It's other people's problems—whatever they want to do.
Shen Rui: Are there any poets who are homosexual or bisexual in China?
Wang Jiaxin: I don't know. I never heard of anyone. Though in the West, many poets were and are homosexuals, such as Walt Whitman, Rimbaud and Allen Ginsberg.
Shen Rui: How about Chinese poets? Don't you think that is quite strange that no Chinese poet or intellectual has candidly claimed his or her homosexuality or bisexuality? Does it mean that no Chinese poets or intellectuals have different sexual orientations from heterosexuality? Or maybe that Chinese social reality does not allow them to be "different"?
Wang Jiaxin: I don't know. How can I know about that? I never think about that kind of thing. That is other people's problem, not mine.

Conversation 3

(July 7, 2004, Beijing/the USA, by telephone)

Hu Min is a female photographer, born in 1964. She is married to Wang Jiaxin.

Shen Rui: I just asked Wang Jiaxin why no Chinese poets or intellectuals have come out in China. He has no answer to that question. What do you think? Do you think in China there are no homosexuals or bisexuals?

Hu Min: Well, I don't know if they exist in China or not. But I think because sexuality is a private issue, those people do not want to let other people know their private lives.

Shen Rui: But privacy is a new concept in China. To the contrary, homosexuality and bisexuality are a part of our cultural tradition. For example, we have the terms *longyang zhihao* (love for the dragon's penis) and *duanxiu zhijiao* (the relationship between two who wear the same kind of clothes). Both indicate a male homosexual relationship. That means that this phenomenon has existed so long that they have become phrases in the Chinese language. Only in the middle of the twentieth century, especially after the Communist Party took over China, did homosexuality seem to disappear from public life.

Hu Min: In fact I did hear about homosexuals in China but not bisexuals. I am not sure what that word means. I think being homosexual is still considered mentally sick by most of the people in China. It is hard for them to come out. However, sexuality is an individual's freedom. Anyone can do whatever he or she wants in his or her bedroom. I do not oppose anyone's choice.

Rui is Visiting Assistant Professor of Chinese at Gettysburg College in Pennsylvania. She was born in Beijing in 1957 and came to the USA in 1994. Now she lives in both China and the USA.

MAYRA SANTOS-FEBRES
PUERTO RICO, USA

"Different though the sexes are, they intermix. In every human being a vacilation between the sexes takes place and often it is only the clothes that keep the male or female likeness, while underneath the sex is the very opposite of what is above."
—*Orlando.* Virginia Woolf.

I do not know what bisexuality means. I do know that the term has been used to talk about a "medical condition," a social category for identity, and a "solution" to the battle between hetero- and homosexuality. It is indeed a difficult word to use, especially to define oneself. If I have slept with women, being myself a woman, but mainly have relationships with men, does that make me a bisexual? Can a girl "exploring" her sexuality in college, protected by the idea of "sexual curiosity," assume this identity for herself? Or a lesbian who in her youth had relationships with men? And how about an adult woman, who, after a heterosexual break-up, finds herself emotionally "involved" with a woman? What counts as bisexuality?

These questions make my head spin because I have been one of these women who, to her surprise, has found her hand gravitating towards the body of another woman to caress it. It happened once. Maybe it will happen again. I am not afraid of the feeling nor am I afraid to pursue it. But I am afraid of naming with a fixed category an experience that is so fluid. Once I fell in love with a woman, now I am in love with a man. I do not wish to underplay any of the experiences, but what do they make me? Does it matter?

In many cultures "bisexuality" does not exist, although people sleep and/ or love other people, whether they are of their same sex or not. That does not make these cultures "backwards." Neither does it mean that they are beyond the male/female, homo/hetero dilemma. In Caribbean and Central American cultures (the ones that I know best), many men sleep with women and men, sometimes in situations shielded by a particular definition of "maleness" (*activo* vs. *pasivo*, the active rather than the passive role considered "male"); sometimes through "chance" encounters outside their heterosexual marriages; sometimes freely. One has only to read Cuban writer Reinaldo Arenas' autobiography *Before Night Falls* to see the point. In these cultures women's bisexuality becomes even more unnoticed. Since women's sexuality is discussed only in medical terms and among intimate friends, many "heterosexual" women sleep with other women without any concern. Common knowledge holds that sleeping with another woman is not considered "real sex" (there is no penetration, no chance of conception). Shielded by extreme intimacy and secrecy, many share the practice, but none talk about it. I am not arguing that there is no homophobia configuring these practices. I am arguing that a culturally specific type of homophobia is in place and that categories such as bisexuality cannot be imposed, without translation, from the World of Reason, of Civilization, from the First World.

However, I truly believe that most humans' sexual experiences lie not within exclusive hetero or homosexual boundaries, but somewhere in between. I hope that one day homophobia and heterosexism disappear. Maybe that will be the solution to the problem. Without social oppression and legal marginalization, these categories will no longer be so necessary. Loving people, living the instability of desire and emotions, will be considered what it is: a human experience. And maybe, to have loved both women and men will not be looked upon as a "deviation" or a "defect," but as a practice that completed a particular human being's journey through life.

Mayra (born 1966) is a professor of literature at the University of Puerto Rico, and a poet, novelist and critic.

ALICIA VALLEJO LORENZO
CANTABRIA, SPAIN

I had always considered myself heterosexual. But when I was at the Institute, I began to notice women; I remember checking out this girl in a fashion magazine who was wearing a see-through blouse. I believe that each of us has our own personal history and unique experiences, and we live and experience our bisexuality differently: for some it will be about having sexual experiences with men and women simultaneously, and others might consider themselves bisexual without having had experiences with either of the two sexes.

In my opinion **it is only necessary that the person feel that they are bisexual,** that is to say, that they be aware of their feelings. Our experiences, relationships, feelings: each are a thing apart.

Alicia lives in Cantabria, in the north of Spain.

KAZUMI MATSUNAGA
JAPAN

I learned the word "bisexual" from a book about homosexuality. It said that if a person has sexual desire for the opposite sex, that person is heterosexual. If a person desires someone of the same sex, that person is homosexual. If a person has sexual desire for both sexes, that person is "bisexual," literally *ryoseiai*, both sex love.

I became active in lesbian functions, and became one of the founding staff members of a group called "Japan Womyn's BiNet" [in existence from 1994-1996]. BiNet was mainly for bisexuals but many lesbians and women undecided about their sexuality were also members. Every other month we put out a newsletter and every month we held a meeting. While working as a staff member for BiNet, I met many bisexual women and came to know the varieties of bisexuality. It changed the way I understood bisexuality. Before, when I talked with lesbian and gay friends about the difference between homosexuals and bisexuals, I used an analogy with coffee and tea. If asked "Which do you prefer, coffee or tea?" we may answer "I only like coffee," or "I only like tea," or "I like both," or "I don't like either." Among the people who like both coffee and tea, some take milk and some don't, some like it hot and others iced. Like this, the people who prefer only coffee are like homosexuals. Those who drink both are parallel to bisexuals. Homosexuals, whether they are aware of it or not, divide men and women as to standards of preference, favoring one sex. Bisexuals, on the other hand, prefer feelings and style and other kinds of things—the sex of the partner is not a factor. That's what I thought at first.

But when I met other bisexuals, I saw that many had times when they liked men and times when they liked women, and others who would like to have relationships with both at the same time. Many also gave serious consideration to the standards by which they judged men and women. If we use the coffee and tea example again, of course the various flavors and aromas of tea are different, and there are espresso, mocha, and flavored coffees.

Even when it comes to a choice between coffee or tea, many people like both without labeling one as superior to the other. Some people drink coffee in the morning and tea in the evening. Bisexuality is full of variations.

Kazumi was born, was raised, and still lives in Japan.

[Excerpted, and edited with permission, from "A Bisexual Life," in *Queer Japan: Personal Stories of Japanese Lesbians, Gays, Bisexuals and Transsexuals*, Barbara Summerhawk, Cheiron McMahill & Darren McDonald, eds. New Victoria Press, 1998.]

HUR JHSAJ
TURKEY

Bisexual? The word sounds funny to me. It is difficult to fit gay or bi identity into Turkish culture. Many people here in Turkey don't think about identity in terms of labels. Sure, bisexuality exists: it's my life's other side, and we have our club scene, so there are good places to go out and have fun. Things are changing somewhat, though. Slowly.

Hur Jhsaj is 21, male, and, like most Turkish people, Muslim, at least according to his identity card. He studies economics in Istanbul.

BIJAN ETEMAD-MOGHADAM
MASSACHUSETTS, USA

Bijan, right, with husband Matt

Being bisexual to me is the ultimate assertion that there is no such thing as hetero- or homosexuality: we all stand along the vast continuum of emotions that is sexuality. Because of cultural taboos, imposed gender inequalities and all sorts of invented societal structures, the average person is rarely honest about what they like to do in bed. The result: we end up believing that we are perverts unless we are in the missionary position with a member of the opposite sex.

That said, I do identify strongly as a bisexual man. I have been in a monogamous relationship with a man for the past ten years. Before that, I had many lovers, men and women. The biggest turn-ons for me are dominant women with long hair and smooth skin, and sensitive hyper-masculine men. I guess I was brainwashed by society after all.

Bijan, 36, was born to an Iranian father and a French mother and raised in Iran, France and the USA. He has a Ph.D. in Genetics from Cornell University (where he met his husband), and currently works in a small biotech company generating cancer therapeutics. He does not believe in a god, unless it is a truly cruel and obnoxious one. His religion is social justice; he spends a great part of his time volunteering and being an activist (currently in the battle over same-sex marriage). At the moment he and his husband are starting a family.

SARA PONCET
FRANCE

For me, a "bisexual person" is simply somebody sexually attracted to both men and women. But **this sexual orientation also means an escape from the usual categorization—a questioning of society's traditional values.** Many people are irritated when unable to put you in a box. We face a lot of prejudice. The queer community says "Bisexual? It doesn't exist!" or "You must make a choice!" or "You try to hide your homosexuality behind this label?"

I once heard a lesbian wonder why an acquaintance still called herself bisexual as she hadn't had any relationships or even one-night stands with women for 15 years. But bisexuality is an identity, independent of behavior! Would a lesbian stop calling herself lesbian because she hasn't had any sexual relationships for a long time? Lesbians often say, "You're a traitor; you've surrendered to the enemy." In France, personal ads in lesbian magazines often read "no bis."

At least when it comes to coming out, bisexuality has an advantage over homosexuality: parents may remain hopeful regarding marriage and grandchildren (it doesn't occur to many of them that lesbians and gay men can raise children).

For me, dealing with men is more challenging, thus more exciting. On the other hand, I feel safer with women and better understood by them. Our gender conditioning makes it very difficult for adults to understand the opposite sex. So for a rest, I would go to girls; for adventure, to boys!

Sara is a 24-year-old French physiotherapist who spent a year volunteering in a Jewish old people's home in London. There she met her husband. They are now back in France.

CARLOS IVÁN GARCÍA SUÁREZ
COLOMBIA

For me, bisexuality is not alternating between men and women in bed but rather recognizing the affective and erotic potential that I have with women and men. Bisexuality is not some kind of middle-ground between heterosexuality and homosexuality; rather I imagine it as a way to erode the fixed systems of gender and sexual identity which always result in guilt, fear, lies and discrimination. Sexuality is fluid, mutable and creative; no obstacles to the soul and its desires can be justified. It is vital, especially in Latin American countries in which machismo goes hand in hand with widespread but shamed and shameful bisexual practices, to educate the public about what bisexuality is and isn't. Then we will understand and live it not as charade, indecision, immaturity or transition, but rather see it as a vast and fertile field of human possibilities.

Carlos Iván lives in Colombia.

JESSICA
CALIFORNIA, USA

To me, bisexuality is a matter of loving and accepting everyone equally—seeing the beauty in the human soul, rather than in the shell that houses it. Being transgendered, I know firsthand that love between two people can transcend—even embrace—what society regards as taboo. **Bisexuality is a mindset of revolution, a mindset of change.** We're creating a brave new world of acceptance and love for all people, of all the myriad genders and methods of sexual expression that this world contains.

Jessica is a transsexual (M2F) teenager near the beginning of her journey, rather recently kicked out of her parents' house for choosing to transition.

Roberta Gregory

Chapter II:

Coming Out as Bisexual

The official logo of National Coming Out Day—celebrated every October 11th in the United States—is a delightful drawing by Keith Haring of a person exiting a closet. If only coming out were that simple: something done only once, and once done, complete.

To the contrary, coming out is a complex and multifaceted process. We come out to ourselves. We come out to our parents and to our children. We come out at work, to our friends, and to our neighbors, and to our children's friends, our parents' friends, and the friends of our neighbors.

And coming out is not simply a one-time event. It must be performed repeatedly throughout our lives. We must weigh the benefits and risks of coming out to every new friend, family member, employer, coworker and so on. The stakes can be high. Unlike people with gay or straight identities, we must decide when and whether to come out to potential romantic partners and risk a biphobic response. Like transgender people, lesbians and gay men, we must weigh whether to come out to health care professionals. On one hand, we may fear a negative response and poor treatment; on the other, nondisclosure leaves our providers with incomplete information and may put our health at risk. As we age or deal with serious illness, we are likely to face new challenges as we become increasingly dependent upon external support, whether at home or in assisted living facilities. Sometimes we must even come out more than once to the same person, to clarify what we have said, or to overcome their denial.

We may also need to come out more than once if we experience a shift in our own identity. Someone formerly identified as gay may decide that the word bisexual fits more comfortably. Or vice versa. Finally, not only bisexual people must come out. Once we are out to friends and family, they too must deal with questions of whether, how and to whom to disclose information about us.

Why come out? We come out because the alternative to disclosure is misunderstanding. This is particularly true for bisexuals, as we are so rarely seen by others *as bisexual*. We cannot come out by simply mentioning a partner, or by being seen at a "community" event.

The cost of silence can be great. Failure to communicate, to share important information about ourselves, creates a barrier between us and our loved ones. André Gide said, "It is better to be hated for what you are than to be loved for something you are not." We want others to know us not as their illusion of what we are, but as we truly are. Without this, we cannot truly be close.

As Amber who begins this chapter and Elizabeth who ends it emphasize, coming out to our loved ones is a great gift, an expression of love. Here contributors from Australia, Canada, India, Mexico, Switzerland, Turkey, the United Kingdom and the United States honor us by sharing their stories.

—Robyn

AMBER TERRELL
IOWA, USA

Mom, something you said a couple days ago actually prompted me to finally write this letter. You said, "Amber, if you ever try to hide anything from me again, I will kill you." Now, obviously I did not fear for my life. However, I was tired of keeping this secret from you. I know that you two love me with all your hearts, but I felt you loved someone you thought I was or am. You see, this last break up with Colin had a little more to it than I let on. What you didn't know is that before I met him, I wasn't single. I was dating someone and had been for almost nine months. Her name was Tammy. I know you don't want to hear it, but you not only have one daughter who is a lesbian, but you have another who is bisexual.

Now, I know what you are thinking right now… "If only I had stayed away from Jessica and her friends." All I can say to that is that I have felt this way for a long time, as far back as 6th and 7th grade—when I was going to a Christian school and before I would even acknowledge my sister.

I tried to ignore it for years, hoping it would go away. Then Jessica came out. As I was dealing with some internalized homophobia, I got angry at her for making us all face it. I thought, "Hey, I am having some of these same feelings too, but you don't see me telling anyone and you certainly don't see me making mom and dad cry over it."

After seeing everyone's reactions, I chose to remain silent about my own feelings. I tried to get rid of them over and over again, hence the reason I was so boy crazy in high school. Now, don't get me wrong, that was not a show. I like men. I love dating them, and I have nothing against the majority of them, but what I am saying is that I also like women. I have feelings for both sexes and I have had wonderful relationships with both.

Mom, last summer you made another comment when you were upset about me wanting to live with Jess and her partner. You said, "It's just that I don't want you to turn into one of them." I told you, "I won't *turn* into one of them," but what I should have said was, "Mom, I *am* one of them." I didn't turn. I already was. One reason I wanted to live with them was that I was already dating Tammy, and I refused to hide my relationship while living at home. I was not ready to come out to you and Jessica's was a safe place to be.

I know we are finally a family of "no secrets" now that I am being honest with myself. I hope this does not change your opinion of me. You will have many questions, many of which I will not be able to answer, but I will be open to talk about it and will do my best at giving you answers. I want to remind you that I am still your little girl, that you still know me, and that I have not changed. It is just now you know a little more about me.

Colin knew I was bi. He supported it and accepted it. We talked about it often, but we decided when we got together that we would just see how and where it went. I eventually came to realize that I have more feelings for women than I thought I did, and I was with an amazing man. Why was I feeling this way still? I realized that I need to be single as I try to become comfortable with myself and with being alone.

This does not mean that I will never be with another man or that I will not marry one, but it also does not mean that I will, or that these feelings for women will ever go away. All I know is that I am attracted to both men and women and that I need to be with neither right now.

Dad, you warned me of the hazards of "trying to find myself," especially in today's society. You were right. That is why I decided to stop looking and just be me, who I am right now. That person is the daughter you two have raised. The one who loves you with all her heart, the one who appreciates everything you do for her emotionally, physically and spiritually. The one who has looked up to you since the day she was born. The one who values your opinion, the one who respects you and your relationship. The one whom you have watched grow into the woman you see today. The one who loves children, the one who can't wait to be a teacher, the one who graduates in December. The one who adores her family. The one who is getting stronger every day and realizing that she can't please everyone, and that she must make decisions that are best for her. The one who wants to continue to be accepted, but who is tired of keeping this secret. The one who is bi, but who wants you to know that it is only a part of who she is…the one who is scared and yearning for your understanding. The one who will never stop loving you and hopes you never stop loving her.

Your Daughter,
Amber

A 22-year-old recent graduate of a small Christian college in central Kansas, Amber now lives in a small town in the Midwest, is currently dating a woman, and hopes soon to be teaching in her own classroom.

DENISE PENN
CALIFORNIA, USA

I told myself that I wasn't worried about coming out to my son about my bisexuality. After all, he had been around GLBT people all of his life. But when the issue came up, I realized it had been a nagging fear for a long time.

He was nine years old and we were in the car, on the freeway, talking. He asked about a lesbian friend of mine who had recently had a baby. "Mom, I don't know how she can take care of the baby alone," he said. "She needs help. Maybe she should get married."

"To a man? That will never happen," I said, laughing at the thought.

"Why?" he responded. "Doesn't she like men? Is she a lesbian?"

After I gave him an affirmative response, he wondered, aloud, if we knew any other lesbians. He began guessing who was, starting with the most butch women we knew and working his way through all of our female acquaintances. Finally, came the BIG QUESTION:

"You aren't a lesbian, are you?"

"Not exactly," I said, holding my breath.

"But you like them, and men too—what is that called?"

"Bisexual," I said.

"I knew that, I just didn't know what it was called," my son responded. It was just that simple.

Denise is a journalist and a social worker. She lives in Southern California with her teenage son.

NANCY LECLERC
QUEBEC, CANADA

Many of my friends feel that there is no need for children to know that one, or both, of their parents are bisexual. They reason that what goes on in the bedroom is of no concern to children. They assume that a bisexual identity directly correlates with sexual activity and that divulging one's bisexual identity is tantamount to describing one's sexual practices. But explaining bisexuality to children does not entail giving elaborate and graphic descriptions of sexual activity. It simply entails explaining the different ways that people have of loving each other on the emotional, mental, spiritual and sexual planes.

Hiding our bisexual natures from our children merely helps propagate the notion that bisexuality is an anomaly, or a perversion that should be avoided. I see a contradiction in wanting to teach open-mindedness on the one hand, while pretending to be heterosexual on the other. Being comfortable with our own identities and showing our children that they will be accepted regardless of whom they love is an important step toward building a tolerant and free society.

My son is only five years old and therefore too young to understand the nature of sexual and emotional attraction. Someday, he will be old enough and he will realize that Mommy is capable of loving a man and/or a woman. I am comfortable with that and will make sure that he is too, regardless of his own future orientation.

Nancy is a 31-year-old gender-blended bisexual woman and an anthropology teacher living in Montreal with her son. She has been involved in local bi activism for two years.

MEDINA JOHNS
ARIZONA, USA

How did you turn bisexual? Why did you turn bi? When did you turn bi?

These questions always seem very bizarre to me. They are the equivalent of asking me why I am black. I just am.

Being bisexual is as natural as laughing and crying. Growing up, seeing a beautiful woman affected me as much as seeing an attractive man. I thought everyone saw people the way I did, that women looked at men and women and men did the same.

I knew what gays were, I knew people saw them as Problems. But I'm just Medina. I go to school. I have a few friends. I am a good friend. I have a home and an older brother. My mom works hard and she loves me. I have a dog named Max. I am normal I am normal I AM NORMAL.

Never has being bisexual defined who Medina is, what I stand for. It never seems to be as important as my name. In a way I have felt shame for thinking, seeing, wanting—for being what I am. I've always been different, and admitting that I am bi would (in my mind) make it final. Everyone would know. It would add another oddity to my already long list: she listens to weird music, she dresses funny, she says strange stuff.

Being different has always been a problem for me. Everyone who cares about me tells me that it's better to be different. But that idea is hard to swallow at a young age. It sounds like "You can do anything you put your mind to." Or "Sticks and stones may break your bones but words will never hurt you." But words do hurt. And to have this desire is twice as heavy a burden at school as just dressing weird or listening to different music. It makes high school a bigger hell than it already is.

But the thing is: I'm 16 now. I'm older than I was when I felt ashamed. Now I understand I can't let people make me feel I am less of a human because of what I am, how I dress or what gender I like. I always hoped that when I grew up all of this childish stuff would go away.

I was wrong.

Medina is a teenager and a member of her high school's gay/straight alliance. She recently came out as bi as a speaker at a rally to commemorate the 50ᵗʰ anniversary of Brown v. the Board of Education (a Supreme Court decision ending racial segregation in the USA) and the start of same-sex marriage in the state of Massachusetts.

DEBORAH WOODMAN
NORTHERN IRELAND & ENGLAND, UK

If I woke up,
And everyone knew,
Would I lose the rest of me?

Half in, half out,
The eternal optimist,
My glass half full.

Not so much a closet,
More a shadow,
Where only the knowing see.

Deborah is a 31-year-old clinical psychologist, originally from Northern Ireland, who works and lives in London. She likes walking and being out of the city, but is most likely to be found curled up with a good book.

SIMONE PANTALEO
VICTORIA, AUSTRALIA

It was a normal day at work. We all were eating lunch. A few hours earlier I had placed a pamphlet on a notice board we have in our tearoom. I thought no one would notice. Boy was I wrong! One of my work mates said, "Who put that up there?" and read out the heading: "Internalized Biphobia. Did you put that up there, Simone?" I said "No," and walked out of the tearoom. I was so nervous, trembling almost.

Next thing I knew I heard my phone being buzzed. It was my boss, who asked "Simone, are you bi?" I said, "Yes, do you have a problem with it?" (As always, my feistiness came out when I least expected it.) I hung up the phone and started to cry, afraid I was in trouble.

Then they all came back and hugged me, saying that my coming out as bisexual wouldn't change what they thought of me. It was a huge relief. But one of my work mates asked me if I had had sex and I said no. She turned around and said "If you haven't had sex, then how can you call yourself bisexual?"

I call myself bisexual because I feel I have the capacity to love both sexes as much as members of a heterosexual couple love each other. It's not about "swinging both ways" or "being promiscuous"; it's about my capacity to love both sexes equally and fully.

It's that simple to me.

Simone, 23, has identified as bisexual since she was 16 years old. When not studying for her diploma in Community Services at Kangan Batman Technical & Further Education, she is trying to create awareness around sexuality and mental health topics. She lives with her parents, brothers and sister in a small northwestern suburb of Melbourne.

ERIKA SMALLEN
CALIFORNIA, USA

Simple flirtation prompted my coming out four years ago! I would have come out much sooner if a woman had been so forward with me before that time. My previous attractions to women had been brief moments of mistaking a woman for a man. I dismissed crushes on women, usually more butch or androgynous-looking, with the thought, "Oh wait, she's not a man!" Never mind dry humping nearly all my childhood girlfriends from ages 5-13; one of us would always play the part of the guy.

Fast forward to life in San Francisco. **At the age of 27, there was no question in my mind that I was straight.** I was working in the financial district and she started flirting with me. It hit me one day when I saw her in the elevator. She gave me that smile, my stomach jumped, and after my usual response—"Oh wait, she's not a man"—I finally got it—"Ooh, she's not a man!" No woman had ever flirted with me so brazenly. Was I more open? Was it her? Either way, I joyously embraced my new-found attraction to women. I briefly questioned my het identity, but quickly understood that I was bisexual. Although I have only had relationships with women since that time, I do not discount my previous relationships with men, nor would I discount having relations with straight men, transmen, genderqueers, and/or bisexual men in the future!

Born in New York, Erika has lived in California for seven years.

GREG RODGERS
VICTORIA, AUSTRALIA

My bisexual identity developed over a number of years—sort of like putting down a wine to age—and in mid-2002 I accepted it.

I was introduced to the concept of bisexuality by three different girlfriends who themselves identified as bi. One was publicly bi, and the other two did not wish me to tell others. This was before I had come out, even to myself.

My first sexual encounter with a guy was unplanned. We had gone for coffee and a meal and had talked until quite late, so he offered to let me sleep on his couch. I suppose we had a few drinks. Our topics wandered and we somehow ended up mentioning that we both had an interest in guys, which at that time neither of us had explored.

We decided to go to bed, and have a joint and watch a DVD. We discussed the idea further and put on a porn video. We both got into bed. I was just wearing jocks and a shirt and he was in jocks. Not surprisingly, things got sexual.

We spent the night together a few more times and I realized that I liked guys as well as women. At first I was not sure what to do, so I looked up bisexual material on the net and found a bi group in my town.

I kept it quiet from my family. Being single, I had no partner to tell, but I was not sure how to inform family members. I had originally planned to mention it when the family got together at Christmas, but the right moment never seemed to occur. That year had already been a big one as one of my brothers had come out as gay.

In January, while taking a walk with my mother, I told her I am bisexual, and that evening after dinner I told my father, my straight brother and my sister. It has not been as difficult as I expected. Only two people have responded poorly. My mother told me that my gay brother said to her that I could not be bi "because it is not normal." She also said that we should keep my bisexuality and my brother's homosexuality from my grandmother to avoid upsetting her (ignorance is bliss?). My gay brother believes that there are two groups, heterosexual and homosexual, and that it isn't possible to exist in "both worlds." He believes that being bi is like being gay but being in the closet. Ironically, my straight brother, cousins and other family members have been accepting, seeing sexual orientation as just part of a person, and my mother has come around. My gay brother and I have not spoken since Christmas 2002.

I do not consider myself a 50/50 bisexual but rather have a 90% preference for women and 10%—and sometimes less—for men.

Greg is single, male and 36 years old. He lives in Bendigo, a large rural town. He writes poetry, short stories and plays and hopes to write a novel.

SUNG YUN LEE
MASSACHUSETTS, USA

We met at the College Student Womyn Leaders Conference at Georgetown University the summer after my first year in college. I was heavily involved in anti-racist organizing with students and faculty on campus. Some white lesbians were allies, and I got to know one in particular with whom I felt safe enough to ask about sexuality. She answered the questions that had been rolling around in my head, but I did not connect personally with what she said.

At the conference, I stood up in a room of 2,000 womyn and made a rousing speech about the lack of womyn of color in attendance and the disproportionate representation of

white womyn. Many womyn cheered. Afterwards a white womyn came up to say she liked my speech. She told me her great-grandmother was Native American, which is usually a big turn-off for me, but for some reason, she intrigued me. Maybe it was her stories of the influence this great-grandmother had on her. Maybe it was because she was impossibly cute.

She reeled me into her plan to give the leftover conference pastries to the homeless people in D.C. It turned out that the homeless guy with no teeth wanted pork chops, but I still felt we had done a good deed! The next night, we met up to have dinner at a Caribbean restaurant. As we walked down the hill, she came out to me as bisexual. **Something shifted inside me, something I had known all these years but had been afraid to acknowledge, give a voice.** Recognition clicked. It felt like such a magical moment. Finally, someone else was speaking my language.

She told me, "I have a boyfriend."

Hmm, I thought, I have a boyfriend, too! And I am attracted to her…could that possibly mean…?

The meal was incredible; it was like a scene from *Like Water for Chocolate*. Every bite of our food, every breath of the sultry air pulsed with sexual energy. The rest of the night seemed like a dream. It didn't matter what happened, only that I felt so alive and happy.

Now, almost ten years since my initial coming out, I am much more sexually experienced and much more sure of myself, though there have been many bumps in the road. Understanding my bisexuality, all the memories I had previously ignored and buried—seducing my kindergarten playmate, and a high school friend almost seducing me—came together in a more holistic perspective.

Even writing this essay, I still feel the twinges of uncertainty and lack of safety coming out in a world determined to be confused and titillated by bisexuality. When I reflect upon my past, I wonder…would I have been attracted to boys at all if I had been allowed to pursue my feelings towards girls as a child? But we cannot change our decisions made as a small child, constrained by the intense pressures of heterosexism, classism, sexism and racism. And I have come to accept who I have become today, knowing that I am an ever-changing art form.

Sung Yun was raised in a Korean-speaking, working class home as the child of immigrants. She is a Korean-American activist, realtor, artist and world traveler. A resident of Boston, she is a member of Queer Asian Pacific Alliance, a steering committee member of Asian Sisters in Action, a model and a cabaret performer.

DAVID ERTISCHEK
MASSACHUSETTS, USA

For most straight men, having a bisexual girlfriend would be a fantasy come true.

But for me, dating Sung Yun has never been about the possibility of having a threesome with some cute blonde. I just happened to fall in love with a woman who is bisexual.

Her sexual identity seems more important to everyone else than to me. I've always felt it important to acknowledge and embrace her sexuality, because I would want her to embrace such an integral part of me. But I would love my girlfriend no matter what—whether she likes both men and women, just women or any combination. That's who she is, and I accept and love her.

I've never thought that she was going to change, or that her bisexuality was a phase of any sort.

But when I tell other people that my girlfriend is bisexual it brings up a host of questions. How do I deal with it? Do I worry that she's going to run off with a woman? And with whom am I going to have a threesome?

Well, I don't need to "deal" with it. I mean the gay pride parade is one of the coolest things out there to do on a weekend. And no matter who you're dating you can always worry about them running off with someone else.

As for the threesome thing? Not all bisexuals are running around like some porn star trying to bed every Jane or Joe.

I've noticed that I feel much more comfortable telling female friends and coworkers about Sung Yun's bisexuality than their male counterparts. I think males will inevitably bring up the threesome question. Or worse, think that they will be able to have sexual relations with my girlfriend.

But just because someone is bisexual doesn't mean that they have loose sexual ethics. It doesn't mean they're a swinging cat. It just means that they're attracted to men and women.

Although I must admit that I can never comprehend what she sees in butches. But then I'm a straight man who loves feminine women—long flowing hair, sultry legs, and curvaceous bodies.

But I must admit I worry about the future of our relationship. At some point will she tire of my maleness and want a more sensitive person, i.e., a woman? But I've always been willing to take that chance because I love her so much.

Although I've told my sister about Sung Yun's bisexuality, I have not told my parents. I'm not sure why. I want them to accept my girlfriend in her entirety, but they are rather naïve when it comes to sexuality. And telling them that my girlfriend is bisexual may just confuse them or make them worry needlessly about the future of my relationship.

And relationships, whether involving heterosexuals, bisexuals, transgenders, lesbians or gays, are hard enough as it is.

David grew up in the suburbs of New York City in a straight male-dominated world. He is now a journalist in Boston and always pursues the chance to write, as an ally, about GLBT issues.

ANDREA TOSELLI
SWITZERLAND

I don't like words like heterosexual, homosexual or bisexual because they define you according to your relation to someone. The corresponding definitions can only be murky, imprecise, and therefore meaningless.

However, when I think of the word bisexual, I can only smile, remembering the day I met Frau Jeannette Fischer, a therapist who helped me for three years here in Zurich. I was going through quite a rough time then. I had recently moved from New York with my wife Paola and my two-year-old daughter Martina, and had during the past year finally accepted that I was attracted to men. I had recently fallen in love with a Swiss man, Thomas, and was torn between my love for him and my relationship with my wife, which was not really working anymore.

Having realized that I needed help to sort things out, I was interviewing psychiatrists. I had already seen one to whom I had spent an hour telling the story of my life. He concluded that it was not really a question of Thomas or Paola, but that these two were only images of two parts of me I had never managed to reconcile. Other people had already suggested this concept.

Frau Fischer was different. Instead of letting me talk about my past, she asked me what my problem was at that moment. After explaining to her that the choice between a man and a woman was tearing me apart, that I was feeling depressed and suicidal, and that I did not know what to do, she said, "In my opinion, you are scared of the power that bisexuality gives you." I looked at her, my mouth open. I honestly had no clue what she was talking about. I thought, "But wait a second, aren't you supposed to make me think over the two parts of me represented by Paola and Thomas?" Seeing my puzzled look, she repeated the concept, a little bit slower, as if to make herself clearer, but with exactly the same words. My look did not change. She had nothing more to add and the session was over.

I left. Who the hell was this crazy woman who instead of giving me some serious insights about my choice between a family and the love of a man had come out with that absurd concept of the power of bisexuality? Something I could not even relate to...I thought.

Well, guess what, she was right. I know it now and I felt it then, deep inside me. I left my wife, who was not able to accept who I am, but not my daughter.

Thomas soon left me, unable to keep up with a situation (and a man) that was evolving so fast. After three years of dating and falling in love with men, I recently met a woman in a bar and found myself attracted to her—and scared, of course.

Bisexuality (whatever that means) for me is about the ability to relate to all people at a deep emotional level. It is an openness of the heart. It is the absence of limits, especially those that are defined by the other person's sex. It is about not needing to choose. Who said that to love someone you have to renounce something? Bisexuality is the realization that you can indeed have it all. It is the power of not giving yourself limits.

Andrea is an Italian mathematician living in Zurich. He studied engineering in Milano, soon realized that the work of an engineer was too applied for him, and then earned a Ph.D. in Mathematics at New York University. He is a happy divorcé and the father of a beautiful five-year-old daughter.

TALIA ERINNA
MASSACHUSETTS, USA

I have only identified as bisexual for a little over a year.

I got my heart broken by this guy and vowed that I would never find another man like him. So I wanted to venture to the "other side," as I sometimes like to call it. Some people say their feelings were always there or they've known they were different since they were children. That's not the case for me. I totally decided to be this way and now that I have had the chance to be with another woman, I realize that this is who I am.

However, this realization has brought some difficult moments to my life.

Luckily, I am not from the typical super-religious Hispanic family—in fact, my family is very Americanized. My father was born in Panama and my mother, my siblings and I were all born in the United States. My parents are very young-looking and young-thinking. We can communicate about a lot of things going on in my life—except when it comes to my new-found love of both women and men. I have not been able to gain enough courage to tell them that I am bisexual.

My problem is that my parents will not understand how this came about. I was so guy-crazy during high school and the first three years in college that my parents have jokingly said, "You change the guys you like as often as you change your underwear." So, I know they will have no idea where my new feelings have come from.

It's also tough because I did date a woman who identifies as a lesbian, and whom my parents knew. We were best friends first and then became something more. They will think that this woman had something to do with me liking girls. Knowing she was gay, my father was never too keen on me hanging out with her, but I tried not to let his personal feelings stop me from choosing my friends. He started asking, "Why do you hang around Deb so much? I don't like the fact that you hang out with her a lot. Why did you have to bring Deb with you on your vacation? Why couldn't you have taken a different friend?" (In other words, someone straight.) Then one day, my father flat out asked me, "Are you gay?" My heart skipped a beat. I was shocked that he asked me this question so bluntly while he was watching television. I had to think on the spot and I said, "No, I'm not." He didn't ask me the right question. He failed to ask if I was bisexual. Even to this day, I don't know if I would have admitted it to him that day.

Now, my parents have laid off from asking me so many questions, partially because I've been away at school. They have no clue what I've been doing with women or that I've been to several gay clubs and drag shows. Also, I still manage to talk about guys here and there to get them off my back.

I know my mother would be OK with me being bi. Her sister is gay and lives with her partner of six years in Atlanta. So I'm not concerned about her reaction. However, my father is very old-school when it comes to gay issues. Not long ago, he said to me, "I can't imagine two guys holding and hugging each other. It's just something I'll never understand." So, knowing how he feels about gay/lesbian situations, how can I tell him his innocent, first-born daughter is bisexual and has even been in a sexual relationship with a woman? It would break his heart. I know I need to live my life but at the same time, I couldn't stand to know that I've hurt my family so much and possibly lost a lot of his respect.

I'm sure one day I will get the courage to say something to them. But as long as I live under their roof and need their support while I begin the difficult task of joining the workforce, where it can be ruthless and cutthroat, I want to come home to people I know care about me and will not hate me.

Talia is a 21-year-old bisexual woman who graduated from college in the spring of 2004. She is Cape Verdean, Panamanian, Native American and also Italian. Her identity varies depending on the people she's talking to but she mostly identifies as Hispanic or Cape Verdean.

DIANA MILILLO
CONNECTICUT & NEW YORK, USA

When I was first contemplating coming out to my parents as bisexual, I thought it would be a one-time deal. I would do it, we'd talk about it, they'd be confused and ask questions, but nonetheless profess their respect for my identity and any other decision I'd make in the future. I prepared for months—I even celebrated in anticipation with a coming out song, and reveled in the sweet irony of those times my mother and I would sit side-by-side in the car, both mumbling Sarah's words: "Momma, can't you see I've got to live my life/the way I feel is right for me/Might not be right for you."

Well, when the time came, it wasn't that glamorous, as coming outs usually aren't. No, in a fit of tears, anger and humiliation from the previous night's first encounter with college homophobes, I sought solace and support from the one who thought she knew me best—my mother. My long-awaited, well-practiced announcement shattered into a few choppy words caught between sobs: "I think, uuuh, I might want a, uuuh, a girlfriend…" I never uttered the word bisexual. Once it was out of my hands, I watched quietly as the wheels in my mom's head hunted for momentum and churned out a few oft-cited excuses, or causes, as she calls them: "Was it _____ (asshole ex-boyfriend)? Do you think your women's studies classes are making you mad at men?" **She searched for days for overlooked clues from my past, obvious traces that she missed. But I'd always had boyfriends!** She didn't believe it (though "it" was certainly ambiguously defined). She became upset, and I decided not to touch "it" again. I needed her as my mom.

Over the next few years, my family never knew about the women I met, only the men. I began a relationship with a beautiful, loving man, and resorted to the idea that I could be bisexual in many ways. I still frequented lesbian bars or events, my circle of friends became more queer and I kept taking those Women's Studies classes! Indeed, my steady commitment at school to LGBT issues, academic and not, was my own little public invitation for others to go ahead and question my sexuality—I'd be ready to tell. I call this subtle, omni-present inundation with facts, lectures and stories my second coming out. Although I had a boyfriend, I felt that I could still get the message across that I was queer.

I sit here now reflecting, mad and disgruntled after my third (and failed) attempt to come out to my parents. I'm in the midst of a two-year relationship with said boyfriend, and of a time when I feel the outside world is more than ready to catapult my identity as bisexual into any open closet, and crown me Queen Heterosexual. I'm mad at myself for allowing them to believe that I'm confused, not knowing if I'm a lesbian. I'm disappointed by my failure to annihilate their assumption that once I was with a man they could erase all I've said to them before. I'm frustrated that I couldn't give them answers to questions like, "Do you know who you're going to end up with?" and angry at them for asking.

My bisexuality offers the remarkable capacity for many forms of expression. It also puts me in constant limbo to the people and situations I'm around, which I think we bisexuals learn amazingly to navigate around. As for my parents, I don't know how many times I'll have to reinvent the wheel, but I do know that we need to be honest and open with each other—albeit in doses. I'm working on it for my next coming out.

Diana is a 24-year-old bisexual woman and graduate student. She teaches psychology and women's studies classes, and has bi-residency in New York and Connecticut. She practices yoga and shares a birthday with her favorite female folk singer.

CHERYL B.
NEW YORK, USA

My mother thinks it's perverted.

"But how can you like both?" she says to me every time I try to explain my sexuality to her. "Lesbian, I can understand. But when you say you like both, it's, it's…" She never finishes, but I know what she's thinking. "Can't you just pick one?"

In my late teens I thought I had picked one: girls. I'd always been woman-centered and I was elated to hang my hat in a community of fierce, young baby dykes.

When I was 24, I met a guy through a straight female friend. We became friends and eventually we fell in love. Throughout our two-and-a-half year relationship, people—especially other straight people—assumed I was now straight. I would explain that I still identified as queer and they would look at me strangely.

I'm in my early thirties now and in love with a woman. Unlike my girlfriend, who has been out since high school and has never been involved with a man, I wasn't quite sure where to place myself on the queer continuum. I'm bi and I identify as a lesbian. Since lesbian-identified bisexual can be a mouthful—no pun intended—a friend and I came up with an acronym, LIBI, for lesbian-identified bisexual, and we use it to describe ourselves.

I'm currently editing an anthology, a collection of personal essays entitled "Coming Out of the Closet Again: Queer Women on Loving Men." Reading the submissions, I realize there's a vast and varied world of women like me out there. My goal with the anthology is to bring these voices together, creating a new territory for queer women.

Cheryl is a writer and spoken word performer whose work has appeared in dozens of publications. She lives in Brooklyn and online at www.cherylb.com.

SARASWATI BRYER-BASS
CALIFORNIA, USA

I was 13 and madly in love with a girl at my middle school. I took a few days, read *Rubyfruit Jungle* obsessively, and came out to a lesbian family friend. This sounds easy, and in a certain way it was. I was happy to know what I was, and because my mother was an out lesbian I had a label for my crush on the soccer star. I was a happy, very out, baby-dyke for the next few months trying to figure out my life in the way only an intentionally precocious teenager can. Then came high school, and JJ, and I fell madly in love again. The big problem was that JJ was a guy, not a femmy guy, or a pushy aggressive guy, but a sweet boy who was gamely trying not to have feelings for me because he knew I was a lesbian. I was simultaneously trying not to have feelings for him. I knew lots of people who had previously been straight and were now lesbians, and a few women who had previously been lesbians and were now straight. What was clear from the people I knew was that it was an either/or. **I could either like girls or boys. The problem was that I seemed to like both** and now I had to prioritize and choose.

On the one hand I was very attached to my queer identity. I liked the queer youth group I went to and the friends I had made there, I liked the sex and safe sex information I was getting. I was doing public education speaking as a lesbian and I loved it. On the other hand was this boy whom I loved—we were very close and spent almost all our time together. Finally almost six months into our platonic love affair I told JJ that I was attracted to him. A few months after that, I found bisexuality as a sexual orientation, not just a bridge from one identity to the other.

Saraswati is a 25-year-old bi-dyke in a committed non-monogamous relationship with a woman. She lives in the Bay Area.

LITTLE SQUIRREL
TURKEY & USA

Most girls are straight until they're not...I never even thought about the concept of "gay" or "bisexual" until I became close with a girl. Before that I was always spending time with guys. I thought I could never be real friends with girls, but then one became my best buddy, and we realized we had a chemistry for more than friendship...and boom! First I freaked out, then I began a huge searching and networking process. Until then I hadn't known or met a single gay person.

I have never liked putting a label to myself. I go with the flow, and think about sexuality as chemistry between two people. I believe in monogamy and always argue with people who think being bisexual means being with a girl and a boy at the same time, or think that you are calling yourself bisexual because you want to keep your options open.

Maybe I was lucky because right after I came out to myself I came to the US and started searching for websites and people. I met many people from Turkey online, and when I went back to Turkey for vacation I met some of them. First I wasn't out to my friends here or there, but after a while I didn't want to hide it. I'm out to almost all my friends in the US but not in Turkey—not because this makes me nervous but rather because my life is in the US right now, and will be at least for a while. I don't want to deal with friends' adjustment while I'm not near them. My friends here in the US are all straight and even the Turkish ones have become very comfortable with my sexuality. I never tried to explain, but day by day they saw my lifestyle, learned my thoughts, and came to respect me.

I don't think the Turkish understanding of bisexuality is much different from the USA understanding. Well, people in the US are much more tolerant and respectful since they're becoming used to living in the same environment with gays. But I've met so many conservative and narrow minded people here as well. For Turkey—I guess it'll take some time. Homosexuality is something people don't talk about. It is always hidden, so it's still a taboo. But Turkey is the most open-minded country with a 90% Muslim population. Our lifestyle, especially in cities, can never be compared with other Muslim countries.

Little Squirrel was born in Turkey in 1977, and grew up in Istanbul in an intellectual, educated and open-minded family. She came to the US for graduate studies in engineering in January 2002 and is currently living and studying in the Boston area.

RAJIV DUA
DELHI, INDIA

One evening when I returned from work and was having tea, my mother approached me. She said, "If I ask you a question will you be offended?"

I replied, "Please do ask, the issue of getting offended or not rests with the kind of question!"

"But assure me that you will not feel offended."

Sensing what was in store for me, I replied, "Mama, no question is right or wrong, so do ask."

She paused. "Have your friends turned you gay?"

I did not know what to answer. I have lots of friends, gay-identified, bi-identified, people living with HIV/AIDS and many others. They come to my house and my mother knows about many of them. After a moment I said, "You know that I have had sex with other men, but I am not gay."

She heaved a sigh of relief. "That means you are normal?" She deemed my sex with men an aberration and believed my marriage to a woman made me "normal."

I paused and said, "Well after having sex with men, how can one be normal?" She looked confused. And I began the journey of explaining my bisexuality to my mom.

This incident sums up the attitude of many in Indian society. Identifying as a bi person has not been easy. In the monosexist society of urban India, I was seen as either a heterosexual or a homosexual. I tried to meet people like me. Heterosexual friends welcomed discussions until the moment they veered toward same-sex relationships. With homosexual friends it was the same. In a gay support group meeting I was told not to talk about my relationship with women.

A whiff of relief came with the internet. Access to e-groups brought me in touch with other bi people and slowly I started coming to terms with my sexuality. It has been a Herculean task to ensure that bi people meet. The only success was bi-mumbai—a group that met six times in the city of Mumbai (formerly Bombay) before disintegrating. The group was based on bisexuality as a behavior rather than as an identity. That was the closest one could get to a common platform. People attending the meetings were kothi, panthi, crossdressers and bi-identified.

Though gay people believe that identifying as a bi person is easy in India, bi people themselves do not share the sentiment. Bi people attending gay groups do not talk about their bi identity, for fear of losing what little support they get in these spaces. With heterosexual friends they either hide their bi identity or ridicule their same sex-partners. This way they think they are able to hide their same-sex preferences under an umbrella of exception rather than preference per se.

Rajiv is a bi-identified person who hails from Delhi and currently lives with his parents. He is Hindu by birth and comes from a middle-income background. For the past sixteen years he has worked in non-governmental organizations across India.

Editors' note: for definitions of "kothi" and "panthi" see page 152.

MAGDALEN HSU-LI
WASHINGTON, USA

Coming out as bisexual? Mostly it was all about confusion for me. Then again, growing up as an Asian American in the rural South, facing ignorance and racism every day, and navigating through the tricky waters of "unfilial piety" in my semi-Confucian, southern debutante-like upbringing gave me plenty of challenges during my "formative" years. I didn't have any time to think about my sexual orientation. I was too busy just trying to stay alive.

I didn't realize I was bisexual until after college. I never even considered labeling myself because I thought it was pretty normal to be attracted to both men and women and to have relations with both. I found it hardest to deal with the fact that my attractions varied. I was more attracted physically to females and emotionally to men. Why were my attractions split like that? I could not understand. Neither could my partner or counselor at the time. Since I was already performing as a musician and had a public life, I was forced out publicly before I was ready. I was afraid that lesbians would hate me for dating a guy—that they would not understand. I used to try to hide my partner from the queer-identified groups that would bring me to do concerts...to no avail. I'll never forget the first time my partner and I were outed at a gig by accident. I was so ashamed. Everyone was so tickled that I hadn't come out yet—they made jokes about it and teased me—but I was so ashamed. My coming out process didn't get to be in my own time and of my own choosing. Everyone had an opinion about who they thought I was or what they thought I needed, but no one cared to listen.....to ask me questions about how I was feeling...to ask me who I thought I was or how I defined myself. I had wanted my coming out to be a process that I could do privately and at my own pace—ultimately it was a very public experience.

Looking back I can see that the biggest problems were ignorance and misinformation in myself and in those around me, and a lack of role models. Growing up in the South (at least in my hometown), you just didn't talk about being queer. No one was really openly out. So who were you to emulate? My parents, as immigrants from China, had a hard time understanding. Bisexuality is so out of their range of comprehension. In their mind, you just aren't gay and Chinese. The two words are not compatible. OK, Koreans have it worse...but seriously...it's just not OK. If I can do anything to help others it would be—just by my presence being out there—to help people find that moment of clarity—of identity—where they go, "Aha...I am like this person. I identify with her, what she is saying, and what she has been through."

I know what I am. To me that knowledge of self-identity is so much power. Because from there you finally have a place from which to approach the world and say, "I know who I am—unfailingly and unshakably. And nothing you can do or say can take that away from me."

Magdalen is a music artist, painter and activist based in Seattle. Her most recent albums are Fire *and* Smashing the Ceiling.

GEORGINA ANTILLÓN
MEXICO

Let's see, well, I discovered myself
bisexual
at fourteen but it was
quite frankly terrifying since I never accepted it and
tried to deny it and
rationalize it when I caught myself looking at
girls or, say, when I
saw myself attracted to them, I used to say that
what I experienced was untrue
that they were mere fantasies, this lasted almost five
years even though my
relationships with my friends were quite frankly
close, obviously not erotic
but with so closely knit a bond of friendship to
the degree that I'd write them letters
in which I'd say how much I loved them and
"within this friendship" it was

always reciprocated and I knew myself loved by them,
until nineteen or twenty when
I had a sexual experience with a
friend from the university itself that was
wonderful to me and at once with enormous
guilt and a profound negation since
I told myself as justification that I had
lost my senses,
since we had been drinking a few hours prior,
therefore it neither was nor should
be significant to my sexual orientation,
it was then that I cancelled that
part of myself and I dedicated myself (forcefully) to
relate with men
(exclusively) so I led my life until three years
ago in which necessity
and dreams accosted me with many
erotic fantasies of women
and in a course on sexuality I was able to accept my
orientation, afterwards
I've let myself flow more and now I enjoy noticing
how much I'm attracted to women and
in fact I've been able to have erotic relationships with
women without shame and without
fear, I can say that I didn't need therapy
but the course was a great
help in my accepting myself, and in the
same way I cannot say that
I have totally owned it to the degree of going around
spreading it around the world but
I think it's coming along

Georgina lives in Mexico.

ADENA GALINSKY
PENNSYLVANIA, USA

The biggest challenge and joy of acknowledging my bisexuality was realizing that most of what I'd been taught about sex was wrong.

Lie number one: The healthy, clear-thinking, and honest version of you is either attracted to men or to women but not to both. Some of my mentors told me this, straight out. TV shows confirmed it. Even the members of my religious community, who had reconciled their own seemingly contradictory identities (feminist American intellectual/traditional observant Jew) had limited imagination when it came to sexual preference. Some of them could accept a nice Jewish girl who was also a lesbian. No one could imagine a nice Jewish girl who was both straight and a lesbian.

Lie number two: While you're figuring it out, if you're female, don't expect sex to be any fun. High school sex education portrayed teenage sex as the challenge of avoiding STDs and pregnancy while engaging in penis-vagina intercourse. Magazines, movies and advertisements presented an even starker picture. They scolded, "If you ever want someone to desire you (which is far more important than feeling pleasure) you'd better get busy buying stuff that'll fix your disgustingly flawed self. Not that you'll ever be capable of feeling pleasure the way guys do. Not that it matters. Not that you deserve it anyway."

Lie number three: Once you realize which you are attracted to, you will have determined a multitude of other aspects of yourself and your life. Everyone knew that girls who admitted to liking girls stopped being whatever they were before and became a cross between a lumberjack and a punk-goth-anarchist.

Coming out as bi meant I could stop struggling to stay afloat in this swamp of corrosive nonsense. It meant I could stop wasting energy trying to pretend that I belonged to either of the two proffered categories. It also meant that sex became a lot more fun. Finding the clarity and courage to know and ask for what you want will do that.

Best of all, I've discovered that I don't have to stop being me. I'm the same person I was before—except that I'm more self-aware and less likely to accept conventional wisdom. I used to think that I needed to deny parts of myself if I wanted community and companionship. Surprise! I'm a member of a fantastic, progressively traditional Jewish community. I've also fallen in love with an unbelievably wonderful man who understands and loves me for who I really am.

So look out world! I'm energized and I've got plans. I'm going to do everything in my power to ensure that the next generation is better prepared. They deserve to be taught how to figure out what kind of sex they want—and how to engage in that sex responsibly, with love and respect and skill. I also intend to reach out to those who are feeling as alone and confused as I was. I want them to know: it's possible to be healthy, to think with clarity, to love and be loved, to be exactly and entirely who you are—and be bisexual.

Adena has lived all 20-something years of her life in the Philadelphia area, and currently does so with her life partner. She just recently discovered the color of her parachute and so, leaving behind the technology consulting industry, she is preparing for graduate school in public health.

She loves me...
HE Loves me...
She Loves me...

Roberta Gregory

ROBYN WALTERS
WASHINGTON, USA

Actually, it was a late-in-life hormone thing, a shocker. After 60 years as a very heterosexual although not at all macho male, my transition to female was very pleasant and satisfying. The first shock came about six months after beginning a hormone therapy regimen of Premarin and Spironolactone.

The sun ruled over a cloudless blue sky when I saw him walking down the road toward my car. As I zoomed by this young 'gardenboy,' stripped to the waist and without an ounce of fat, my inner self thought, quite loudly, "Oh, my, that's nice." I almost ran the car off the road. It was just the shocked reaction to feeling sexually attracted to a male for the very first time in my 62 years of life. Even though I wasn't equipped to handle the attentions of a male at the time, it certainly gave me pause to wonder. Hormones. Had to be the hormones.

Five years later, I am long since female and have a wonderful husband. But my strongest sexual attraction remains another woman.

I was a male attracted only to females; now I am a female attracted to both male and female. I've always been a monogamist; so I'll always be faithful to my husband.

At 67 years old, my instantaneous fantasies when seeing a beautiful woman or a foxy man are quickly forgotten, and I return home to fix dinner.

Robyn is an older woman who lived too much of her life as a heterosexual male. Now living west of Seattle with her husband, she considers herself a transactivist and a non-practicing bisexual.

RUSS STEIN
MASSACHUSETTS, USA

For me becoming bi was a non-miraculous epiphany late in my life. As a young adult, I had recovered from stunning depression—we are a small and so far secret band—and that was a miracle!

My high school and college years were straight, shy, dry and non-sexual. Moving to New York, I met the love of my life, a woman painter who took my 28-year-old virginity and introduced me to the Art Students League. Our love affair, art, and later a spiritual grounding in the Human Potential movement opened me up.

Returning to Boston in my thirties, I began volunteering intensively in state mental hospitals, and eventually became a rehabilitation counselor, thus embarking on a new career. At night, I lurked in gay bars, another new career of sorts. At last, in 1982, at age 56, I came out as gay. I have few lovely memories of my 17 years as a gay man, much of which was tangled up in booze. Less and less do I buy into the clichés of gay and straight thinkers. After a particularly moving exchange of confidences with a stranger who may or may not be gay, I realized hey—I'm bi! **I started calling myself bisexual in my seventies,** which is where I am now.

Russ is a 78-year-old licensed psychologist with a specialty in individual and group psychotherapy. He lives in Franklin. He is an artist, a long-time gay/bi activist, and a former board member of SpeakOut, a GLBT speakers' bureau.

JULIE HARTMAN
MICHIGAN, USA

Lots of people talk about having crushes on girls or somehow just "knowing" they were gay early on in life. I had a few crushes, but I also knew I *really* liked boys. A lot. So I knew I wasn't a lesbian. Faced with the categories of gay and straight, I always just figured I was straight. I had heard about bisexuals, but those were just "nymphos" in porn movies, or people who were "AC/DC" and flashy—musicians like Elton John. Bisexuals were weirdos, and I wasn't one of those. I was just a straight girl…who kinda liked girls. I never acted on any crushes on girls because I never thought that was really an option. If I made out with girls then I would be a lesbian, but since lesbians don't like men, and I definitely liked men, I figured I must be straight.

In college I let my imagination wander more and actually thought of my attractions to women as "crushes." I had a huge crush on that cute punky grrl in my philosophy class—the one with the black framed glasses that were so intellectual-looking. And that quiet one in women's studies with the long hair. Yeah, I had lots of crushes on women, and I even started thinking maybe I was a dyke, except for one little problem—I still liked men. A LOT. I had heard of the Kinsey scale, and about the continuum of sexuality between heterosexual and homosexual, but the continuum never quite made sense to me. **I didn't feel like I was somewhere in between two points, I felt more like I was somewhere off the scale entirely.** It wasn't like I was part heterosexual and part homosexual. I'm not part anything—I'm just all me!

Then I went to grad school and during second semester I went out dancing with friends. That's when I met Ruthie. We met in the ladies room of the club, reaching for the last paper towel. (She tore it in half so we could share—how chivalrous!) We danced together all night, took turns buying each other drinks, and even introduced each other to our friends. At the end of the night she gave me her number and asked me to call her. I never did. I realized at that moment that I liked boys *and* girls. Both. A LOT. I spent the next few weeks staring at that slip of paper with Ruthie's number on it. I threw it away. I rescued it from the trash. I threw it away again. I'm straight. I'm gay. I cried. I'm straight… I'm gay…. I sat there and tried on both words and neither seemed to fit quite right. So, like any dorky academic I turned to the dictionary for help. "Bisexual: having attraction to or characteristics of both sexes." Hmm…no nympho porn stars or flashy pop stars. Just attraction to both sexes. Simple and yet so complicated. That's me. I'm bisexual…I took a deep breath and let it sink in.

The word seemed to fit in a way that straight and lesbian never had. This word contained possibilities. Possibilities for all kinds of love, all kinds of sex, all kinds of relationships. I felt kinda proud—I had finally found a word that seemed to fit me. I had found a word that meant it was OK for me to like boys *and* girls. Finding the words allowed me to start looking at the way I felt, no longer limited by the dualistic concepts of straight and gay, neither of which fit me. Before that moment I had had bisexual desires, but I never acted on those desires until I had a vocabulary for my identity. People underestimate the power of language. Language gave me the avenue to *be* bisexual. Until that moment I was just a straight girl who never felt totally straight.

I never did call Ruthie. (Sorry, Ruthie, wherever you are now. You were so cute and a great dancer.) Though I never really knew her, she changed my life.

Julie is a 24-year-old Ph.D. student in sociology at Michigan State University. She's still not quite sure if she's a sexuality researcher who studies identity, or an identity researcher who studies sexuality, but her main research interest is bisexual women's identity and community.

MARCELLA BUCKNAM
NEBRASKA, USA

I lived for years alternating between calling myself a lesbian and slipping back into the het world, depending on whom I was dating. But every identity I assumed was a lie and I always felt guilty—whether expounding the wonder of sex with women or talking about how much I liked men. I didn't really fit either category and I dreamed of lovers of any gender. Like so many other bisexuals, I feared I was the only one in the world who felt that way. I finally reached a point where I could no longer live with the lies, and I told a friend about my secret attraction to both genders. I was terrified I would lose her friendship, but the pain of the lie was more terrible than the possible loss. She looked at me and said, "Oh, you're bisexual! OK."

The look on my face must have been interesting. Inside I was faced with a sudden realization. I had never told anyone about my feelings, yet there was a word that described how I felt! There must be other people who felt as I did—other bisexuals!

The simple fact that a word existed not only gave me an identity, it opened up a whole world of new possibilities! And even though several years passed before I met another person who identified as bi, everything was different after that moment. Sometimes I hear people say they don't like the word bisexual. They feel it has negative and limiting connotations. **But for me it will always be a cherished doorway to a new world. It represents freedom, honesty and self-realization as no other word ever has.**

Marcella is a former national coordinator for BiNet USA, currently living in Omaha.

JENNIFER WILLIAMS
CALIFORNIA, USA

For me, coming out as bisexual was as painfully simple as discovering the name, finally, for a decade of desire. In hindsight, I did a terrible job in coming out to my parents, and they returned the favor by responding with homophobic bile. Over eight years later, when my wife and I first got serious about our relationship, I was torn. To whom in my family was I was willing or interested in disclosing our relationship? I had actually been in the process of drifting away from many of my dearest relatives because I suspected that their Deep South sensibilities wouldn't mesh with my radical queer politics and sexual activism.

In the long run, I decided that if I was going to lose them anyway, for lack of contact or content in our relationships, I might as well give them the chance to decide how to react to my primary partner. In the end, I finally came out to my 80-year-old Southern Baptist grandmother, and had the amazing experience of her acceptance of me, my sexual identity and my partner. **The sad thing is that for all of those distant years, her main worry was that I might be alone; whereas mine was that she might reject me for how un-alone I really was.** She loves my wife, she loves me and I can finally give her real updates on my life again. This is my happy ending story, and the one that I hold onto in the face of biphobia and other bigotry. I like to share it whenever I get the chance.

A resident of Oakland, Jennifer is a 34-year-old disabled student who has been out as bi for 14 years. Over the past ten years, her bi identity has taken half a dozen different turns, each positive in its own way. Most recently, she finds herself a student of psychology and human sexuality. She lives with her partner of seven years, roommates, cats and fish. In 2002, she co-coordinated the First International Queer Disability Conference.

OLAMIDE MAKINDE
NIGERIA/UNITED KINGDOM/SOUTH AFRICA

I'm 23 and just finished my law degree. I'm a black female originally from Nigeria and have lived most of my life shuttling between the United Kingdom and Southern Africa. I first started to identify with the term in my first year of university when a friend told me of it and guessed that I was bisexual. This was about the time that I had my first experience with a woman, but I chucked it away as an experiment. As far back that I can remember I have felt an odd resistance to women, and most of my friends were and still are men.

I recently fell in love with a woman. The experience triggered all my suppressed fantasies of women and thus sparked confusion over whether I was gay. The lesbians I knew tried to convince me that I was gay and in denial, and my straight friends felt that I was just experimenting. These reactions only further confused me. As a result, I started researching the term bisexual. I don't have any particular inclination to one sex, but I do find that at particular times in my life I have a strong inclination for one over the other.

I started working for the Equality Project in February of this year. I aspire to be a human rights lawyer and working here has been one of the best experiences I have ever had. I'm a very strong feminist and believe in the protection of human rights for all. My sexual orientation only heightened my devotion to this cause, as in my home country there aren't equal rights for the LGBTI sector, leading many to believe that there are no gay people in Nigeria.

There are very few resources about bisexuality in South Africa. LGBTI organizations in South Africa are really progressive but the bisexual side of things has been really left out. The bisexual struggle is still mainly seen as a homosexual one and you would be surprised by how many people, even within my organization, do not understand bisexuality. Many people struggle to come out as bi because there are so many misconceptions and a general fear toward us. Even as an out bisexual I struggle to find answers to my confusion because neither my gay nor straight friends is able to help me with it.

I recently spoke to a lesbian woman who told me that she had never met a bisexual before! When I told her that I was bi, she started to pour out her heart. She told me that she actually hates bisexuals because they never come out as being bi. It turned out that she had a relationship with woman who identified as lesbian for five years and then one day found out that her partner was pregnant. I receive the same sentiment when I talk to other lesbians.

When I came out as bi to the woman I'm in love with, she told me that it was easy to be bi. This totally crushed me, as she did not take me seriously and totally disregarded my sexual identity as genuine. This in my point of view is why many South African bisexuals do not come out as bisexual; they are shunned by the gay community due to stereotypes and misconceptions.

I would like to make a stronger and bigger bisexual community in South Africa because the deeper I research the more harm I see coming out of the invisibility of our sexuality.

Olamide is currently a legal intern at the Equality Project, which works to achieve full legal and social equality for lesbian, gay, bisexual, transgender and intersex people in South Africa.

ELIZABETH J. ANDREW
MINNESOTA, USA

Sue shifted in her rocker. "Would you like a practice run-through?" she asked. "I know what I'd ask my daughter were she to come out to me."

I nodded.

"I'd want to know who you've slept with," Sue began. "Are you in any danger? Do you have AIDS?" I began shaking. The questions easiest to answer (no one; no; no) hurt the most. Twenty-six years of being my parents' daughter and they would no longer see me as Elizabeth but rather *this word* with all its connotations. "What are your feelings about monogamous commitment? How do you know you're bisexual? What does bisexual mean?" Sue continued ruthlessly when I didn't answer. The hard questions left me flushed and speechless, my ears ringing. How could I explain?

I was on the sofa across from this barrage, eyes closed and hugging my knees tightly. Not for the first time, I wished I was in a relationship that might justify the torment of telling the truth. If I had a lover beside me, coming out would be less personal. It would then be an explanation of the outward commitments—of my relationship with a man or a woman or of my "lifestyle," whatever that was. Instead, I was turning myself inside out, making the sexuality of a single celibate person an issue without due cause. I was choosing to say, *Fundamentally, even alone, this is who I am.* It reminded me of my audacious decision at the end of high school to apply to only one college, in the middle of the prairie, where I had never visited. Everyone thought I was crazy for not having first checked it out. But I knew it was where I belonged, just as I knew now, without having been in an intimate relationship with a woman, that the capacity resided inside me.

I imagined my parents receiving the dreadful news. Their hair was gray. The porch light shone too brightly and tree branches brushed against the black outsides of the screens. I took a deep breath, imagining the aftershock of coming out. Slowly the shakeup of Sue's words settled into quiet.

"What is the gift you most want to give your parents?" Sue asked, more gently now.

I kept my eyes closed. "An invitation," I said. "I want them to join me on my journey. None of us should ever be alone like this. I want us to be together through hard times." It occurred to me that this was why I had to tell my parents first, before even my most accepting friends. I couldn't think of any greater gift.

Elizabeth is a writing instructor and spiritual director living in Minneapolis. She is the author of Swinging on the Garden Gate: A Spiritual Memoir *(Skinner House Books, 2000),*

Writing the Sacred Journey: The Art and Practice of Spiritual Memoir *(Skinner House Books, 2005), and* On the Threshold: Home, Hardwood, and Holiness *(Westview Press, 2005) a collection of personal essays. She is a recipient of a Minnesota State Arts Board artists' fellowship and the Loft Career Initiative Grant. She teaches creative writing at the Loft Literary Center, United Theological Seminary, and various religious communities in the Twin Cities.*

Excerpted with permission from *Swinging on the Garden Gate: A Spiritual Memoir* (Skinner House Books, 2000)]

Alex Hirka

Chapter III:

Why Bi?

Why bi?

Most bisexual people hear endless variations on "Why do you call yoursel
bisexual?" Whether spoken aloud or present but unvoiced, the question usuall
implies that identifying as bisexual is unusual, unnecessary—or worse: an ac
of disloyalty, a sign of immaturity.

Often the question accompanies a personal attack: "Why do you cal
yourself bisexual when you are committed to so-and-so? When you never dat
men? When you haven't had sex with both men and women? When you'r
celibate? When you've never had sex? When all your partners are women? Wher
all your partners are men? When you aren't polyamorous? When you don'
feel 50/50?" All of these questions draw on stereotypes and misinformation t
discredit bisexuality or limit it to someone else's personal definition.

Which brings us to a more interesting question: why do so many individual
embrace their bisexuality in the face of overwhelming negative pressure? Afte
all, we confront not only an overwhelming lack of openly bi role models, but
surfeit of models who acknowledge attraction to more than one gender yet insis
on a gay or straight identity. This curious fact demonstrates that even withi
the categories of lesbian, gay and straight, individuals define their sexuality in varie
ways (some arguably bisexually). Yet the phenomenon passes undiscussed, anc
members of these communities are presumed to be both the same as everyon
else and 100 percent attracted to one gender/sex. The presumption is tha
everyone with the same label experiences their sexuality in the same way.

By contrast, the bisexual community engages in a healthy and active
discussion of these very topics: What does it mean to call yourself bisexual? Wha
do you gain or lose when you embrace this word and this aspect of yourself
We employ tools (like the Kinsey scale, the Klein grid, and the Storms scale
to aid the discussion. Above all, we understand that these questions are critica
to our self-identity and expression.

When we proposed themes for contributors, the topic "Why Bi?" received
an overwhelming response, proving the most popular subject. Because one
of the most common attacks on our collective identity is the declaration
that bisexuality doesn't exist, most bisexuals appear to have a ready persona
response to this question, and to its implied disparagement.

These answers are as varied as the community itself, and serve to underline
an important point: although our common identity unites us, we differ from
each other not only in the usual categories—race, gender and gender identity
age, ethnicity, social class, ability, religion, nationality, and the like—but in the
very bisexuality that brings us all together.

Many bisexuals will explain that they are attracted to more than one sex
or gender, but even this simple definition encompasses those drawn to all

genders and those to a select few—for example, a person attracted to women and female-to-male transsexuals but not to genetic males. Others note that their attractions to one gender are stronger, most lasting or more intense. For some, attractions to different genders feel qualitatively different—some more erotic, some more emotional, some encompassing both love and sex. More and more people identify as bisexual because they are attracted to more than one gender *within* the same person. Still others note that they have been attracted to different genders at different part times in their lives. Indeed, many people declare their bisexuality to claim their personal history. They don't want to erase previous lovers (or crushes, or even a really hot fantasy) and parts of themselves to buy acceptance.

Others respond to the question, "Why bi?" by affirming the many perks of being bisexual. Many of our contributors find a deeply rewarding, sometimes spiritual wholeness in looking beyond gender in their partners, lives and sexual imagination.

Others enjoy actively engaging with gender and experiencing its range. Many bisexuals also find their lives enriched by the bisexual community, the larger LGBT community, or both. They forge strong friendships and a sense of purpose, and credit the deeply diverse and welcoming atmosphere with aiding them and broadening their lives. Still others see power in the act of naming themselves. They claim their bisexuality as part of a larger mission of making the world a wider, more expansive place, in which people with diverse gender and sexual expressions will be welcome.

Varied though their voices are, these pieces from Australia, Belgium, Canada, Germany, India, Ireland, the Netherlands, Peru, the Philippines, Spain and the United States often return to the freedom to love, the liberation of being true to one's self and the rewards of being whole.

—Sarah

CAROL QUEEN
CALIFORNIA, USA

Why bi? I'm sure I'm bisexual because I can't ignore the allure and loveliness of a wide spectrum of people—differentiating by gender never seemed attractive or even logical to me. I've been bi since high school, even through a ten-year spate of lesbian identification (trust me, it seemed like what I had to do at the time if I ever wanted a girlfriend). For me bisexuality means I don't stop attraction, caring or relationship potential based on gender; I can have sex, flirtation or warm ongoing love with anyone (not everyone, okay? That part's a myth).

We have enough trouble in this world connecting, loving, getting pleasure and finding our true adult families of choice without cutting half the human race out of the project. That's why I'm bi. And we have enough trouble splitting the human race into two halves, assigning mandatory characteristics, and then torturing people to fill arbitrary roles—I consider that a wrong and inaccurate way to understand human potential, and that's also why I'm bi. Men and women are different? Honey, everyone I've ever met has been different. I think being bisexual lets me see each person as an individual. That's the way I want others to see me.

Carol has a doctorate in sexology, is a worker-owner at the famous sex toys shop Good Vibrations and is a much-published author.

STEPHANIE BAIRD
MASSACHUSETTS, USA

I consider myself bisexual for many reasons—most importantly because I am sexually attracted to women and men. I came out to myself at age 18, after people began asking me questions about gender and sexuality, prompting my own epiphany that both were indeed fluid. My theory was way ahead of my reality, until reality slammed on its brakes, giving me whiplash.

The best class I ever took in college, Human Sexuality, confirmed the validity of my identity with discussion of the Kinsey Scale. I find the Kinsey Scale a useful tool to gage where I am currently, compared to the past. I love fox-trotting between the hetero- and homosexual ends of the scale, subtly fluctuating my footsteps and placement throughout the years, depending on my romantic situation and peer group. This continuum dance is like a trusty old weathervane creaking back and forth with the wind.

The professor of that class, bisexual herself, perfectly captured the essence of bisexuality: **"It's not a set of genitals walking up to me, it's a person."** I think of this quote when I wonder whether the word bisexual describes me best. Perhaps I could use pansexual, omnisexual or allsexual (like allspice). I am definitely attracted to more than one gender (thank goddess infinite permutations are available), and am also turned on by nature. However, I stick with "bisexual" simply because I have had romantic experiences with people who term themselves female or male, and because bisexuality as a term still gets a bad rap in some hetero- and homosexual circles. But I love conversing and mingling with gender-savvy folks, providing pleasant opportunities to use the more fanciful and inclusive terminology. Love and sex are possible with any individual. The world is our oyster, and (bi)sexuality is the butter that makes it go down smoothly.

Stephanie is a trauma/violence therapist in central Massachusetts. Originally from Texas, she enjoys motorbiking, snowshoeing, camping, hiking, knitting, writing, bass-playing and merry/mischief-making in scenic New England.

DANIEL M. OCAMPO
PHILIPPINES

Bisexual is the only appropriate term to describe my emotional, physical, and sexual attraction to both women and men. Not limited by heterosexual societal norms, I have been involved with women and men of different backgrounds. To me, being bisexual means you do not look at another person as a woman or a man but see them for the real person they are. I am bisexual because **I do not choose to have attractions to only women or men. I have more options of finding people with whom to explore life.**

Daniel lives in the Philippines.

MARCIA DEIHL
MASSACHUSETTS, USA

Why bi?
Three words: **Truth in advertising.**

Marcia has been a musician, writer and activist in the Boston area for 30 years. She co-wrote a chapter with Robyn Ochs in Homophobia: How We All Pay the Price *(Beacon, 1992) and contributed to* Blessed Bi Spirit *(Continuum International Press, 2000). She has written music, theater and feature articles for* Sojourner: A Women's Forum. *Along with Robyn Ochs, she co-founded the Boston Bisexual Women's Network in 1983. She's a member of the Cambridge Lavender Alliance and a book reviewer for the Harvard Review.*

DARRAGH DOHERTY
IRELAND

In some ways, the hardest part about being bisexual is talking about it to non-bis. Not because I'm in any way confused about it—I'm not. Nor because there's so little to say—there's lots. The problem is that bisexuality is many different things to many different bis, and to explain it away in a few lines is next to impossible. Most of my friends are bi, yet I can't think of two who are bi in the same way.

I'm a bi guy out for six years, with a strong queer identity. Some people are even visibly shocked when I mention a girlfriend, because I identify so queer. I socialize in the scene. I'm active with Bi Irish. I'm out at work, and to most of my family. I do occasionally sleep with people who identify as straight, but very rarely, and the last one was a man.

So why identify as bi? What's so important? Why classify? All very good questions, and often asked by people who are bi in practice but not identity. For me it's an assertion, mainly political, but also social. My last straight (in both identity and practice) girlfriend was and still is a wonderful woman, and put up with a lot from me, our relationship having started six months after I came out. I would still describe her as homo-friendly, and a very supportive person. However, about a year after we split up I mentioned that I'd started going to Bi-Irish meetings.

"That's just stupid!" she said. "Surely you're straight when you're with a woman and gay when you're with a man." At times like that I realize the vast differences between straight and queer understandings of identity.

For me, either of the monosexual identities are worlds apart from mine. That's not to say that I can't identify with their sexual appetites. Nor does it mean that there are no limits to my appetites—that they are in some way the sum of hetero and homosexual desires all rolled into one person! It's just that a person's gender doesn't make me more or less attracted to them. It's like the straight guy who fancies someone, and then finds out it's a drag queen. Or the gay guy who fancies a lad and crosses the dance floor to talk to him, only to find it's a butch/boyish-looking woman. Both men (so the script goes) are likely to recoil with varying degrees of horror or squeamishness. If they don't, they have more than a little explaining to do with their mates the following morning. But for me, there's no reason in the world it should matter, and that's something I choose to celebrate.

Identifying as bisexual does not mean that I mightn't be attracted to one sex more than the other. Nor does it mean I don't end up in relationships with one more than another. It does assert that when I'm with the "less frequent" sex, that it's not some sort of an aberration, that this relationship is as valid in my mind and heart as any other. It asserts that being with a member of the opposite sex in no way dilutes my queerness, that my feelings for men remain as strong. It means telling my gay friends that I don't believe that my attraction towards men should impose new limits upon my desires. It also means telling my straight friends that no, that girlfriend doesn't mean I'm "cured," or "through with that phase." It's me being me, not some prescribed behavioral pattern.

Is it equidistant between the hetero and homo worlds? Well, sexually it can be anywhere along that continuum, depending on the person. But politically it's queer as fuck. Just as someone from a biracial background suffers racism as much as other members of the black community, homophobes hate bisexuals as much as our lesbian and gay brothers and sisters. In many ways, we're worse. We're even more stereotyped as hypersexual superswingers, more interested in emissions than emotions. *We could* live the straight lifestyle. We upset their world view even more by crossing borders, and "spreading" this evil into "their" community (as if such a thing exists!).

The current Blood Transfusion service [blood bank] ad at Dublin bus shelters announces, "It's your type we're after." Bi men, just like gay men, know that they're not talking to us. At least, not yet.

Darragh is 36, a civil servant and a member of the Irish bi community. He spent 2003-2004 based in Brussels, Belgium, doing EU-related work in the field of social security.

LIZ
NEW JERSEY, USA

I have chosen to identify in so many ways since I was a child, but bisexual only became important to me when I realized how much it was belittled by those I love and admire. There never seemed to be a reason to identify. I was so content just being a sexual being, loving and admiring all genders. Once I started to truly explore my sexual attraction to women and was blessed by a loving but brief relationship with one, there was no turning back. I embrace the bisexual label because I know that I am just right as I am. It has never felt so normal to me as when I opened up to loving men and women. As a Latina married to an amazing man who embraces me in every way that I am, I know that that I can be me, bisexual, *sexual,* loved. I tell my story because there are so many people like me who need to accept themselves and enjoy the many possibilities in this lifetime. The personal becomes political in order to end sexual stigmas. We need to normalize sexual behavior and accept the endless ways one can be partnered and sexual. I have been living a bisexual life for ten years. I look forward to updating this in another ten and talking about my bisexual life as a continuously evolving human being.

Liz is a sexuality educator and speaker on Latina and youth health issues. She has a Masters in Public Health from Tulane University & a B.A. in Political Science from Rutgers University.

RONAN WATTERS
IRELAND

I am a 31-year-old, Irish, queer activist, socialist, bi guy who is sometimes into kinky sex. I can be all or a mix of these at any one time. These identities link me to other people in communities and friendships—they are part of who I am. But importantly, none of these identities are fixed; what those words mean to me now is different from what they meant a year ago and in another year's time they may have a different meaning again. I don't know the reason but I have always felt more at home with things that aren't fixed and static. **I have always liked having a range of very different projects and plans on the go at any one time.** It both keeps me interested in what I am doing and gives me more room to move about. When I was younger I did this because I didn't know what I wanted to be or do when I grew up and settled down (as I was told I would have to). Now, while I still don't know what I want to do in a few years' time, I do know I still want to have as many options as possible open to me then as now.

Ronan Watters is involved with Bi Irish.

COLLEEN D. MCCARTHY
YUKON TERRITORY, CANADA

I call myself bi because I prefer to give my same gender relationships/flings/crushes/whatever the same weight of acknowledgement as my "opposite" gender ones. I may be only a two on the Kinsey scale and have had far, far fewer female lovers than male, but I still prefer to call myself bi rather than straight (or bi-curious or whatever). **I think I left "curious" behind years ago!**

Colleen, 40, lives with her family in Whitehorse. She maintains the Gay and Lesbian Alliance (GALA) Yukon website and also serves the organization as a board member.

AXEL GRIESSMANN
GERMANY

Why not? It is my firm belief that **all humans are born bisexual.** It is just a natural thing to be bi.

Axel lives in Hamburg. He works in the computer and communications business. In his little spare time he likes listening to music of all kinds and building, restoring and riding his motorcycles.

ANTONIO FERRERA
SPAIN

A lesbian friend once told me that when she came out to her brother, he asked her, "How do you know that you don't like men since you haven't been with any?"

"How do you know you are not gay since you haven't been with men?" she replied.

"Because I don't feel the need to be with men."

"Me neither," she said.

I call myself bisexual **because I feel the need to be with both men and women.**

Antonio is 36 years old and has a Ph.D. in physics. He is fond of good meals, good wines, flamenco dancing late into the night and anything related to having a good time.

GINA WERTZ
INDIANA, USA

I started watching porn when I was eleven or twelve. I went into my parents' room and turned on the television and there it was: nude women making love. I found it attractive, but I told myself it was because the scene was sexual, not because it involved women.

Throughout middle and high school, I tried hard to be feminine and heterosexual to prove that I wasn't gay. It wasn't that hard. I like boys. However, I've also always found girls attractive too.

At this point in my life, I've been an out bisexual for over two years. **I haven't yet been in a relationship nor had a real kiss with a woman. However, that's irrelevant to my sexuality. I am attracted to both men and women and that makes me bisexual.**

I'm not sure if I am more attracted to men or women. I date men more often than women. Meeting men is easier than meeting women for various reasons. Heterosexual men greatly outnumber gay/bi women. Also, I find it hard to evaluate my chances with women I meet in public and thus I am less likely to pursue them. To meet women, I have to go to gay-frequented places or meet friends of my queer friends.

Dating men more often may mean I have a male preference, but to me it's the result of social circumstance. Maybe someday our society will support equal and open pursuit of both homosexual and heterosexual relationships.

Many people brush off bisexuality as a shameful stage on the way to proud homosexuality or heterosexuality. However, I think that mentality greatly limits our understanding of human sexuality. Unless the opposite or same gender completely disgusts you, never rule out the possibility of being attracted to someone outside your "sexual orientation."

If everyone would look at human sexuality and gender as continuums, there would be no labels. I would no longer be bisexual. Simply sexual.

Gina lives and works in Bloomington, where she is pursuing a degree in Social Work from Indiana University.

ADIA
PERU

In questions of sexuality, I prefer not to use labels to define myself. But as we live in a society that needs these damned labels, I prefer to use the term "bisexual." Considering my personal preferences, **calling myself "bisexual" covers a wider territory regarding my capacity to fall in love** and to share the life of a couple with another person without taking into consideration questions of gender. Like all labels, bisexual has certain disadvantages, because there exists a widespread prejudice that bisexuality implies promiscuity. This idea exists in hetero as well as homosexual groups. One suffers certain discrimination from those who believe that bisexuality represents an easy out, when in reality, for me it has to do with an open perspective.

Adia is in her 20s, has a B.A. in literature and lives in Lima.

ALEX LI-HUA LEE
CALIFORNIA, USA

I am bisexual by default, in that it is the only word in common usage that approximates my sexual orientation. To me the word implies the existence of only two genders or sexes, when I believe there are many more. **I am attracted to a wide range of gender expressions,** and many times the only way I can describe myself to people who still believe in the binary gender system (the idea that there are only male and female genders) is with the word bisexual. I use this identity with reservations, as the word itself is inadequate and fails to challenge the traditional oppressive model of sex and gender.

Alex is a twenty-something Taiwanese/Chinese American law student who has dedicated his life to fighting for the rights of low income people, people of color, immigrants, transgendered people and others.

SPARROW
IDAHO, USA

I began by thinking I was a lesbian. That identification fell apart when I admitted to myself that I found men attractive as well. Then I identified as bisexual. That identification fell apart when I fell in love with a gender-bending transsexual who had decided, halfway through the switch, to stay "in the middle." With an attraction to three sexes, how could I be bisexual? Trisexual? No, that's the punchline of a bad joke. For a while, I adopted the seventy-something-year-old term "pansexual" but I got tired of defining the word for people. Too many aspects of my life appear cryptic to most people; why intentionally add another? I want a label that brings people closer to me, not one that sends them running for their dictionaries.

I've found freedom in the term bisexual even though it hints at a simple dichotomy that I've long since discarded. Like most symbols, the word bisexual is an icon that depicts a transcendent reality, a meaning too large for that symbol to effectively capture and box away. When I label myself bisexual, I am calling myself open. **Open to possibilities, open to the ebb and flow of people past the shores of my life.** Though "bisexual" contains the word "sex"—a vast realm itself—to me this identity is about so much more. It's about opening my heart and my life to the winds of time and learning to love as much as I can, as long as I can, as full and deep and wide as an ocean.

Sparrow is a 36-year-old bisexual person who used to be a lesbian before she came out of more closets than you can shake a stick at. She lives in southeastern Idaho with a lover and pets. A retired sex worker, Sparrow now writes erotica and non-fiction under the pseudonym Magdalene Meretrix.

ANDREA ZANIN
QUEBEC, CANADA

Bisexuality as a term has its problems.

Some say the stem word sexual makes it sound like we're all about sex. Some say there aren't just two genders, so why use such a binary word? Others prefer pansexual, homoflexible, queer. Still others choose to go with gay or straight.

Plenty of people out there have sexual or romantic fantasies, attractions and involvements with people of more than one gender but for any number of reasons don't claim the term "bisexual"—because it scares them, because it doesn't fully represent who they are, because they don't like labels. And plenty of people out there feel that bisexual (or queer) is the right word for them regardless of who they sleep with—to them, it's a political statement, a challenge to the norm, an indication of their openness to possibilities.

I believe there are genders and sexualities out there far beyond our current abilities to define them. With such limited vocabulary at our disposal, the words may not yet even exist.

Even for those who do claim the term, trying to define what bisexual actually means can get a little complicated. We are a diverse bunch with many ways of seeing ourselves! So no, bisexual isn't the perfect term. It doesn't do justice to the full range of sexual expression that we are capable of, and it doesn't convey the nuances of how our practices and identities can change over time.

But for now, the word bisexual has one big advantage: it's recognizable. In a world where different sexualities are so often silenced and ignored, claiming the word "bisexual" is a stark reminder to mainstream societies (both "straight" and "gay") that there are other options—and people know what it means. Certainly not in all its depth, not with every variation and subtlety, but they usually get the general idea.

The very fact that there are sometimes hostile reactions to the existence of bisexuals is proof that we're challenging something very important. If our society is built upon rigid divisions–black/white, gay/straight, woman/man, evil/good—then simply by voicing the existence of another possibility, we are opening the door to all sorts of questions to be asked and answered, and changes to be made. The word bisexual is just the beginning.

As for which words we choose to name ourselves, that's up to each of us. Right now, I'm comfortable with the term bisexual, among many others. I use the word often, loudly, clearly, proudly, because who I am, unfortunately, is not written on my face; and I use it in the hopes that, as much as humanly possible, I will not find myself hiding behind either heterosexual privilege or lesbian appearances.

And one day I may change my mind. Because we can do that.

Andrea is a 26-year-old activist in Montreal. She runs Tip of the Tongue, a social group for lesbian and bi women, serves as the president of Quebec's Gay Line and is an active member of the BDSM community. She also writes a column on queer sexuality at www.attitudes.cc.

CHERYL DOBINSON
ONTARIO, CANADA

Not everyone likes the word "bisexual." And I'm not talking about biphobia here (or prejudices against bis). I'm talking about people who themselves may be attracted to more than one gender, and other folks who have no issue with that kind of attraction but find "bisexual" a troublesome label. I totally understand their perspectives and I've definitely struggled with the term as well.

At this point I've come to accept the term as a useful shorthand for explaining something about who I am when I don't have the time, energy or desire to get into the specifics of my life. **Getting involved in a bi community has also changed my perception of the word, and I've come to see it as a cultural identity rather than just a clinical term.** However, it would be nice if we had another word, the way gays and lesbians can call themselves, well, gays and lesbians, instead of homosexuals.

I like the abbreviation "bi" as a cultural term. It's more apparent that I'm talking about an identity and not just sexual behaviors. I like "queer" as well—but I often find I have to explain how I fit into that because a) people assume it means I'm a lesbian, or b) it causes confusion to those who see me with my male partner. So I use bi most of the time, especially when I don't feel up for giving an explanation of my personal flavor of queerness. And I leave it to others to define themselves (or not) in whatever way they see fit.

Cheryl, a bisexual writer, educator and activist, lives in Toronto. She is the creator and editor of the bi women's zine The Fence *and co-founder of Fluid, a group for bi youth.*

HILDE VOSSEN
NETHERLANDS

I call myself bisexual because I love people and I especially appreciate it when the person to whom I am attracted has mental and physical characteristics—ones traditionally described as female or male—balanced in himself or herself, and is totally satisfied with that.

Once I had a beloved one, whom I now describe as a "feminine man." When he called me a "boyish woman," he touched me in my soul, because I most eagerly wanted people to look at me like that, physically as well as mentally.

In 2004 I celebrated my seventeenth year as an out-and-proud bisexual. This is the clearest way for me to make visible to the heterosexual and homosexual world that my sexual identity is not limited to one specific gender.

Hilde was chair of the Dutch Bisexual Network from 1998 until 2002; one of the organizers of the first European Bisexual Conference, which took place in June 2001 in Rotterdam, the Netherlands; and is one of the co-founders of the European Bisexual Network.

RAMKI RAMAKRISHNAN
INDIA & TEXAS, USA

To me, the word bisexual has evolved in meaning over the years. I originally used it to describe my being attracted to some men and some women, regardless of whether I chose to act on that attraction. But nowadays I use it to mean my being attracted to very specific kinds of people—those who challenge, and occasionally demolish, the limits of gender in their lives. Specifically, I find myself attracted to feminine males, butch females and other transgendered people. **My awareness of androgyny in myself has led to my reclaiming the older meaning of bisexual** (two sexes in the same body) and a political position from which to tackle the institutions of gender and heterosexism, and the way we marginalize some people and privilege others based on their gender-role conformity.

Ramki is a biologist, musician and queer community organizer who calls both Austin and Madras, Tamil Nadu home. He is a founder of Trikone-Tejas, a pan-Asian queer-straight alliance at UT Austin, and a founder/member of LGBT-Madras, a new community group in Chennai/Madras.

BRAD DETTMER
CALIFORNIA, USA

I identify as bi because it's easy. It doesn't affect my gender. I mean I can change my gender without having to change my sexual identity.

My dad told me he was bi when I was twelve. He sat me on the couch in the living room of our redwood house. It was awkward. Why was he telling me this? Obviously it was a big deal but I didn't think it was. It was supposed to mean something. It didn't. I knew he was fucking men the whole time he was married to my mom. Only I didn't know. I pushed it deep inside me. Along with all the other sexual abuse he imposed upon me.

So the first bi guy I knew—my father—was a total dick to me, which has made it hard for me to embrace my own bi identity. I went from bi to asexual, to heterosexual … in high school I changed my sexual identity every week.

I've finally come to terms with not needing to know who I am. Do I like women or men? Am I gay or straight? I asked myself those questions every night. I had to know. But now I just don't give a fuck. Why does it matter? And why are there only two to choose from?

Struggling through my bi identity has helped me struggle through my trans identity. I no longer need to know if I'm a boy or girl.

I'm tired of bisexuality. I'm over it. I'm attracted to all genders. So what? Bisexual implies that there are two sexes. Bisexuality conflicts with so many aspects of who I am and what I believe. Yet I'm bi.

My name is Bradley (not Brandy).

Bradley is a 23-year-old bi tranny boi who just earned a bachelors degree in women's studies at University of California, Santa Barbara. His 'zine, Fence sitter, *focuses on bisexuality, gender identity and all in-between spaces.*

SKOTT FREEDMAN
SOUTH CAROLINA, USA

i do not define myself so it's easier. so people will understand me better. so my partners won't flee the scene at the beginning of our relationship. so at last i will have chosen a side. i am bisexual and therefore i identify as bisexual. i don't care if it's easier or harder. it is a part of my identity just as i am jewish. just as i am a vegetarian. just as i am a human being with the same basic need and desire as every other human being: to be loved. whether i am loved by a man or woman or both or neither will never change the fact that i am bisexual. i am proud to be bisexual. i am proud to be able to live my life so at the end of it i will be able say i have loved and was loved in return. by men. by women. by both. by neither.

Skott is a 24-year-old nationally touring singer/songwriter and bisexual speaker. With his music and his lecture "Battling Biphobia and Bringing Bisexuals Back to Both Communities," Freedman reaches thousands of people a year.

LES DAVIDSON
NEW SOUTH WALES, AUSTRALIA

3 reasons I love bein' bi:

One:
yr in the fruit an veg section f yr local and a hot bod's chekin out the produce just like u r, and their partner walks round the corner an th're even hotter

Two:
These days there are women who are my friends and always will be and there are women who are my lovers
These days there are men who are friends and always will be and there are men who are my lovers

Three:
Since I've been out to my family, there are no untold stories, no secrets, no lies, different from a lot of older brothers but I can be me. Now that I have my self-respect, we all have ours.

Les is a parent living in Sydney with two guinea pigs. After stepping in and out of the closet for years he is currently very out. He has recently become active working with Bi Pride Australian, Bi New South Wales, Sydney Bi Men, the Bi Performance Group and Biversity, and he loves dancing in the kilts that he makes for himself.

ERIC
TENNESSEE, USA

I have always been aware of my "non-heterosexuality," just not always comfortable with it. In times past, like many bisexual people, I feared my same-sex experiences would dictate my identity as gay, a label which scared me—and didn't really address my other-sex desires. And the term "queer" absolutely horrified me. I knew of the term "bisexuality," but didn't understand how that could relate to a person who tended toward monogamy. A little education on my part was in order.

I did, in fact, marry my life and soul mate and came out to her very early on. But I knew her gender did not dictate my sexual orientation. With lots of reading on the subject, I discovered that there were all types of relationships that bisexual people could opt for, including opposite-sex partnered monogamy. After much discussion and a little bit of trial and error, we mutually arrived at a conscious decision to maintain an exclusive relationship for just the two of us.

There was just one catch. The thought of everyone assuming I was a straight married man began to suffocate me. I told my wife that I had to know that she didn't see me that way and that I needed her support for me to do something outward, positive and constructive with my bisexuality. It was at that point I decided to start a support group (with the help of the *Bisexual Resource Guide*) and get involved in the queer community. And I have not looked back!

Why the term "bi"? Because I own it. And, because I've earned it!

Eric was an Army brat, raised all over the USA. He now lives in a small town in Tennessee. He has been married for 15 wonderful years to his wife, Laurie. Eric founded and continues to facilitate a support group for bisexual men and women called Bi The Way – Nashville.

LAURIS LEDI
BELGIUM

I have always felt attracted to different kinds of people. Their gender wasn't that important. When I was eight years old, I had a friend, a boy from class. We hugged and kissed in the garden at his home. When I was about 16 years old, I discovered a term for feeling attracted to both boys and girls. As this fits me quite well, I called myself bi (bi-relational, bi-emotional, bisexual and bigender). In general I felt myself attracted to boys and girls. This fluctuated from time to time, but overall I felt attracted to both sexes equally.

Slowly I started to feel worse and worse about the categories of sexual orientation or gender. I don't feel male or female, I can't be put in a simple box. I am also convinced that dichotomies are very limited. I think there are more possibilities. In a narrow bipolar gender system I refuse to take a position. **The range of my gender and sexual feelings is wider even than the image of a continuum between two extremes. I would prefer the image of a field, space or universe.** All individuals take gender position in the universe or in the field. The traditional position of man and woman are not extremes, but two of the many unknown possibilities. A universe doesn't have a beginning or an end, anyway. All possible positions are equal, regardless of how many exist. There is no hierarchy whatsoever!

No position is fully static. People live, have contact with others, develop, are on the move. Everyone carries their experiences as baggage or as a basis for further development. Gender positions (for example, man, woman, transvestite, transgender or transsexual) and sexual orientations (e.g., homosexual, bisexual, heterosexual and pansexual) are ambiguous. Identities are necessary to create a social and political basis. But in fact every individual is unique. Though we share points of similarity, no two bisexuals experience bisexuality in exactly the same way. When you listen to pure personal life stories, the gender, sexual and other identities blur.

In my personal life I want to be, without being labeled. I want to love someone without being identified as hetero, bi or whatever. But I realize that a bisexual identity is needed to build a collective front to fight for justice.

Lauris (b.1981), a Flemish gender activist, was active in To Bi! (the bisexual workgroup of Wel Jong Niet Hetero) until 2004, and is currently active in Dubbelzinnig (the bisexual group of Antwerp).

BRIAN DODGE
NEW YORK, USA

Emiko and Brian

When I was 13 years old, I injured my ankle and my mother brought me to a medical center. While we were in the waiting room, I noticed a sign on a door across the hall that read "BISEXUAL." I asked my mother what the word meant.

She paused for a moment and then said, "I think that is a 'unisex' restroom ... but usually it means a person who loves both women and men."

"Oh," I said, "that must be what I am."

It's been pure bliss ever since.

Brian, who lives in New York, is a post-doctoral research fellow, a self-identified bisexual man, a fabulous husband and the father of two dogs.

DONNA HUEN
MANITOBA, CANADA

Calling myself bisexual was a long and often troubling journey. In a world that persists in seeing sexuality as dichotomous, I came to see bisexual **as the most honest representation of who I am sexually.** I am active in anti-homophobia work in my community, and find that maintaining this label, while confusing and even abhorrent for some, is necessary for me. In some small way I am a role model for young people who might otherwise be too scared to call themselves bisexual.

Donna is a resident of Winnipeg.

JUDE
IRELAND

My mother used to tell me that when I was about five I would point at the cherry tree in our garden and say, "When I was a boy, I used to climb that tree." I was 21 before I realized that my attraction to women was about more than platonic bonding and I wondered for about a year whether I was gay; I certainly enjoyed hanging out with like-minded gay men and women, but would catch myself looking at men and thinking rather lustful thoughts about them. **My best female friend came out as bisexual around this time and all of a sudden I had a whole new set of referents in which I could frame my identity.** I came to realize that the label 'bisexual' is the only one that fits me—for now. The important thing about my identity (for how can I speak about the identity of any other bisexual?) is not who I have a relationship with or how I choose to have that relationship, but rather an attempt to understand love better, and an attempt to unlearn many linguistic/conceptual categories which are taken to be universal Truths. I try to remind myself that most binary categories we use are relatively modern, Western, dominant-male ones, can be related to power differences, and that I am free to use the same categories in different ways if I choose, or make my own categories if I need to.

Jude lives in Dublin and has recently completed Ph.D. studies.

JENNIFER WILLIAMS
CALIFORNIA, USA

When I first fell in love with a boy, in ninth grade, in Knoxville, Tennessee, in the early 1980s, I was also in love with my best friend, who happened to be female. It took me five years, and a 700-mile move to the big city to finally find the concept of bisexuality. When I first acknowledged my attraction to other women, I was terrified about what it might mean about my committed relationship with a male partner. I was very clear about my feelings towards him, and yet felt that I might not be able to keep him if I was actively attracted to women. In the long run, he, not I, stumbled upon bisexuality—as well as gender bending, sexual politics, and queer community—and brought this knowledge home to me.

In hindsight, I've discovered that the majority of my pre-coming out lovers were, or are now, bisexually identified. I guess we lacked the language, or perhaps simply weren't ready to find bisexuality before we did. I try to keep this in mind as I am vocal as a bisexual sex radical. **I try to remember that people discover things when they are ready to,** whatever may be under their noses, and that we all grow and change as our lives progress. Bisexuality fits me today, and has for many years. Maybe tomorrow there will be something else that I am ready to discover.

Jennifer, 34, is a resident of Oakland, a student, and a disabilty activist.

TONI
WASHINGTON, USA

I came out as a lesbian at 16 years old. This process was particularly difficult because I came from a devoutly religious Jehovah's Witness family. At the time, I was only able to come out to other queer-identified folks or those I knew to be allies. At that point in my life, my relationships with men were more born of competition and hate than any acknowledged or unacknowledged affiliation. As I neared my 35th birthday and began a process of introspection and reflection, I reconciled many of the personal reasons for the anger that I felt towards men. **I realized that although I continue to have a strong lesbian identification, my history of four connections with men in 19 years meant that I was other than lesbian.** I now currently identify as a bisexual lesbian as I feel that this expresses more completely my identification. If there were such a thing, I'd be a Kinsey Scale 5.5, having relations with and being predominantly attracted to women, but very occasionally physically and emotionally attracted to men. I am happy here.

Toni is a 35-year-old professional living and working in the Seattle area. She finished a master's degree in physical therapy in 1995 and loves her work in this field. She has a second career in real estate which she also enjoys. Her passions include good theatre and film, womyn's music, spoken word performance, humanistic art and traveling.

SOPHIE VERHALLE
BELGIUM

I have been calling myself bisexual since the age of 14 when I came across the word in a dictionary. For me, **one's sexual identity, however contradictory that may seem, is more than a sexual thing:** it involves feelings, social contacts, friendship, etc. At first, I assumed I was 50-50 (50% for guys, 50% for the girls), but now I realize my life is more complex than that: I am more easily attracted to girls than boys. I don't often fall in love with guys but when I do, it's "serious." I am now in a monogamous relationship with a girl and find it very fulfilling. I certainly have no need for a man. I am more attracted to girls on the whole but identify as bisexual since I have had some meaningful relationships with boys in the past, because that might happen in the future (if my girlfriend and I ever broke up—God forbid!), and because guys still seem to interest me.

Sofie is a former regional editor of the Bisexual Resource Guide.

JO GERRARD
NEVADA, USA

I'm about the least likely bisexual you'll ever encounter—I don't currently have sex, have never had sex, and generally regard the idea of sex with suspicion—like handing a small child a glass of grape juice: you just know the end result is going to be messy. And I'm not super-fond of labels anyway. So, why bi?

Part of me wants to turn the question around and say, "Why not bi?" but that would be cheating—it's always harder to "prove" a negative.

It's easier to say bisexual than "Well, most of the time I don't actually want to engage in the sexual act, but when I do think about it, or fantasize, or read porn or what have you, I'm as likely to imagine a woman as I am a man." Leaving aside, for the moment, complications of gender expectations, bisexual explains me pretty succinctly.

In a way, it's a non-label label. Yes, some gay and lesbian folks out there will say that we're fence-sitters who need to make a choice. Some of us will, ultimately, in whatever our relationship ends up being (those who are polyamorous and bisexual don't necessarily have to make that choice).

But just because I might settle down some day with a loving woman won't mean I have to stop drooling every time I see a hot guy. Or vice-versa.

A resident of Northern Nevada, Jo is a recent graduate with a bachelor's degree in multimedia and in English. Currently, her only mammalian companions are two rats named Zig and Zag.

Chapter IV:

Life Stories

When we meet someone, we get an external view of a life at a specific moment. This snapshot view flattens complexity and often renders bisexuality—and many other things—invisible, outside the frame. When we step back and view a person's story as a landscape over time, contours, patterns and contradictions may emerge that are not visible when viewing life as a still photograph.

This chapter provides the reader with diverse landscapes to explore. Some contributors look back over long lives, while others focus on a few critical years or come to us at an early stage of their journey. Some have traveled widely without leaving their place of origin; others have transnational histories or have experienced moves within one country as pivotal moments in their development.

Topics range from childhood crushes to adult relationships. Many contributors describe a process of moving from confusion to clarity, from self-doubt to self-discovery—a process of integration, of embracing all of themselves. From Australia, Belgium, China, Ghana, Mexico, Sri Lanka, Turkey, Uganda, the United Kingdom and the United States, these stories map out many possible lives.

—Robyn and Sarah

CISEM KUNDUPOGLU
TURKEY & USA

I don't know how to start my biography as a bisexual Turkish person because I have always denied both parts of my identity, even though deep inside I knew I was Turkish and bisexual—something I felt I always needed to hide from lesbians and cute tarkan-looking guys.

Now I think that being "biturkish" is the most natural combined identity in the world. Here is my reasoning: Turkey is located between Asia and Europe. It has traditional roots in Asia and "westernized" modern roots in Europe, but is part of both continents. I am both—combined—loving dearly both genders. I am Turkish and bisexual. It is hard to say it, but I say it anyway.

I don't remember coming out to anyone in Turkey except my best pal, Feride. She understood what I meant by "any form of love." However, to my other peers, being bisexual meant being confused. I remember having a big crush on this cute short-haired girl, yet whenever I was asked whom I would like to go to the prom with, I always answered, "Oh, this guy from my PE class. He is the cutest ever..."

My bisexuality was there, but hidden inside my skin. Only God and I knew how I enjoyed girls and guys at the same time. When I was 12 years old and playing with my Barbie dolls, I pretended to be my Barbie's girlfriend. I would kiss her, yet dream about this handsome soccer player. Then I would ask myself, "What am I doing? Am I OK? Maybe I am crazy." I loved both girls and boys, Barbies and soccer players. I had to stop kissing Barbie dolls.

As a sophomore in high school, I moved to the United States and started something totally new. Instead of hiding, I was going to stop being bisexual and start my new "straight" life, which involved volunteering for HIV/AIDS. However, as I volunteered, I learned that back in the 1980s HIV/AIDS was erroneously considered a gay disease. This made me angry. Something inside my skin hurt.

In February 2002, I was in Dallas, Texas for a Youth HIV conference. I guess it was my first time feeling so free; I looked at one girl as she kept looking at me. Again, something inside my skin hurt. I could only say, "Hey, would you like to go out with me?" She said she would. That was the day I took off my mask and shed my skin. I was in love with the cutest gal. (She was neither a soccer player nor a doll!) As I returned to my home town in California, I was lonely. But I was myself, at last: bisexual and Turkish.

I discovered a few online Turkish GLBT discussion groups such as Legato. There I found many Turkish bisexuals who blamed themselves and were uncomfortable. When I was in Turkey, I blamed myself too. Some people still believe in the Quran which, like some other religious books, says being homosexual or bisexual is an act of evil. In a community as involved with religion as "secular" Turkey, it is hard to come out and show "the evil act." However, some transgender singers such as Bulent Ersoy have modeled GLBT power and tried to show that changing genders was normal—not an act of evil. I hope everybody appreciates her in our LGBT community. I love her personally; she is braver than I am. For example, I cannot say both my name and I am bisexual in public. I still don't know why.

I am 20 years old now. I am studying to be a cancer researcher at one of the best colleges in the United States, and hope to show the world that cancer does not discriminate against people on the basis of sexual identity, even though society does.

Cisem (not her real name) is a Turkish citizen, currently attending university in California.

KIM
USA

My story, I am sure, is like many others. I grew up a confused young girl with no one to share my feelings with. I believed if I told my family or friends that I was attracted to other girls, they would be upset. So I never said a word.

Throughout my teen years I liked boys yet also felt attraction to girls. Believing I was the only one like this, I pushed my feelings deep inside and kept them secret.

At 16 I married and began a family. I knew I was too young but I was in love. I married my best friend who listened to me and showed me love like no one else ever had. Yet close as we were, I never could tell him my little secret. I was afraid he wouldn't want me if he knew.

Years went by, our kids were born, and by age 21 I was a mommy of three. Life was good, yet my secret feelings for women grew so intense I felt I could literally explode!

I put on so much weight after having my kids and having this family life that I became unhappy, and somewhat depressed. Even with the perfect marriage, a loving, caring husband and three great kids, inside I felt alone.

One day I ran into an old friend from middle school. We talked, and she mentioned that she and her man were not together anymore because he wanted things that she didn't. I asked, "Like what?" She responded that he wanted to have a threesome. My mouth dropped. Then she said she would love to be with another woman but did not want her man to do so. When she said another women, I felt so free. I wasn't the only one! She said she believed it was natural for women to be curious about sex with another woman. I took a breath and told her that I have been curious as far back as I could remember.

We got off the subject when the food arrived at the table, but made plans to meet the next day at my house. When she came over we talked for a long time, then she leaned in to kiss me. I was both shocked and excited. Yes, I was attracted to women, but not this one. She left a couple hours later. Nothing happened beyond the kiss.

When my husband returned from work, he could tell by my face something was wrong. I told him what had happened. He asked me how I felt. I told him the truth. I broke down and told him how I had secretly felt for all of these years. He hugged me and held me in his arms. I felt so loved.

He asked why I never shared my feeling towards women with him. I said I was afraid of losing him. He said, "You will never lose me." He wanted me to figure out if my desires were real or just curiosity. I repeatedly asked if he was sure, and he said yes.

In the next months, I felt like a ton was lifted from my shoulders. I felt free. My attitude was so much better. *I could be me.* I met a woman. We started talking every day and eventually it became sexual. She was also married and we had a lot in common. We both wanted to be with a woman and have friendship and closeness without leaving our men. I talked with my husband a lot and he knew about her and was content with the situation. He always reminded me that he loved me for all of who I was and would never leave me because of my feelings.

It has been almost eight years now. We are still happily married, and I am a bisexual woman. I have great kids and a great husband and wouldn't trade who I am for anything in this world. I am me, proud of whom I am.

I have met many other women in similar situations. We are not alone. I feel bad thinking of all of those years I was so upset and scared. I truly am happy now. And my family is much happier now too as a result. Honesty and communication are the key.

Kim is married and a mother of three.

LIONEL GANBILL
CALIFORNIA, USA

I grew up, like most American men, convinced I was heterosexual. At age 20 I could not imagine having sex with another man. Yet I never felt comfortable with my socialization into American manhood. I despise violence; I dislike arrogance; I always bridled against expectations to compete with other men, especially for women; I've never been interested in sports; I had no interest in taking charge of other people; and in my childhood I liked girls.

I had sensations that didn't fit the pattern. I've always loved to be naked, especially outdoors. It was a turn-on, a feeling of freedom and vulnerability. By the time I was seven I felt sexual arousal not only as an erection but also as an intense anal craving, but didn't guess what might satisfy it. My childhood was so sheltered that I didn't learn how to masturbate until I left home.

I was 20 the first time I had sex with a woman. She was 17 and had been sexually active since she was 14. I loved it, thrived on it. I enjoyed the intimacy and all the skin-to-skin loving every bit as much as I did getting off inside her.

Over the next couple of decades my heterosexual experiences varied from exquisite to so-so. I loved fucking, loved tasting a woman, loved having a woman take me in her mouth. And I wondered what that felt like to her. If I could have managed auto-fellatio, I would have. I think most men would if they could. I began to fantasize about giving head to a man, but when I'd look at an actual guy and try to imagine it, the idea still repelled me.

Then a male friend set up a situation in which he and I would share a bed for one night. In my naïveté I didn't think about the implications until hours before the denouement. When I finally did think about it, I knew he would come on to me, and I knew how I'd respond, and I felt a rush I'd never before known.

When I took him in my mouth it was as if a door opened into the lost half of my sexuality—of myself, really. I met the feminine in me, welcomed it, relished it, and celebrated it. I've had too few chances to repeat that experience, but

I continue to change and to feel more whole. I now believe that masculine/feminine is richer and much less mechanically symmetrical than the familiar yin/yang symbol. I think the feminine underlies all sexuality, including the masculine.

Part of what I experienced in that night of discovery was an ever-deepening serenity that at the moment of my partner's ejaculation became pure solace. Never before had my ego boundaries so completely dissolved. Never before had I consciously felt feminine; never before had I felt submissive. And it was ecstatic and blissful.

Beyond seeing myself and others as a mixture of feminine and masculine in varying proportions, I've begun to feel at ease with perceiving myself as feminine. I'm still playing with that notion. I don't feel as if I was born with a wrong-gendered body. I like my male body, just as I like the female bodies of women I love. Next year I may feel differently, but for now it pleases me to be a feminine man.

Lionel, a senior citizen, grew up on the East Coast and moved to California in the 1960s. He has been a writer and editor, and is now involved in many attempts to make the world a better place socially, politically and economically.

CARMEN L. OQUENDO VILLAR
PUERTO RICO, USA

Queerness was not foreign to me when I was growing up in Puerto Rico. My parents, who were very conservative in sexual matters, never mentioned the subject; however, my closest childhood friend was a gay boy. We both hung out with a young lesbian who worked in a record store and told us that Debbie Harry from Blondie had a dick. I took her comments literally and spent hours staring at the record's cover trying to find it.

Later, when I went abroad to college, I had a lesbian roommate who lived her sexuality in a very open and unproblematic way, which made me view the LGBT option as a very natural alternative. However, I still never thought of it as a possibility for myself.

I first experienced my bisexuality when I was about 23 years old. Until then, I had only dated and been in relationships with men. All of a sudden I received a different gift of love: intense emotional and sexual feelings for an amazing person who happened to be a woman. My feelings for her were of such intensity that I thought I needed to assume a lesbian identity to be true to my heart. I was truly in love with her. Even today I can still say that our connection has been the most intense relationship I have ever been blessed with. However, the label "lesbian" did not last long because my partner was not troubled by labels, which was a great relief to me. If anything, we identified as bisexual women.

Today I consider myself a woman who identifies with women, who connects with women, who likes to date women, but who has not shut off the possibility of finding a life partner in a man. I guess that is what bisexuality means for me.

Carmen is a Puerto Rican gal currently living in Massachusetts. She is a Ph.D. student in Latin American Literature and enjoys foreign languages, films (popcorn a must), salsa dancing and exercise.

JENNY MARTINEZ
ILLINOIS, USA

It's not easy for me to call myself bisexual sometimes, mostly because of my family, culture, and religion. Growing up, I was not exposed to many kinds of difference, so when I first came to college I was surprised at the diversity I found.

Ever since grade school I knew I was attracted not only to the opposite sex but to the same sex too, but I kept those feelings to myself because I was scared. In fifth grade I realized that my feelings for certain girls went beyond friendship. I thought it was normal until I realized my other friends did not feel the same way. In high school I lost touch with those feelings until my junior year, when my boyfriend at the time told me his brother was gay. Finally knowing that there was someone else who felt the same as me, my feelings returned.

I found the LGBT group on campus and started to attend meetings because I wanted to figure out all these different feelings I had inside, and became friends with some of the girls. Some were friendlier than others, but I became attracted to this lesbian who didn't like bisexuals (no one warned me). She really hurt me and killed my faith in the "open" gay community. I closed myself off to the gay community on campus until my junior year when I met a nice girl named Kate. We became really good friends in the blink of an eye. I was so happy to finally be with such an amazing and beautiful woman. Two years later, and through many ups and downs, we are still together. She has helped me feel more comfortable calling myself bisexual. I'm not sure if I will always use the term bi, but for right now it fits. Many men have made me happy in the past and they have changed my life, but I am with Kate and I couldn't be any prouder than I am right now!

Jenny is a 21-year-old Puerto Rican from Chicago. She is currently pursuing her B.A. in Business Management at Northern Illinois University and preparing to work towards a Masters in Higher Education.

EMILE MINTIENS
BELGIUM

In 1955 I turned 18, and left my parents' home and town to attend university in Brussels. I was stuck both in the area of feelings and sexuality and in my learning process and social life, so the doctor in charge of the health service of the University in Brussels easily convinced me that I should start psychotherapy, although this was quite unusual at the time. During this treatment I discovered the nature of my sexuality.

I had first hetero, then homosexual relations. A short flame for a fellow student made me think I was gay. His fears and inhibitions, and his lack of love for me, rapidly put an end to our relationship. After about nine years of therapy, the psychotherapist could not tell me whether I would turn out gay or straight. I stopped treatment at about the time I completed my medical studies. I then worked for about five years in an Arab/Muslim country where prejudice against homosexuality is far tougher than most foreigners realize. A few short-term relationships with local girls appeared equally dangerous. I decided to leave.

By the end of my stay, I had met a fellow countrywoman whom I immediately "liked." She had been married a few months and was already completely disappointed in her husband. We both left, traveling through Morocco and France back to our homeland. We had a really good time together. For the first time in my life I had a real sensation of release. We lived together for about five years. During this period I had no homosexual relations, although I missed these sometimes. Then a casual argument turned violent, and I threw her out of my flat. To my great disappointment she did not try to come back. I started to spend every weekend in Amsterdam where I could spend all my time in gay cruising saunas with no risk of meeting any of my Brussels patients. I had at most two boyfriends with whom I thought I was in love. But that feeling never lasted more than a few weeks. And nowadays, I can hardly remember what I truly felt.

At 40, I decided to marry and have the children I had always wanted. I had an affair with a woman with whom I really enjoyed sex and who seemed to like me too. We lived together two or three years. She got pregnant and we married. During that period, our sexual relations satisfied me. Nevertheless, I started to cruise gay men. To my surprise, having homosexual relations during the day enhanced my desire for sex during the night with my wife. Of course she never knew what was truly going on. I knew from previous experience that women cannot stand the idea of their mate having homosexual relations. I guess the absence of real love led us into arguments. We divorced after five years. Even so, I remember this period as satisfying and even happy.

Seized by anger again, I went back to the promiscuous life I had had in Amsterdam. I met a man cruising; it turned from a short encounter to a ten-year relationship, although the experience was hardly satisfying. We did not live together. Love, tenderness, kisses were still unimaginable for me. Meanwhile I went back to the first woman I had lived with, who had also divorced. She again became the mainspring of my life. But, although she was ten years younger than I was, she died suddenly. For the first time in my life I experienced what mourning meant. For two years I cried whenever I thought or spoke of her.

At 55 years old, I was thrown back onto the meat-rack of availability in the "love and sex" scene, still uncertain of my sexuality. To allay loneliness and idleness, trying to socialize with people similar to me, I launched a group for bisexuals. I fell in love with a brilliant, witty, good-looking young member of the group. For the first time I got aroused just by speaking to someone, by recognizing his smell or remembering his smile. Too late, of course: he fell in love with a younger guy.

The homosexual affairs I have had did not make a strict homosexual out of me, nor did the straight life that I have led make me a heterosexual. My feelings for both men and women are highly fragile and furtive. Exclusively male gay society turns me off. I can have multiple sexual relationships, but love and its chemistry are subtle. Without identity references, without trustworthy experts, without reliable tests, conditioned as I am through family values and taboos, through biased psychotherapies and social pressures, how can I make up my mind?

For so many of us, wherever we are born, raised or spend our lives, there is nobody to tell us who we are, where we belong, and how (if ever) we are going to evolve. There is little space, little tolerance for allowing us to experience our real selves, leaving us to wonder who we are, whether we are lying, and if so, to whom. For many of us, contrary to what is frequently argued, bisexuality is a long flirtation with doubt, lack of self-trust, moral questioning and even suicidal tendencies.

Emile was born in Antwerp in 1935. He worked as a medical doctor from 1962 until his retirement in 2000.

JESSICA AMOS
NEW SOUTH WALES, AUSTRALIA

A woman I met recently says, "You're confused. I'm bisexual." I love it. I love being bisexual...now. For around ten years, I thought I was a lesbian. Then I read Pat Califia's short "The Surprise Party" and I decided I wasn't uninterested in men after all. I met my partner Damian. I left the big city. I moved to Wollongong—a regional town where he lived. For three years I didn't talk about my past and I didn't make any friends. But the more I tried to efface all trace of bisexuality, the richer my fantasy life became. I had mildly odd experiences like this one.

I was late. My shoes clapped along the pavement and into a small Wollongong Art Gallery. I was there for the "Forum on Public Perceptions of Sexuality." In a small room, twelve people in black were seated in comfortable chairs around a small coffee table. I descended as discreetly as I could onto a small camp stool behind a goth woman. The speaker was intense. She had glasses like mine. I felt awkward looking at her. We were alike—she couldn't afford a hairdresser either...words, words, words—her words were succulent—treasures for me—words like Foucault, heterosexual, lesbian, bisexual (together the speakers must have said lesbian forty times). My speaker with the glasses went on—porn, porn, porn, porn, sex, sex, sex, sex, bad dirty outside. Her hands shaped her words and feelings. They quivered, drew arcs, shut invisible doors, vibrated. Her hands—one cupped her face. The other stretched out and she admired it absently...shapely fingers—neat, olive, pale pink cuticles, cream moons at the top, each beside another. She sat in the best blue chair. She said she was bisexual.

She spoke about fantasy. I guiltily wondered what her sexual fantasies were. I looked around. Was I one of the few women there who had had sex with a woman? But surely they all wanted to or had. One of the speakers handed around photocopies of exhibits from the gallery that transgressed the boundaries of "public." "How was the boundary of 'the public' articulated?" she asked in her speech. People looked through the photocopies quickly, the sort of look which says, "I'm just observing, taking note." When they got to me, I wanted to look closely. The first one was a line drawing of a woman masturbating while she sucked someone's cock. All the genitals were in full view. "Obscene" radiated through my mind. Don't look too long, I thought. But I wanted to. This was something I did with my partner Damian when we first met.

"Are there any questions?" the convener asked. I desperately wanted to ask a question of the woman with the hands. Some women talked. The convener asked for further comment. The woman with the hands looked at me. I looked around. I looked at the convener, her face like pillows with a second chin, a smooth forehead, her mouth neat like a rosebud. I couldn't ask. The words would have stumbled out. I wanted to ask her how did fantasy change as it became public if fantasies are usually hidden? I thought of her going back to Sydney on the train tonight or tomorrow.

That night I dreamt I wore a dildo. In the dream I was at a leather party. It was dark. Someone put it on me. But it was curving downwards and I tried to say—Look, the shape is wrong. It was red and laced with gold. I wandered around. There were lots of women and some men there. I began to feel more and more embarrassed. I was clothed in black. The dildo was on the outside. I might have liked to approach some of the women but I was too embarrassed about the dildo—so bright and red and so obviously big and curved downwards.

During those three years in Wollongong, I lived in my dreams. Now I live back in Sydney. This last Gay and Lesbian Mardi Gras I helped out with the Bisexual Float and damn it felt good! I joined the Parade. I carried my banner. I felt so fine. I no longer scold myself for desiring men and women. I am becoming whole.

At 33, Jessica has only recently accepted her bisexuality. She lives in Sydney, where she is working on an MA in journalism for which she has written a documentary script. She has made one short film and loves painting and writing. She works as a nurse.

JUDY PINSKER
ENGLAND, UK/CALIFORNIA, USA

It took me a long time to acknowledge my bisexuality to myself, let alone anyone else. I've been close enough to the heterosexual end of the scale to make it appear easy to shrug off feelings of attraction to women as part of a phase, or something I can take or leave.

I was always attracted to males and females, but I had no frame of reference for my attraction to women. I didn't know how to express those feelings and I felt confused by them, afraid to admit anything. My longings remained dormant until my early 30s when I met a man who encouraged me for his own purposes. We played with several women together, him taking the lead.

After I moved from the UK to the United States, I experienced a long period of adjustment and then a steady six-year relationship with a man. He was horrified when I told him about my attraction to women so I suppressed my feelings again and focused on work.

After that relationship broke up, I met my second husband. He professed to be attracted by my same-sex interests and I never questioned what this might mean for our relationship as it progressed. After seeing a counselor, I finally realized I needed to face my attraction to women and decide how to manifest it in my life. I took the momentous step of finding and attending a local Bisexuals and Friends discussion and support group. I was so afraid to go. I didn't tell my husband until a few days after my first meeting. He was furious. He felt left out and wanted to know what I was doing. Everything was too new for me to explain. It was just something I had to do. We didn't stay together to try to work it out. I needed to explore and meet like-minded souls without having to bring a disapproving husband along.

In my 50s my bi side finally burst out. Self-realization still is a challenging business. I've redefined my choices and embraced change yet again. **By facing truths about myself, I've been rewarded by finally experiencing moments of peace in my soul.**

Divorced for the second time, I wonder why it has taken me so long to accept and celebrate my desire to appreciate both sexes emotionally and physically. I still wrestle with how to live a fulfilling life that includes both.

I want to embrace my bisexual nature and express all aspects of myself with joy. My bisexuality is only one aspect of who I am. It's like everything else…a question of balance.

Judy has a Ph.D. and has published widely in the field of pharmaceutical drug development before turning mid-life to nurture her artistic side. A UK native, she now lives in California and runs a jewelry business while crafting novels with romantic themes.

ANN TWEEDY
WASHINGTON, USA

for two girls from childhood

i.
first there was sheila. her almost
black hair and shock-white skin
were the prayer of snow white's mother
answered, my first worldly
prototype of beauty. in third-grade,
when freckle face down the street
called her fat, i beat him up
even though she wasn't. we met on schedule
at the bus stop. my uncut nails
made it hurt to curl my fingers
in a fist, but it was worth it. i pinned him
to the ground. before i did, he yanked
my hair so hard clumps came out.
at home, victorious with my sore
scalp, i wondered why i did it.

in fantasies, sheila and i ran
away to the woods and i always got
to take care of her, scrounging
food and cooking it on a campfire.

ii.
from fifth grade through high school, there was
my best friend eléna: thick waves of brown
hair, brooke shields eyebrows, and tannable skin
i let myself envy even while our meticulous
god watched me. she wore her brother's hand-
me-down corduroys till the ribs ground
to a sad shine. when her mother screamed
at her for some minor housekeeping
failure or she couldn't go out on a date
without her brother, i wanted to save her.
when she found a boyfriend who ordered
her to do laundry and cook supper, who got drunk

and punched her, everyone said
she could do better. secretly i knew
mankind would fail her: the better
she could do lay elsewhere

iii.
now, when embedded verdicts flash:
not dyke enough, married, bisexual, i remember
the girls i loved earliest,
before we understood what to call ourselves
or what that meant the world would think of us

Ann's poetry has been published in Clackamas Literary Review, Berkeley Poetry Review, The Drag King Anthology, Harrington Lesbian Fiction Quarterly, *and online at* Xcp: Streetnotes. *Ann lives north of Seattle, along the Skagit River, where she works as a lawyer for an Indian tribe.*

XIAO MEI
CHINA & USA

I grew up in China as a "normal" girl. I dated a few boys in high school and college but I always enjoyed spending time with my girlfriends. The first time I ever heard of homosexuality was when we had an English teacher from England. She told us one day that she was surprised to see Chinese girls walking hand in hand and boys shoulder to shoulder on the street. She said she thought those people were lesbians or gays until some friends told her that this is quite a normal expression of friendship in China.

After I moved to the United States, I finally met some real gay people. To my surprise, they seemed quite normal. As I continued to have a "normal" life, I had some very disappointing relationships with men. It was then I became more interested in women. But some women were boring or evil, worse than men, so I had to swing back and forth.

At my first job in the States, I couldn't get along with a particular male co-worker. He always found fault with my work or argued with me for no reason. Later on I discovered that he was gay and jealous of me because I was attractive to the men in the office. I laughed and laughed. But I also noticed he was trying to get my attention too, and it dawned on me that he was bi!

Am I bi too? I think so but I can only tell a few best friends. The last bi friend I met before coming back to China was a Mexican guy who looked obviously gay as he wore earrings on one side and walked in a feminine way. For some reason, we didn't get along at first. One day he told me he really liked his girlfriend's daughter and would be a good stepfather. "Are you becoming straight?" I asked. He said he was confused and liked both men and women. That's exactly how I felt—drawn to both sexes.

As China is becoming more open, homosexuality is gaining more understanding and acceptance. But still bi people don't like to expose themselves except in a small circle. In the old days, if two women lived together, people would call them spinsters. Nowadays, if two young women live in the same apartment, people would think they are friends unless they behave strangely in public. Some girls pretend to be lesbians in the pubs to get attention. Real lesbians know how to protect themselves. I have a public life and a private life. I have had a few lovers but I always have to be very careful—I don't trust people easily. I don't take revenge on men just because some men have hurt my feelings in the past. I don't turn to women just because I hated some men. For me, it's becoming more of a natural thing and it helps keep a balance both emotionally and physically.

Mei, a Chinese native, went to graduate school in the USA and currently works for an American company in China.

JULIEANN
NEW SOUTH WALES, AUSTRALIA

It's hard living a lie and expecting everyone else to buy into it, to understand why and how it is that you can be attracted to both women and men. Now this doesn't mean at the same time—it just means that your heartstrings can be pulled in either direction when it comes to love.

The first of my female encounters, which started me on this quest called life, was at the age of 13. I had a very close best friend. We did everything together. One night she asked if we could kiss. She had been feeling this for some time and wanted to act on her feelings and see if they were real—if in fact she was more attracted to girls than guys. We had always said that if we were going to lose our virginity we would do it together. We kissed just before going out with our boyfriends and we could not believe what we felt: a strong feeling I now know as love. Hence, we didn't end up going out with the boys that night; we stayed home and experimented with our bodies in a way that at this stage of our lives we didn't really know much about. All we knew is that we liked touching each other and that it felt right. We stayed together and eventually dumped the boyfriends. But the relationship ended when she moved back to England, as her parents were involved in the import/export business. I never saw her again. We kept in contact for two months, but after that the letters stopped.

I then at the age of 15 found solace and friendship with the very same boy I had dumped two years earlier. I found myself attracted to him and for the first time I kissed a boy. It felt OK, but I was a bit confused, wondering how I could go from liking a girl so much to liking a boy. A transsexual friend helped me to understand my feelings and introduced me to the world of bisexuality. This friend explained that it was OK to feel this way, but I should be careful who I told about it as it was harder for people to accept bi people. I decided that I was not going to tell anyone. The relationship with my boyfriend lasted for three years until a fatal accident took him from me.

I then moved towns (it was to hard for me to stay where he had been) and met a girl who understood me. We developed a relationship based on sex alone and survived some tough years. I was scared of commitment and scared to come out to my family and friends. "Sharon" wanted me to open up and be honest with myself but I couldn't. My family was pressuring me to marry and settle down and have a family. I was so afraid to upset them that I decided to live my life as my family wanted—the worst decision of my life. So I got married at 21 to a guy I had only known for six months, had a child and divorced, all within three years. I wasn't a well person. I then lost my child when his father and my in-laws said I was too unstable to raise him. At 25, feeling pretty washed out, I moved towns and met another man. He was strong and able to help me through. Still living my life for others in my family, still trying to please everyone but myself, I settled down with him and we now have a lovely daughter.

I have tried to contact my son to regain his trust. He is happy with his foster parents, but he knows that I am here for him.

The moral of my story is to think of yourself, to be open with the people that love you, and to be yourself. I am now stuck in a comfortable but not necessarily happy relationship just to make my father happy and keep the peace in my community. I am bisexual and have lived that way all my life, but people in my family do not understand or know. I live behind closed doors hoping that one day I can find a way to open them and let them all know how I feel and what I want.

EDITORS' NOTE: A few months after receiving Juliann's essay, she wrote again to report that "no longer am I fighting with my family or lying or cheating on myself..... just so you know—I opened that closet and now I am living my life for who I am and not for everyone else."

Julieann is 38 years of age and has had two serious female relationships and two male relationships. She has a daughter who lives with her and a son who lives with foster parents. She is a full time student, mother and office manager and lives in a small mining town.

JIAO TIAN
CHINA & USA

I was born in China an illegitimate child. My grandma brought me up. I moved to America at age 14 and lived with my mother and stepfather for four horrible years—my mother treated me badly, hated my natural father and even wished me to be a whore. My stepsister hated me too and I had to eat leftovers. I longed for a man who would love me and give me fresh food and a decent life. I ran away from "home" at age 18 and never went back.

Luckily I got a loan to go to college in Boston. I worked while in school and made it through. In college I met H—the first guy I ever dated. He was very attractive, but it was hopeless as I knew he didn't love me. Then I met J, a 26-year-old guy with a Ph.D. from MIT. J loved me and spoiled me.

One day H told me that he had a girlfriend. Completely disappointed, I went to New York with J, who took good care of me and provided for me so I didn't have to work. But one day he told me I had to move out because he found a girlfriend that he wanted to marry.

One after the other, H and J destroyed my self-esteem. I found a job and met G at work. We lived together for eight years, and started a successful business. However, G didn't want to marry me either. He even told me he wanted to marry a "better" woman!

I went back to H after ten years of not seeing him and found out he was gay. I couldn't believe it until I saw his white boyfriend.

My heart was broken. Then I met R, a lesbian who had had 14 girlfriends before we met. She was a very successful businesswoman and very self-confident. I didn't really like her in the beginning because in my eyes she was *too* self-confident. Yet life twists in interesting ways. When R started asking me for a date, I rejected her. But she was very patient and persistent. She was sincere and cared about me more than any man in the world.

R and I made love on Valentine's Day that year on an island off Boston. It was sweet, passionate and yet relaxing. After we started our romance, I became "famous" in the New York Chinese gay community.

I'm now back in China doing business and living an "abnormal" life. I know one day I will probably have to marry a man because that's the tradition in Chinese society. But I'm not sure yet. Why should I care about other people's opinion? I'm living my life.

This essay was narrated by Tian to Yang Li. Tian was born in China, came to the United States at age 14, graduated from a college in the Boston area, and currently lives in China. Yang Li is associate chief editor of China Press in New York.

TREVOR
SRI LANKA/USA

The very minute I could leave home, I left. Not across the country, not across the city, not even across the street, but halfway across the world to America. Why? To get far away as possible, so that I could not only pursue my education, but a lifestyle that nobody at home would understand.

Most men who want to knock boots with each other in Sri Lanka prefer bisexuality over homosexuality. Some continue the path of denial after their late teens or early twenties, getting married and living a straight life. Some continue to knock boots with each other behind their wives' backs, or even with their tacit support. So the Sri Lankan gay man is virtually non-existent. Instead a bi culture has evolved in a vacuum. In this culture, gay men take "less masculine" roles such as crossdressing and transsexuality while the "more virile" and "more masculine" man turns to bisexuality. The culture and the society condone such a man in a hypocritical manner as masculine and butch, and consider him the lesser of the two evils.

So where do I fit into such a culture? This is a difficult question. Of course, finding the answer has been a gradual process and at times very painful. I was extremely uneasy living in Sri Lanka. I knew I was "different," not in any flamboyant way that would make me stick out, but in my dating patterns. I would have preferred to date both boys and girls, but where would anybody find a guy who would want to date another guy, especially in Sri Lanka? There definitely have to be some around—if I looked at the right places, but again—where to look? Mine was a protective family. While we had the freedom to visit with friends, go to places and have fun, my parents kept a close tab on whom we went out with and what we did. Sometimes they even read my journals and diaries. Furthermore the upper middle class and the upper class are so close and insular that if something happened within this circuit, everybody would know in a blink of an eye. The best example is my careless, adulterous cousin who got caught cheating when he parked his car overnight in front of his mistress's apartment. The awareness that I was constantly being watched and the difficulty of finding like-minded people brought me to a decision: I would have to leave home. Living under the watchful eyes of an extended family and within a community that expected self-sacrifice for family honor and the betterment of the whole group was too much for me. Should I describe myself as selfish? Maybe. I would rather pursue my individual happiness elsewhere than live in such a demanding and restrictive society.

The culture shock I expected fizzled out once I arrived in the United States. The area where I went to school in upper Minnesota was as conservative as Sri Lanka even though I found a group of like-minded men. The only difference was that I was starting fresh and had no family or anybody who knew me. But still I was cautious about opening the closet doors wide open. Changes were gradual and I tiptoed cautiously. Chat room visits evolved into chatting online and, in time to meeting and dating. Several friendships that started as dates turned out to be full-blown relationships that I wouldn't have imagined a few years ago. It was kind of surreal to realize that I was living an alternative lifestyle that a few years ago I thought was impossible and had discarded as a mere dream. I now felt in control of my life.

Growing up I was adamant that I was born gay, though I never mentioned it to anyone close to me. Numerous people that I dated or got romantically involved with here in America nearly brainwashed me into thinking that bisexuality didn't exist. So what makes me embrace bisexuality? Definitely I'm attracted to both men and women, something that I had been in denial about for a long time. The fact that I want to start a family someday and that I want to meet like-minded women forced me to get over that denial.

Having lived outside of Sri Lanka for five years, it will be hard to readjust to the culture and lifestyle that will be expected of me when I return. It is hard to imagine my family getting used to the idea that I am attracted to both sexes. I believe in myself and know that life is full of choices. Finding the terms of one's sexual preferences is a life-long process and being bi is the lifestyle I have chosen.

Trevor is a 28-year-old medical student who is the oldest child in a progressive and well-to-do family in a large city in Sri Lanka. He is a Buddhist and also learns from other religious traditions.

MELINDA BROWN
TENNESSEE, USA

So you may wonder how this fat and often sassy, pagan, white, sex radical, polyamorous bisexual ended up in Nashville, Tennessee (often called the buckle of the bible belt due to the large number of bible publishing companies here). The answer is easy: I was born here in Tennessee, and though I escaped its conservative clutches for a long while, I found myself falling in love with the land again when looking for employment about five years ago.

Things had changed quite a bit from when I left Nashville in the 1980s, though not as much for the city as for me. I left Nashville a monogamous lesbian with a lesbian partner and came back to it a poly bisexual with a heterosexual male primary partner. **Never in a million years would that transition have been imaginable to my 19-year-old almost-lesbian-separatist self.**

Though I often feel restricted by the conservative attitudes of people here, including those of some LGBT activists, I am glad to be back. Housing is much cheaper here than on either coast. Nashville is becoming more international with an influx of people from all over the USA and the rest of the world. I live within five minutes of Thai, Vietnamese, Ethiopian and Honduran restaurants and a number of Middle Eastern, Latin and South Asian groceries. Plus, we're less than an hour from Short Mountain, Ida and Pumpkin Hollow, three very different Radical Faerie communities.

Our longstanding local LGBT pride event has doubled in attendance for each of the past three years. Two of the largest employers here, Vanderbilt University and Deloitte & Touche, have domestic partner benefits for same-sex couples. Despite this visible community and support, the city council recently defeated an anti-discrimination proposal based upon sexual orientation. Even so, we continue to see progress here.

On the personal front, I was able to be with my sister when she gave birth to her daughter, and I'm living close to my aging parents. I've recently joined a Reclaiming-style coven, and we'll be involved with our local pagan pride day (and that's a whole other coming out in this neck of the woods).

I love the folks I've met at our local bi group and count many of them as good friends. We are all over the political, religious/spiritual and relationship style spectrums, and we are still able to have fun and talk about things that are important to us. And have a great time at our local LGBT pride event!

Melinda is a bi activist in the southeast USA where she's doing her best to unbuckle the bible belt.

SALVADOR CRUZ
MEXICO CITY, MEXICO

Growing up in a province, in a conservative country, it is difficult and complicated to feel freely and without guilt desires that can at times be contradictory, but are very intense and honest.

When I was fifteen years old, desire—primarily sexual—presented itself to me in a palpable form: desire for women, for men. Opportunities were few, and the external pressures were overwhelming. In my city, the option to have both was nonexistent. The sanctions were frightening, and the ridicule, the rejection, and exclusion were evident. It was necessary to define oneself and follow the only existing "path," that is to say, to be heterosexual, or to follow the road of social transgression and be homosexual, with its corresponding costs, the stigma of being different. Erotic desire wasn't only my need to share with women; I also felt affection and tenderness. Why was it necessary to decide on only one of the two sexes? Why separate desire and emotion by sex/gender? My relationships with men took a sexual form: cold, quick, and with no emotional component. In my experience, relationships with men have never been characterized by deep affection, caring, and commitment, but I also consider it wrong for women to have to take responsibility for the emotional side of life. Through my own experience, I understand what a tremendous influence social pressure has on our experience of passion and tenderness toward other living beings; it controls all of our emotions, obstructing, for each of us, our basic humanity. Nevertheless we learn to live and to adapt to a world that is less than ideal, and we continue forward, living and giving love to the people we come across in our daily lives.

Salvador is a graduate student in Mexico City.

SENSPA
UGANDA

"Are you bisexual?" Ask this question on the streets of Kampala today, and you will more than likely get a puzzled frown. "Bi what?" It is not generally known what a "bi" is.

Ask whether one is homosexual, if you are unwise enough. You may be hit for daring to insult a person's sexuality. That term is known. The general public holds it in contempt. The papers and radio ridicule it. The (Anglican) Church of Uganda is at war with this "vice."

"Men who have sex with men"—a newer term, encompassing both—may be a more apt description of us. We are believed to be homosexuals, though in reality and practice, quite a few of us are bisexuals.

For a lifestyle that is socially condemned in Uganda, there is an incredible show of interest in it, judging by the amount of press the issue generates at the moment. Most columnists mention us to deride and condemn. We are considered only fit for prison, and ridiculed. The Church is particularly riled at us, especially since one of their own, Retired Bishop Senyonjo, had the courage to say he did not think it was "wrong"; and since the American church province elected a gay bishop.

Positive voices are few and far between, and they rarely get positive press. The political stage is not yielding, too. Once the president, in a heated speech, railed at "homos." He ordered the police to "hunt down and imprison them" (the penal code punishment on the books is life imprisonment). Only after an international furor did he rescind his remarks, though he made no such retraction in Uganda.

Growing up bi in such an atmosphere is not easy.

Growing up is tough. And it is tougher when you are different. Being bi is different. Being gay is different. Yet we grow up what we are. Our minds, our bodies are true to ourselves, true to our feelings.

Quite a few of us suppress the "condemned" feelings. We may want to express them; necessity decrees a lid on them. Physical contact between pals and friends of the same sex is a matter of course in Uganda. Friends touch, hug and hold hands, even on the streets. To those of us with a secret desire for more, suppression of emotion is the cross we have to bear.

One can adapt. One can get the needed contact. The straight world is open, and noisily big. In comparison, other orientations are unseen, hidden.

Yet we do exist in Uganda, and have been very adept at adapting in our beautiful homeland. To the general public, homosexual relationships seem unimaginable. The public is hostile, so we Ugandans of a different orientation have developed well-practiced camouflage. We blend in, we merge into the general background, and we do thrive. To have the appearance of "normalcy," we pretend to be straight in public. We date the opposite sex. For the guys, we beget a few extra-marital children, as is the norm. We then get married, happily consummating one part of us. We go to church, and listen to sermons against the vice of homosexuality.

We then leave our families at home, and move to the other world, filling the emotional needs of our hearts. We move between two worlds, one hidden deep in another, unable to be acknowledged. To own up to this in public would be suicide.

Camouflage is easier in Kampala, a bustling city of more than two million and a melting pot of multiple tribal groups. It is harder in the rural areas. It is presumably much harder for exclusive homosexuals, who have to go the "bi" route. We all face clan pressure to have children, to make the clan and family bigger and stronger, and to blend in and appear normal.

Harsh choices? Maybe.

Are we cowards not to stand up and be counted? Maybe, again. And maybe not.

Ugandan society is not insular to the changes occurring in the rest of the world. Social tolerance, and acceptance of different lifestyles may not be present now, but the dialogue caused by our presence will continue. It may not happen in my lifetime, but acceptance will come.

Senspa (not his real name) is a Ugandan living and working in Uganda. He has experienced the different conflicts and pressures expressed above.

NANA KWAME
GHANA

One man who has managed to live a happy life in Ghana is 36-year-old Nana Kwame, an educator. "I would not say I'm full gay because I still have some orientation towards women," Nana said. Nana is bisexual and was married for almost 17 years. He is now divorced and has three children.

Nana realized his preference for men when he was in secondary school form four. "When I went to the university in Cape Coast, I realized that it was not me alone who was gay, but that there were many other people," Nana said.

"I have not encountered any problems with the community or the law because I have a permanent partner that I have been living with for the past three years. The problem arises when people have to go hunting for partners," he said. Nevertheless, Nana feels that he must hide his lifestyle for fear of discrimination: "When someone in Ghana gets to know you are gay, his mindset changes. He looks at you as if you were evil."

Nana also admits that he is afraid of losing his job as an educator if he were to come out in the open. "I need to hide that part of me. I have been extra careful," he said.

Nana stressed that being gay or bisexual is not a choice. "They think we are evil, but I think it is neither here nor there. If a child is born that way, it is not the fault of the child," he said.

Nana's family does not know he is gay, except for his younger sister. "My younger sister knows and accepts it. She supports me," he said. "People who are gay in Ghana need to be given the freedom to do what they want, free from discrimination. They have a lot of scriptures to lambast you. It takes somebody with an open mind to accept you for who you are."

Excerpted from an article on ghanaweb.com: "Is Ghana Ready for Gay Rights?" 5/6/04. Reprinted with permission.

ZHANG JING
CHINA

Beijing, June 21, 2004
Dear Shen Rui,

The trip to Shanghai was really pleasant! The most interesting nights were those two when you were our companion. We talked as our thoughts flowed, as the train headed either toward Shanghai or back to Beijing. That conversation on the train among three women condensed then released our experiences—a really good feeling.

I believe that most people in Mainland China would not think that the word bisexual relates to their lives at all. Scholars and the masses have very different understandings of the word. Even different scholars have different layers of understanding and knowledge about it, but the concept has not actually received significant attention. Its definition is unclear.

To reflect upon the issue, I asked myself, "Have you ever loved women, as well as men? With what kind of sexual desire is this love associated?"

I have asked myself this question before, but not as a serious matter—it was more or less as a "joke." Sometimes I ask questions like this to understand my experience growing up or to see the experience from different perspectives. I would like to recall my past experience to you whom I trust, and share my feelings.

When I was four years old, my parents sent me to a kindergarten where we had to take a nap every day. Unlike the other kids I was full of energy and did not want to sleep at all. However, I wanted to be obedient, so I lay there pretending to be asleep. After the teacher passed my area, I would open my eyes and daydream. One day I did an extraordinary thing. It is quite embarrassing to talk about the thing I did! I discovered that the girl next to me was also not asleep. She seemed half-asleep. Over the bed bars, I opened her legs with my trembling hands and studied her private parts. In fact, I had a wish for quite some time to see my own private parts, but I found it quite difficult. I neither thought to use a mirror, nor felt it to be appropriate. So, on that particular day, I did it. I felt quite excited, touching her body gently. That part of a girl's body was not as beautiful as I thought it would be. It was not white with purity. It was not lovely pink. It was dark red and had a strange smell. My touch kept her awake, and she turned her head, looking at me calmly. Her sense of calm seemed to encourage both of us. It seemed that we were not doing anything criminal, but just playing. Then, her hand pushed my hand away, so I turned my back to her, hoping she would do the same to me. But when I looked at her, she seemed to have fallen asleep already. Suddenly I, too, became very tired and fell asleep as well. It seemed that I was satisfied after finishing a task.

I had not thought about that event until we had talked for awhile in the train. All of sudden, the memory came through and I remembered. In retrospect, I believe that I was quite brave back then, and now I find that I am actually quite grateful to that girl of whom I have no memory except her private parts.

Her silence protected me. Otherwise, I would have been ashamed, both publicly and personally, for the rest of my life.

I really wish to thank her! Really!

Another thing I did not want to recall was also meaningful to me, though I do not feel that good about it now.

My high school was an all-girl school. Though we had just reached puberty, we did not feel that sexually frustrated, since everyone wanted to study hard. I was the chair of the students' association of the school and the class monitor. My grades were always among the best, so I was the favorite of many people. I was modest enough and knew how to behave appropriately such as "praising of others for everything and blaming myself for anything wrong" or "getting along with everyone and being a friend to all."

In our class, there was a girl who was good at sports, especially track. She had long legs. I seemed to instinctively like long legs very much, so I became a good friend of hers. She became my most trusted confidant and I gave her many favors. For example, I offered to help her study and brought her with me when I went to participate in my activities. When we went to lectures I always sat next to her. Other classmates all knew that "she and Zhang Jing were good friends." We never heard any whispers about homosexuality, and I was such a good student that I would have found the concept, especially if it involved me, horrifying. Sometimes I would touch her arms and feel love for her. I admired her running figure so much! For a while we both indulged ourselves with this relationship. Looking back, I am not sure if she knew what the nature of our relationship was, but I was just happy to be all over her.

We broke up. It was a winter day. She hurried into the classroom. Her nose and ears were red, and snot was smeared on her face! I suddenly felt that she looked too shabby and dirty. I felt terrible, as if I had just eaten a fly! From then on I refused to talk to her and stopped all intimate behaviors toward her. She was shocked and could not comprehend what was wrong. I did not want to tell her what was in my mind, so, we became distant to each other. After a while, we treated each other like normal friends again, but our intimate past made the loss unbearable for me for a long time.

As of this writing, I am getting along very well with my current boyfriend of one year plus, though we have had some fights. We can do things and reflect on our relationship in an interactive way. We feel the other is as important as a family member.

Looking back on my experiences with the same sex, I realize that I could be attracted and express my feelings to a person, no matter their gender, as long as the person is beautiful and attractive to me. Because of Confucian tradition and education, we only can have feelings, but no action. I believe that the love coming from the heart of an individual is like a seed. If the environment is friendly, the seed of love could grow. The love for an individual can ignore the other's sex. Human beings do not have natural sexual tendency toward the opposite sex. It is education and socially and culturally accepted norms that make us so. Everyone is a mystery. Each individual is different. And the original desire in our body still needs to be studied and understood. Therefore, I support heterosexuals, as well as respect and support homosexuals and bisexuals. I think that everyone has the potential to be bisexual. That is my supposition.

Thank you, Shen Rui. You helped stimulate me to discover myself a bit deeper. Telling you the stories is also a pleasant thing! How good I feel. At the age of 25, I show my strength again!

Best wishes for your trip to Beijing!

With Love,

Zhang Jing

AMY PAYNE
INDIANA, USA

Growing up, I was aware of only two worlds: the straight and the gay. But when I was 24, I dated a man who bent that concept. He loved me, yet was physically attracted to men as well. It greatly intrigued me and somehow also seemed very natural.

Soon I realized that I too felt drawn to both men and women. I told my boyfriend, and later the man I would marry. Both readily accepted this part of me, but for the most part I kept these thoughts buried inside. I wasn't completely comfortable having these "gay" thoughts.

It wasn't until I moved away from my family that I began

to explore my other side. Around this time I first heard the word bisexual and its meaning. Some ten years after my first same-sex attraction, I finally had a word to describe myself. **This was the middle ground I never knew existed.**

Still, I wondered whether I was the only bisexual in Indiana. I searched the internet and found bisexual.org, a chat room with bisexuals from all over the world! These people became my community, my support.

Much has changed since I first found that website. I have now experienced women both physically and emotionally. I feel comfortable in my own skin and embrace the bisexual label. I was instrumental in rekindling the local Indianapolis bisexual support group in 2002. Currently I am one of the main organizers of Indy Bi-Versity.

Also, I discovered polyamory. I have maintained my beautiful relationship with my husband while also loving another man, who lives in Toronto.

One more important change has now occurred. In 2002 I finally got the courage to come out to my then 17-year-old son as both bisexual and polyamorous. He immediately accepted me and thanked me for trusting him enough to tell him the truth. Finally, I have complete freedom in my own home.

Amy is 38, happily married, and thoroughly enjoying her life as both bisexual and poly. She is an active leader of Indy Bi-Versity.

TOÑO
MEXICO CITY, MEXICO

When I was seven years old, I remember looking at my mother's magazines: *Vanity Fair, Cosmopolitan* and others like that. My penis was completely erect and I stared at the photographs of half-naked men and women advertising different products; I liked to imitate both. I would take off my shirt and I would strut like a macho in order to then strip completely and wrap a towel around myself striking a feminine pose, simultaneously feeling something vague for both…it was not until I turned twelve that I fell deeply in love with a female classmate who was popular, fun and intelligent and I started to have sexual fantasies involving her. Shortly afterwards, I had my first experience with a man which was very pleasurable. It was then that I learned words like homosexual, bisexual and heterosexual and I even classified myself in this last category since I thought that the person you fell in love with was most important when it came to identity. Three years later I fell hopelessly in love with a man ten years older than me and whom I saw only once at a mall, where we talked for four hours. He told me he was openly gay and had just broken up with his boyfriend; it was only then that I realized you could date someone of the same sex. I then began to doubt my heterosexuality and thought that I was really homosexual, but shortly afterwards I had my first sexual encounter with a woman and loved it…then I began identifying as bisexual.

At twenty, I entered the gay scene and was fascinated by it. Five years later I started to identify as "gay bisexual" which does NOT mean that I like men more than any other gender or that I have eliminated women as a romantic option. (I have spoken to other people who identify the same way and do so precisely for this reason.) It means that I feel that I belong to a "gay community" and that I would like to build a "bisexual community" and that I want to alternate between both and that if I have a relationship with a woman I would like it to be outside a heterosexual framework.

I had an excellent therapist who helped me with various aspects of my life but who unfortunately was biphobic and thought that I should identify as either gay or straight. The straw that broke the camel's back was when I began to tell her about my transgender experiences (I liked to dress in drag occasionally and for political reasons I am about to stop identifying as male).

My attractions have co-existed since I was 16, and although sometimes I like certain types of people more than others I don't stop liking the others, nor do I ignore them as romantic and sexual possibilities. At twelve, I liked feminine women a lot more than anyone else, at sixteen it was effeminate men, at twenty very masculine men, currently I prefer androgynous men and women, and I hope this keeps changing throughout my life. In the last two years, transgendered people have begun to catch my attention (before they didn't). I pay a lot of attention to genders and like them all. I am excited by the masculine (in men, women and trans) and the feminine (also in men, women and trans). I have had monogamous romantic relationships and been sexually polygamous with men, and I would be willing to be in a polyamorous relationship (with myself and/or my partner having several significant others not necessarily of different genders). I think it all depends on the circumstances. For the moment I don't have a particular preference. I don't believe that men have something which woman don't or vice versa, and I don't like dividing the world up into men and women. I like people who are strong, independent, sensitive, educated, intelligent, sensual and sarcastic, and I look for these traits independently of gender. I currently have a tendency to look for feminine men who want to be protected and conquered and for independent and daring women as partners, but I think this tendency might change in the future.

Toño is a 26-year-old student of psychology who lives in Mexico City.

RAYMOND SCOTT
CALIFORNIA, USA

In primary school, I realized that I was attracted to both females and males. Fortunately, my early crushes responded in a positive manner. Thus, by the onset of puberty, I was very comfortable embracing bisexuality. But those in my gay environments were not, and I simply found it easier to label myself as gay within these contexts.

I came out as a gay male shortly after puberty and at that time found out that my sister-in-law was engaging in a covert same-sex relationship. She subsequently helped me to begin to find ways to negotiate my bisexual attractions despite my overt adoption of the gay male identifier.

As a young adult, I began to seek out bisexual experiences and began to find more emotional and psychological balance in my life. I eventually married and received support from my wife to engage in a polyamorous relationship. Unfortunately, the marriage only lasted for six years. Since that time I have remained single, allowing myself the freedom to explore the diversity of my attractions and desires.

Raymond is a licensed clinical psychologist, researcher and educator who focuses on sexual identities, diversity and critical theory.

RON OWEN
ARIZONA, USA

In 1977 I was a student at UCLA when, after years of struggle, I came to the conclusion that I was bi. In 1981 I met a wonderful man who felt the same way and we both decided then that our ideal was to have a relationship with a woman or two women. We were incredibly fortunate to meet a wonderful woman in 1990 and all fall in love. In January, 1991 we celebrated our commitment with a union ceremony among friends. Unfortunately, our family did not attend—it was more than some of them could accept. One of my sisters, in particular, has not spoken to me or my partners since 1990.

We have been blessed with two beautiful children who were born at home and are being raised with three loving parents. They have grown up knowing that they have a special family and our older son is able to distinguish prejudice and bias. We had another encounter with direct biphobia when our son's best friend's parents learned about us and banned him from ever coming over to our home to play. Teachers have been very cool about it when the three of us show up to parent-teacher conferences.

In 2001 we celebrated our Tenth Anniversary Re-union ceremony, officiated by the minister of our church. We came together out of conscious intention and feel that we practice conscious parenting to create our ideal family. I don't think we could have reached this stage without the foundation offered by the bi support group networks that started in the 1970s. They created a movement of human consciousness beyond anything the world had ever known to that point.

Ron has been a bi activist since 1980 and attended the March on Washington in 1987 when the first group of bi activists from around the country gathered. He also founded BiNet AZ and ran BiNet LA in the late 80s. He has spoken at conferences and college campuses to let people know there are many lifestyle options available.

ROBYN OCHS
MASSACHUSETTS, USA

Robyn and Peg

Funny, my bisexual life, when viewed as a snapshot, doesn't look particularly bisexual. I have always been monogamous in my relationships. It's not a "moral issue" for me—I'm fully supportive of my friends who choose other options—monogamy is just what works best for me. Peg and I have been together for eight years now. We married—legally—on May 17, 2004, and we intend to stay together. To the onlooker, we must look like just another lesbian couple.

My life only begins to "look bisexual" when you pull back the camera and see the broader landscape of my experience. Looking over time, you see the long string of boyfriends in high school and in college. In college I fell head over heels for a woman, who to this day still doesn't know! But I did acknowledge—to myself—that I had both same- *and* other-sex attractions. Then, at 23, my first real live Girlfriend! From then on, it was serial monogamy: another woman, a man, a woman, a man… This was followed by six years of intentional celibacy, a condition I fondly refer to as being in a primary relationship with *myself*. Then, at age 38, I met Peg.

People sometimes ask whether I miss being with men. My answer: no more than I miss being with any of my former partners. I miss Pat's eyes, Chris' voice, Woody's sensuality, Fred's intellect, Shawn's intensity… But what's past is past, and I'm happy to be where I am, in the present. I'm grateful for each of my past relationships, even the ones that were difficult, because I learned from each of them, and each has influenced the person I am today.

It doesn't matter what my future holds. My story will always be a bisexual one. And I have identified as bisexual for 29 years. So far…

Robyn lives in Boston, is legally married to a woman and is the editor of this book.

YASMIN GREENHALGH
NEW SOUTH WALES, AUSTRALIA

Phase: a period that can last an entire lifetime"
Bi Dictionary — www.bi.org.au

1991. Murwillumbah, small service centre town, camphor laurels and clover chains, hare krishnas and banana farmers, hitchhikers moving through cane fields, second generation hippy girls in velvet skirts attending monthly movie sessions at the Civic Centre hall. I spent my time walking round the quiet downtown, dawntime streets. Shops shut, old dudes normally found propped up at Murrays' Bar out walking greying mongrels. A couple of keen bike riders spinning through, the buzz of tires and voices ringing down the street. Watching one of my best mates doing his tennis training in the nets at Knox Park.

I remember calling him aside one day, in the backyard near the chookshed [chicken coop]. I though it best to talk to him rather than to my female friends, just in case they freaked out. I'd been getting these mad crushes on a few of the girls. I mean, I'd had plenty of crushes on girls over the years, and a couple of boys, but this was serious…these were friends…this could mean more. He said "Look, we're only young and this sort of stuff can come up at our age. We're just working out life." I was 15 years old. I gave it a week. Then found him in between classes one day and told him, "Nah, it's not just a phase."

2004. Newtown, inner-west suburb of Sydney, an alternative hub, small streets packed with parked cars surround a bustling King Street with its cafés and pubs and the 'funky' clothing and homewear stores commonly found in gentrifying areas. People greeting familiar faces from last night's party, clutching coffees in cafés, dogs at their feet.

Sitting with my own caffeine, I'm thinking about the emails I should probably write when I wander home.

An ex-girlfriend asked if she could drop in for pre-drinkies and dress-ups before Hellfire next week. We're still friends, but I haven't seen her since we broke up. Damn, she was good in bed. Wonder if there'll be any pangs?

Need to check in with an ex-boyfriend, father of my puppy dog. Been missing my pup like mad since I moved out and the time is ripe for another access visit. It'd be great to see them both. Love my boys. Wonder what's he's up to on the long weekend?

Then there's the new boy, the new maybe. Only saw him yesterday and my head is fuzz and my cunt is sore. Bet his is, too. Damn FTM dream-boy. Am really trying hard to not fall. I can feel weakness in my resolve, though.

But I need a space away from relationships, to be myself in the world away from the buffering comfort of partners. A place where the only justifications I have to make about attractions and lovers are to myself.

A decade and a half on, I know the certainty of myself. Bisexual. Sometimes a partner, often a lover, always a friend, refusing to discriminate along gender lines.

It keeps my brain ticking over. I'll never get bored.

If this is a phase, I don't want it to end.

Yasmin is a librarian in Sydney. Best described as a micro-activist with no sense of politics, she prefers to work on building the bi community on the social level. She's 4'10", is a switch, loves mermaids and old maps, and has a lot of fuckable friends.

Alex Hirka

Chapter V:

Crossing Lines

Bisexuals by definition cross the social lines drawn around sexual orientation. But we are so much more complicated than that. We cross lines of race, culture and ethnicity; we cross lines of gender; we combine identities derived from all aspects of our lives (work, family, politics, religion, geography, and others). All of us, bisexual or not, have diverse identities; no one is defined by only one aspect of their life. This chapter explores the intersection of identities—how different aspects of one's self combine, abrade, affect and reinforce each other.

Many bisexuals are biracial or bicultural, and many are also transgender, genderqueer, or otherwise blur gender lines. Robyn and I see a natural overlap between these groups, all of whom blur boundaries or insist on complicated, less dualistic understandings of our lives. In this chapter, many writers find parallels between the pressure a black-or-white world exerts on their own complicated identities and biphobia. Others write about combining a bisexual identity with other deeply-rooted parts of their selves—race, culture, or another vital aspect of who they are.

These essays demonstrate both rebellion against labels and the desire to reshape them. Boundary-crossers (bisexual and otherwise) are often eager to expand or stretch our existing language, transform the meaning of familiar words, and make them more comfortably fit our lives.

Those of us who cross lines are often asked to choose or prioritize our multiple identities ("Which are you first? Black or bi? White or Chinese? Straight or gay?"). It can be painful to pull disparate identities together in the face of external pressure, but our contributors largely resist these relentless demands. Instead, they persist in seeking wholeness and integration, a place for their full selves.

These pieces, from Australia, Finland, India, Ireland, the United Kingdom and the United States, speak to the messy realities of human experience, which transcends boundaries.

—Sarah

AHIMSA TIMOTEO BODHRÁN
MICHIGAN, USA

was ich bin

for Aurora Levins Morales & Lani Ka'ahumanu

i am the jew   el converso   un judío árabe y africano
ein jude   the sefardí/ashkenazi who does not go ta synagogue
not even on high holidays   who lights shabbat candles in
silence every friday night   not knowing why   bcuz he wuz
hidden   he is a secret   a geheimnis only now unfolding
who hears the shofar   distant   against a backdrop of stars
points of light which guide his people   their lives lived in
exile   along their eternal journey   home
　　i am the catholic   the christian red-headed green-eyed altarboy   irish
priest-in-training   the curandero who does not go ta confession   bcuz he has
nothing ta confess   save his life   which is apparently worth little   here   or in
the hereafter   but who builds altars ta his ancestors in his room   their pictures
on the wall   candles lit   incense burning   offerings at their feet   next ta a
crucifix he himself built   who crosses himself each time an ambulance goes by
a firetruck   a church   each time he hears the passing   of a friend
　　i am the person of color   mestizo   blanco   café con leche   leche con
café   who does not remember racism except his own   bcuz he wuz told he wuz
white n believed it   whose family pulled him out of the sun for fear he would
turn braun   como chocolate   como su papá   como sus abuelos   calling
him el puertorriqueño   making him ashamed of his round body   olive und
braun   who tried ta wash his color away   his mamá always wondering why he
took so long   en el baño   the water always running down   the drain   but
who now longs ta b dark   darker   who waits for the sun ta kiss him   braun
him   burn him   yes burn him   but who does not hate the winters that   pale
him   as he once did
　　i am the queer   the bisexual   el joto   una mariposa   who does not
want ta march in pride parades or go ta bars or meetings or sign petitions   but
instead spread his wings n fly   bcuz he has no name for his love save hers or
his or theirs   nor does he want any   who does not date white people n them
infuriated by this   it being an auction u know n them having already placed
their bid   who just wants ta take care of his gente   his brothers n sisters of color
whom he loves   in whose herstory   he walks   in whose voices   he sings
　　i am the working class person   poor person   struggling person   who
does not talk about class   bcuz the books on marx n capitalism r not written
for him   n he can not afford degrees enuf ta prove   he is an expert on his own
oppression   but who remembers the government food he ate   the bougie white
children he tried ta emulate   who writes knowing his mother can n sometimes
can not   read   who writes knowing besides himself y su hermano y su abuela

y una madrina   no one in his family   reads   whose history   whose traditions
r oral   spoken   n remembered

    i am the disabled   the dyslexic   sin ruedas   who does not use wheelchair
ramps bcuz he can walk "fine"   but with words he has trouble   it is books n
forms   assignments n conversations   that r his barriers   whose disability is
invisible   except ta others similarly blessed   whose gift it is ta always come up
with new words   new ways of speaking   being   the likes of which the world
has never seen   nor heard

    i am the person   who does not fit in   who is alone   who is many   who
is legion   who blends in   who sticks out   who speaks out   bcuz i am often
denied community   i have no home   save this body   n even that   is under
attack

Ahimsa's award-winning work has appeared in Revolutionary Voices: A
Multicultural Queer Youth Anthology, Male Lust: Pleasure, Power, and
Transformation, A Different Path: An Anthology of the Radius of Arab American
Writers, Off the Cuffs: Poetry by and about the Police, *and* Dangerous Families:
Queer Writing on Surviving. *He is a Ph.D. candidate in Rhetoric and Writing at
Michigan State University.*

BEVERLY YUEN THOMPSON
NEW YORK, USA

<u>*Check One Only:*</u> White // Hispanic // Black // Asian or
Pacific Islander // American Indian // or Alaskan Native.

    In grade school, I agonized over which box I was
supposed to check off on their forms. As a child I inherited
my father's last name. Was I also to inherit his white skin
privilege? Or, should I consider myself my mother's child
and check Asian? The four boxes offered did not reflect my
individual identity—I could not be contained.

<u>*Check One Only*</u>: Heterosexual // Homosexual.

    At seventeen, I began to question my sexual orientation. My roommate
came out as a lesbian and, as I got heavily involved in feminist activism, new
ideas enveloped me. Perhaps I had only considered myself straight by default
until this point.

    Questioning my own orientation, the options seemed less clear-cut than
I had previously assumed. Again, I agonized over which box to check. For
two years I felt uncertain before realizing the existence of a bisexual identity.
Eventually, I learned that the problem did not lie in my inability to commit to

one identity over another; the rules of the game did not fit my reality. I had fallen through the cracks of the binary opposition paradigm of identity. Definitions have to change in order to include those who have been marginalized out of the box.

To fight discrimination, many activists want a clear-cut definition of what delineates an ally from an enemy. Biracial and bisexual individuals too often are placed on the enemy side, charged with passing in the dominant society and rejecting their *true* identity because they won't chose a side. The cost of passing is an erasure of history, a loss of pride and breakdown of the sense of wholeness of identity.

Bisexuals face homophobia from the dominant society as gays and lesbians do. But they also face discrimination from the gay and lesbian community. Some lesbians that I have encountered feel that bisexual women are "sleeping with the enemy." People of mixed races, and others who can pass as white, face a dilemma similar to that of bisexuals. They are in the closet in both communities yet are not accepted into either. One must be either white or a person of color. I am both Chinese and Caucasian. However, neither the Chinese or white community perceives my dual identity. In my experience, the dominant society denies me a white identity, yet Chinese Americans who cannot accept me because of my lack of language abilities and my "foreign and Western" concepts and upbringing view me as white. Both communities view me as an outsider, yet I am both and more.

The horizon must be broadened to include those who identify as "both and more." We must fight against the segmentation of identity that leads to the breakdown of wholeness for individuals of mixed races who are denied by both the white society as well as communities of color. We must fight against the alienation that bisexuals face in the gay and lesbian community as well as the straight world. Sexual and racial purity is an ideal that leads only to division and disempowerment. We must work to create pride around issues of racial heritage and sexual orientation, instead of shame and disrespect.

Beverly is currently a Ph.D. candidate in Sociology at the New School University in New York City. She holds an M.A. in Sociology and in Women's Studies. She has published articles on bisexual-biracial identity and the anti-capitalist globalization movement.

PATRICIA KEVENA FILI
CALIFORNIA, USA

Those of us who are not straight or gay, Republicans or Democrats, willing pawns in the stereotypical map the culture has drawn, serve as a reminder that freedom produces multiple flowers. We are living reflections of genuine human behavior. We do not fit into the box neatly wrapped and packaged. We are full of contradictions and irony. In an era of polarity, when challenge and dissent are rare, to know us is dangerous and courageous. As a transgendered woman who is bisexual, my mind, spirit and my body literally, metaphorically and figuratively embody resistance to polarity. I know that my very existence challenges some transgendered people who experience sexuality in one way and one way only. Similarly, my very existence challenges some bisexual people who see gender as this or that, and nothing more.

Patricia is an advocate, writer and healer, and works as a Development Coordinator for an HIV and AIDS organization in Oakland. Along with other activists, she successfully lobbyied the Oakland City Council to extend non-discrimination protection in the area of gender identity and expression. She is presently writing a book on her life entitled "A Fish in the Desert."

MAYA GANESH
INDIA

He stroked himself languidly and sneered, "You'll never be a lesbian again." I ponder my response to this man whom I so love, wondering if his searing insight is in fact true. There is an entire universe of what I want to say. How do I create words where none exist? I polish and oil the shackles of language every day, but when I talk about sex, desire, gender, I wish I were running free.

I don't think anyone is "essentially" anything—straight, gay, bisexual or the many stops in between. Today I live with a man, after having had relationships with women. I've always known myself to desire girls and boys, men and women; despite lashes of guilt now and then, I was always pretty sure that sensuality was a good thing, and all people radiated it. But I cannot think of myself as straight, or as a lapsed lesbian. Unfortunately (or fortunately), the word bisexual is all that exists to talk about who I am.

Way back in childhood I felt being a girl was something imposed from the outside rather than generated from within. I was aware of being someone in a body, but not necessarily or always a girl's body governed by an intrinsic "female" character. I had a feeling of boyishness too. Both co-existed in a shifting sort of way; I wasn't always in control of how to turn into a boy. Sometimes in dark moments I feel like the boyishness was actually a defense mechanism, an internal way of dealing with the terrors of living in a female body. But in the light, I like to think of the boy being the son my father never had and always wanted. At age nine my cousin and I would spend long summer afternoons in a darkened play room exploring our bodies; strangely, there I can't remember feeling like a boy. I felt like a girl.

The human journey of sexuality and selfhood is not restricted to three deceptively neat pigeonholes. Sexuality is like unopened letters in a messy mail sorting room when gusts of wind force the windows open. Sex is an act that serves as a mirror to ourselves, and not as an end in itself. The world being what it is we tend to get confused about this bit. The Self, the individual, beggars itself to the morality of convention by naming itself and slotting itself.

My notion of sexuality is entwined with notions of self-actualization. I find a space for complicated ideas and fantastical imaginings in the thoughts of Jung and in ancient Tantra wisdom. All of us are both man and woman inside deceptive conditioning exaggerates only one or the other. In some unspoken way I have always wanted to discover and feel both man and woman within me. Is it then strange that I would desire both men and women? Tantra thrives heartily upon contradictions. The most ascetic sects live alongside the most sensual, with nothing more than mild philosophical debate between them. The concept of the omni-erotic and pan-gendered deity *Shiva* appears throughout Hindu, Buddhist and Tantric streams of philosophy and ritual. How unusual for a deity to be created in the form of *ardhnareshwar* —half man, half woman. A dope-head, a rabidly sexual and fiery persona, a brooding melancholic mendicant, he is leader of dwarfish denizens of the underworld. He can magically assume the female form to be sexual with another man, or vice versa. The concept of bisexuality here is about being both, living and loving both, so that you distil something that goes beyond both—that is neither? I don't know—I'm still learning—but I think these powerful and sexy ideas are not exploited enough.

I cannot divorce my sexuality from my Self; it is not an act of genital contact alone. But these are also scary ideas, and sometimes awareness, though magical can be a lonely place. I've been told by calling myself a bisexual I'm being "vague" or "playing safe," or that I'm "actually a heterosexual." On good days I exercise the right to be silent and see myself dressed like a goddess astride a lion with four arms and shining chakras, sending out stingrays from my finger tips. On not-so-good days, I call them dirty names.

Bisexuality is the space I have discovered to be and experience everything that is traditionally considered "bad" (lots of sex, pleasure, experimentation choice, alone-ness), as well as what is "good" (love, intimacy, space, togetherness). In Tantra there is no ceiling on sexual desire, only self-transcendence through super-saturation. Therefore who you sleep with and in what position is really the most basic aspect of your selfhood, and your sexuality is only the first step.

I have discovered that I want to be with a *person* whom I respect and vice versa, a person who demands that I strive to be better, and vice versa. A man or a woman? Either can teach you about yourself; either can give you opportunities to love, care, grow, nurture, be intimate. These are the building blocks of the self, of any journey.

> If they see // breasts and long hair coming // they call it a woman
> If beard and whiskers // they call it a man:
> but, look, the Self that hovers // in between // is neither man // nor woman.
> – Devara Dasimayya, 10th century CE

Maya holds a master's degree in psychology from Delhi University. She has worked with women's nongovernmental organizations on prevention and research on gender violence, women's health and sexuality. Now living and working in Mumbai (formerly Bombay), Maya is a writer and consultant to international development agencies on gender, sexuality and HIV/AIDS prevention.

PHILLIP A. BERNHARDT-HOUSE
IRELAND

For most of my twenty-seven years of life, I did not know the word "bisexual." I was sixteen or so when I first heard it, and in the next few years I found that it somewhat described me. However, since my first coming-out moments almost ten years ago, my own definitions have changed even further.

In the last few years, I have realized that I am not a typically-gendered person, and I think of myself now as metagendered, which would be a third- (or more-) gendered person, someone outside the strictly male/female dichotomy which society so eagerly enforces. This second coming out has challenged my bisexual identity because while in reality most of my attractions are to males or females (both of which I consider the "opposite sex"), I acknowledge that there are more than these two possibilities. So what does this make me? Pansexual? I end up, since I've been part of the bisexual movement for so long now, identifying as "bi-/pansexual." In nearly all respects, I am certainly "queer" as well.

Recently, I've started using the label for my gender identity in a light-hearted way to describe my sexual orientation: **since I'm a metagender, I say, "I've never *met a gender* I didn't like!"**

Raised in Washington State, USA, Phillip now lives in Cork, Ireland. Phillip's articles and poetry have appeared in The White Crane Journal, *and an autobiographical piece on metagender identity has appeared in* Finding the Real Me: True Tales of Sex and Gender Diversity.

ERYNN ROWAN LAURIE
WASHINGTON, USA

the land between

to limn the edges with darkness
stray beyond the end of
the known world

here

where crossroads and boundary
are one
who do you love?

if you dip your hands in water
trickling down
fingers and wrists
wet your lips with what's in your palms
is water diminished?

when you stand between day
and night and look to the morning and
evening star
to guide you
past your own horizons
do you love day or night better?

or do you love both, and the land between?

the center is everywhere
no space between man
and woman
each heart at the center
my heart at the center
the edge and the center are one
in love with both
crossing the borderlands

my feet in the land between

Erynn is a professional madwoman living in Seattle. A poet, writer, musician and all around bi poly kinky Pagan weirdo, she volunteers for Multifaith Works and the Multifaith Alliance of Reconciling Communities.

Note: First published in the Canadian bi-zine *The Fence* in 2002

JENNY KANGASVUO
FINLAND

I have a double identity. I am a bisexual woman who researches bisexuality. I am subjective me, a bisexual—and I am an academic who struggles to be objective, to get a forced distance from her research target. Sometimes it feels that my own identity gets lost between these poles.

I am currently doing my Ph.D. on Finnish bisexuality and change of sexual culture. At 19, when I started to form my bisexual identity, I sought all kinds of information, books, articles and websites on bisexuality. I read books mostly written in the USA or Britain, but they felt unfamiliar. In many aspects American or British sexual culture differs greatly from Finnish culture. On the positive side, Finland has a rich heritage of agrarian sexuality that praises sex, especially female sexuality, which was seen as magical and powerful. Sauna culture ensures that nudity is considered ordinary and the naked body is not necessarily linked to sexuality. Sexuality is a part of normal everyday life. But on the negative side, Finnish sexuality has always been strongly heterosexual. There are very few historic references to homosexuality. Even after the decriminalization of sex between persons of the same gender in 1971, the law forbade "promoting" homosexuality. "The seduction theory," which held that people could be made homosexual by seduction or urging, created an atmosphere in which it was almost impossible to talk positively about non-heterosexualities. The aftermath of this is still evident in the self-censoring manner with which the media handles the subject. Thus when I read books written by Anglo-American writers, I didn't recognize the references to political or popular culture, or share their cultural, political or historical framework.

I failed to find anything on Finnish—or even Scandinavian—bisexuality. There was a tiny little section (less than one page) on bisexuality in a huge research report on Finnish sexuality. The report claimed that as few as 0.3% of Finns were bisexual. On the other hand, that meant there were 150,000 bisexuals scattered around Finland. However, the report mentioned only married men cheating on their wives with other men. It was not quite the picture I had of Finnish bisexuality. I had (and have) bi friends, with whom I discussed, ranted, sobbed drunkenly about the unfairness of dichotomies and heterosexism, or drooled over this or that starlet, singer or person.

I studied cultural anthropology and at some point between hectic seeking and frustration I realized I could do my own research. Hey, there was no information on Finnish bisexuality whatsoever! What a perfect subject for a master's thesis!

My professor (whose expertise was on Siberian reindeer-herding peoples and northern fishing customs) discouraged me, saying that it would be difficult to study such a delicate subject as sexuality, especially when there was no prior research. I didn't care. I was the only student in the research seminar who actually enjoyed—no! loved immensely!—writing a thesis. I prowled the literature, found some information on Finnish bisexuality I had missed earlier—and best of all, I interviewed other bisexuals.

I felt almost guilty, as if the research interviews would be just an excuse to get to know other bisexual people. I had great conversations with my interviewees, or "informants"—the proper scientific term for the people who shared their thoughts with me. I got to hear rants that I myself could have given and interesting points that had never had occurred to me. I was surprised by my findings, and I had to turn some of my hypotheses upside down. I played the interview tapes again and again, analyzed, wrote and finally had a master's thesis that was 40 pages too long (a fact that was fortunately overlooked by the professor, who respected my enthusiasm).

But during the research process I lost something.

I started to research bisexuality because I wanted to find out what it could mean to me and other Finnish bisexuals. Now I find myself pondering and analyzing bisexuality not as a part of me, but as a part of sexual culture, public discourse, a commonly shared net of meanings.

I have begun to question bisexuality as a term, as an identity, and to question my own identity. Is there such thing as bisexuality? Bisexuality is a modern formation of an identity- and individual-centered culture that has emerged in recent decades (or in the past century). Attraction to people of different genders in other cultures and times cannot be called "bisexuality," for the term itself is linked to the culture from which it arises.

I have lost the self-evident nature of my bisexual identity. Once I could define bisexuality, my bisexuality, just as I wanted. I could customize it. Now I'm surrounded by the definitions, discourses, thoughts and experiences I collected during the research process. There is no bisexuality of my own anymore. There cannot be, if I wish to continue my research and keep it objective and valid.

So what and who am I now? I keep saying "I'm bisexual." Is the act of saying enough?

Jenny (b. 1975) is a cultural anthropologist working toward a Ph.D. on Finnish bisexuality. She also enjoys Japanese manga and anime, paints, draws and runs.

RACHANA UMASHANKAR
INDIA & USA

Labels are limiting. The need to pigeonhole identities can be as confining as a total lack of suitable labels. This is especially true in terms of sexual identity and orientation.

I am a 22-year-old married woman from India who now lives in the United States. Being married to a man, I am universally presumed to be heterosexual. Yet, I often wonder if this label best defines me. I am sexually attracted mostly to men. But I do find some women very attractive. These attractions are not necessarily sexual; there is just something about them I find very beautiful. Thus, on a spectrum of sexual orientation where one is a homosexual and ten a heterosexual, I am probably an eight or a nine. Yet in America I cannot define myself on a spectrum. I have to be homosexual, heterosexual *or* bisexual; nothing in between. As a happily married woman, any acknowledgement on my part that I sometimes find women attractive necessarily places me in the only available category: that of bisexual. **But 'bisexual' is a powerful term, and I don't think that my mild attractions quite warrant that label**.

In India, and perhaps most of South Asia, the situation is just the opposite. When I say that I find someone attractive or beautiful, my statement is considered an "objective" remark on the particular individual's physical beauty or compelling nature. No one puts me in a compartment, and so I am allowed to be on my spectrum without the spectrum ever being acknowledged. This lack of acknowledgement, however, proves a serious problem for my friends who have embraced the labels of homosexual or bisexual. For them, the total lack of labels within their religion or cultural background makes them pariahs in their own homes and communities. For the majority of their community, their label makes their identities mutant. It places them off the scale of normality. They suffer a sense of displacement and fear of discovery and persecution for their differences. Any attempt to create new labels meets with fear and hatred of both the proponents and the idea.

Thus I find that both water-tight identity labels, the compulsion to place everyone into a pre-designed category and the total lack of any suitable identity labels create restrictions. I find freedom in neither having compulsively to choose from a few identities, nor having no opportunity to choose at all.

Rachana has just finished her bachelor's degree with a major in Anthropology-Sociology. She lives in the United States with her husband.

TOBY HILL-MEYER
WASHINGTON, USA

I've never felt really comfortable calling myself bisexual. Looking back I realize that a good part of my discomfort was biphobia. I wasn't sure how people would react and I felt a lot of associations with bisexuality didn't fit me. But even as I come to terms with that, I still have a little ping go off in my head every time I call myself bi that says, "Does that term really apply to you?"

When I first heard the complaint that bi means two and there are more than two genders out there, I latched on to it immediately. It gave me great comfort to have an actual reason to dislike the term. It also made a lot of sense. As I thought more about it, my attractions became less and less based upon gender. Instead, they were was based on a person's politics and experiences, and my ability to have an in-depth conversation and connect with them. When it came down to it, I was more likely to be attracted to someone because they were somehow queer than because of their gender. The only gender that I found myself fairly consistently attracted to was tranny boys. Bisexual never really communicated that.

Because people are more likely to understand feminism if they are living or have lived as a variation of female gender, I found myself attracted to significantly few genetic men. At the same time, there are quite a few distinct genders I am attracted to. Some want the term 'bisexual' to mean being attracted to multiple genders (as opposed to two). That's a welcome change, but I somehow don't find it realistic; no one understands when I have to explain that I am bisexual, but for the most part I am not attracted to biological men.

For a long time I found it very difficult to discuss this. I found it difficult to admit to myself, let alone to others, that I am rarely attracted to men because I feared my queer community would reject me. As I have been questioning my own gender I have developed a second claim to the queer community. This has enabled me to become outspoken about these attractions.

For all the above reasons, I have preferred to call myself queer rather than bi. It just made sense for me because I'm predominantly attracted to queers. As I begin to understand the full complexity of my gender, I also realize that any relationship I have will be by definition a queer relationship. Yet even with this seemingly airtight case, my conscience kept nagging me: "Are you sure you're not being influenced by internalized biphobia?"

Internalized biphobia can be rather severe. I was once on a speakers' panel at which one of the other speakers identified herself as "a lesbian, but really I'm attracted to men too, I just don't like calling myself bi because then I get reactions like 'Oh, I was bisexual back in college too,' or 'I had an old roommate that was bisexual for a while.'" It's a sentiment I share. Being an out bisexual frequently means having your identity minimized, brushed off, and seen as not real, or a problem. When a friend of mine told people in her queer community about her new boyfriend, they said, "At least you can still be an ally."

I can easily understand why someone would want to find a term other than bisexual to call themselves in order to draw attention away from the stereotypes associated with it. But that's not what I was trying to do. In fact, the more I learn about it, I'm proud of the bisexual community that has challenged and fought so bravely for other types of queerness to be accepted. I know that the bisexual movement that came before me has made it easier for me to be who I am. However, when I think about who I am and try to follow in that history of being true to myself, bisexual doesn't adequately describe me. At the same time, I do not want to disown this movement that means so much to me. The words of Kate Bornstein in *Gender Outlaw* finally helped me in this dilemma: "I'm living my life *as* a lesbian, with many similarities to some lesbians, but I'm not under the illusion that I *am* a lesbian. It's the difference between *being* an identity and *having* an identity." In the same way I describe myself—as bisexual—it is a name I *have* but it is not who I *am*. I *am* queer.

Toby is currently a student at the University of Oregon and hopes to continue writing about sexual orientation and gender identity for many years to come.

DEEP PURKAYASTHA
INDIA

The Playful Body

Everyday and everynight, my body changes.
It changes its shape and its size.
Sometimes its boundaries are soft and flowing, sometimes rough and rugged.
It feels and thinks differently with the seasons.
In the golden sunlight of the tropical autumn, just after the rains have washed the earth green, my body rides away on a horse, like a prince with a sword in hand.
In the spring, when mango trees are heavy with blossom and the forests are ruddy with the blooms of the 'flame of the forest,' my body sings and dances like an intoxicated bard.
My body is magical. It plays by itself, like a child. Self-absorbed and self-forgetful. All at the same time.
A child, who cannot but play because his mother and father are in passionate embrace within himself.
My body expresses itself as male and articulates itself as female.
It transgresses all the thresholds it was told not to cross. It transcends the limits that others etch on it. It transforms itself in the pink and purple of a million dawns and dusks.

The anatomy and the physiology of the body is not the whole truth. It is not even the whole body.

There are bodies within my body. This body nourished by food.

Bodies of vital currents, of feelings and thoughts, of wisdom and knowledge, of bliss and joy. The surface and the core linked in an enchanted bond. My body is One. My bodies are Many. My body is Plural.

My body is the site of a myriad patterns ebbing and flowing without end.

The erotic body and the ascetic body fusing into a heroic body.

Where man and woman become each other all the time, at the same time, for all time.

Evanescent and instituted, my body can only play. It is certain that it will never give up its spontaneity for other people's cartographic impositions.

For it exists in the unbounded and unending ambiguousness.

It knows no other. For all the others have become my body.

The inside and the outside. The above and the below. The left and the right. The sun and the moon. The river and the mountain.

Fire and water. Red and blue. Earth and sky. Gods and Demons.

What is masculine? What is feminine?

When my body plays, I come into existence in all my ambi-gendered freedom.

My body is unable to express what that means.

If it did, it would cease to be itself.

Born in 1970, and raised in Kolkata (formerly Calcutta), Deep is presently involved in child rights and gender equity activism.

PARAMITA BANERJEE
WEST BENGAL, INDIA

Where does one begin a narrative that has neither a beginning nor a perceivable end, and consists of an ever-flowing stream of events, experiences and realizations—fluid by definition and changing everyday?

Capturing the experience of being a bisexual, bi-gendered woman living in India is by no means an easy task. I grew up in a culture that allows a lot of homo-friendly social space, forbids free mixing of opposite sexes, frowns severely on pre-marital sex and erases terms like "same-sex relationships" from public memory. Homo-friendly social space is that Janus-faced custom that renders same-sex relationships invisible even as it approves hanging out with same-sex friends much more than with members of the opposite sex. This complex reality determined that I never quite explored relationships with persons of my own sex during my growing up years and glided towards compulsory heterosexual behavior. It took me nearly forty years of my life—checkered with radical left politics, women's rights activism, two broken marriages, several broken relationships, chance intimate encounters with women and my work with gender and sexuality—to discover that I am bisexual. Every item I have mentioned here has contributed towards that realization.

Bisexuality means a lot more to me than what it is commonly taken to imply—the pleasure of sleeping with persons of both genders. **Bisexuality for me is primarily an attitude, a way of life, a mindset that privileges plurality and dares to tread beyond narrow one-dimensional binds of identity.** In sexual terms, bisexuality has taught me to revere individual sexual autonomy over any specific collective sexual identity. I understand bisexuality to mean an ability to relate to persons as persons—unconstrained by gender roles and norms, allowing such relationships to traverse different spaces, including the sexual.

That brings me directly to the issue of calling myself bi-gendered. Discovering this epithet for myself has taken even longer than the bisexual tag. By calling myself bi-gendered, I mean to imply that I am neither an archetypal female, nor an archetypal male; neither am I transgender, for I am totally comfortable with myself as a woman—body, psyche, spirit etc. Bisexuality and bi-genderism are inseparably intertwined and together they designate an entity whose identity is fluid both in terms of sexuality and gender.

Finding this identity and living with it has been both liberating and harrowing all at the same time. But that is another story to be told another time.

Born in Kolkata (formerly Calcutta), in 1958, Paramita, is a single mother and the founder-coordinator of Discovering Inner Knowledge & Sexual Health Awareness (DIKSHA), which works with children and adolescents living in red light areas. DIKSHA works with a focus on gender and sexuality, offers life skills education and seeks to create safe spaces for its participants. She is also a Training Officer in a mainstream organization that helps the West Bengal State AIDS Prevention & Control Society manage and mentor interventions implemented through nongovernmental organizations.

BHAVANA CHAWLA
CALIFORNIA, USA

My bisexuality is another carving on the wood that is my soul. It is just as creative and deepened by thought, feeling and intensity as is my cultural expression as a South Asian American woman. During my teenage years and still now, I've pioneered a new culture for myself. I've chosen aspects of being "American" and "South Asian" to form my personal identity as a "South Asian American." I value both the independence that marks individuals in the States and the strong sense of community, sisterhood and neighborhood found in India.

When I came out in my early 20s, I embraced my bisexuality as part of the process of forming my identity. At that time, I was surrounded by many, mostly white, les/bi/trans women. Later that year, many South Asian LGBTs entered my life. I felt I had come home, walked full circle, joined these carvings into one bisexual bi-cultural identity.

I am now in my ninth year as a conscious bisexual woman of color. As I look into my soul I see my diverse and beautiful ethnic, sensual, sexual and gendered markings and feel calm. Then I step out into my wonderful neighborhood of bisexual women, and I watch with joy as our cultures thrive, mixing and mingling like leaves on the wind.

Bhavana, 29, has recently moved with her orange kitty, Adriana Katarina, from Boston to the San Francisco Bay Area to start a new career path. She feels blessed that life is opening up to new beginnings.

MIA ANDERSON
MASSACHUSETTS, USA

The intersection of my various identities shapes my politics. I am a full-figured Black woman of Caribbean descent who is openly bisexual. I am also a spiritual person with a strong belief in divine law and doctrine. My queerness informs everything I do: my creative work, my friends, my cultural tastes, even the radio shows I listen to. I currently live in Boston, and I used to listen to The Tom Joyner show on the Black-owned radio station WILD AM 1050 because I wanted hear a voice and commentary that reflected me and my experiences. Last year, after one "gay joke" too many, I switched to another program on JAMN' 94.5, where there are two anchors of color and the mostly hip-hop line-up caters to a predominantly white audience. It was difficult to switch to white-owned radio station but I didn't want to be subjected to another hour of queer humiliation.

My queerness goes beyond just having intimate relations with a woman—my politics inform all aspects of my interactions with men. Regardless of my sexual and (sometimes) emotional attraction to men and women, I feel no affinity to the female–male relationship dynamic of the heterosexual community. As a woman who is largely defined by feminist philosophy, I find it very difficult to deal with men and their me-oriented way of moving through the world. I find straight women are too willing to foster this male dependency upon women and acquiesce to their needs. I am old-school and still uphold the feminist politics of yesteryear that ask how "we" move through this world, rather than the Western, male, capitalist viewpoint of the "individual."

During the same-sex marriage debate in Massachusetts, the intersection of my racial and sexual identities was painful. I stood next to gay white men with no involvement in queer communities of color who held signs that say "We Will Not Go to the Back of the Bus" and faced a group of straight Black and Latina women whose signs read "No to Gays, Yes to Jesus." In this position, I am cut to the core. These white queers are not necessarily my allies. How many times have you seen queers of color on the cover of *The Advocate, Girlfriends, Out* or *Curve?* Further, bisexuals are always dismissed in the discussion of queer liberation. As a producer in Boston for the last ten years, I have had to work twice as hard as my white counterparts for publicity in our local queer papers. My experiences with white, queer non-profits have ranged from good to horrendous.

Yet my sisters of color would look right past me as I stood there with my sign about "Equal Protection under the Law." My community of color will defame queerness but look past the "queen" directing the choir or the butch lesbian chairing the Community Watch meeting.

I have a paid a high price for being an intelligent, queer woman of color who is self-defined in a world intimidated by this identity. I am proud to be a Black woman. I love our history, music, literature, philosophy, politics and our rich language. Our language continues to shape how the *world* speaks. I love the shades of the Black woman, the way she walks, talks and swings her hips like they are the most amazing spectacle on earth. I am enamored of the Black man and his many hues, the way his voice bellows like he is making love to you just by saying "hi," the way he glides down the street like the earth just rolls beneath his feet—and the easy way he does his "gansta lean" makes me scream.

I am also proud to be queer and if this is a "choice" then I am happy with the choice I have made. I would never take a pill, undergo hypnosis or do anything else to change my identity. I like being in a community that is actually a community.

I feel bisexuality is actually the most spiritually centered of all the sexual expressions. I have an open affinity to all of humanity which does not exclude on any particular physical attribute and allows me to approach each person from a place of wonder.

Mia is the producer, director and founder of Mia Anderson's Drag Kings, Sluts & Goddesses, a 10-year-old womyn's cabaret troupe. She is a graduate of Clark University and The New Theater Conservatory. Professionally she has worked with regional theater companies including Boston TheaterWorks, Commonwealth Shakespeare Company, The Theater Offensive, Zietgeist Theater Company, Theater Zone, and Company One, and with Walt Disney Productions. She is committed to socio-economic justice but still has fun dancing and wearing a sexy thong.

BOBBIE PETFORD
ENGLAND, UK

assume nothing

assume nothing of the rings i wear
one may be from a wedding
or perhaps a cheery trinket from that drizzly afternoon
the other belonged to my dead mother

assume nothing of how i'm named
kind and caustic proper nouns set down to resonate and chime
my place in time and family tree
to position me

assume nothing of the clothes i wear
textured suggestion function expression
yet their inverted dangling on the line belies less
of the dresser than the dress

assume nothing of the dears and darlings the company i keep
cup of decaf laugh weep   in all directions
love's potential shines
though at times in a minority of one
i and i   but i spy
between the sequinned flags that fly
one that flies for we

assume nothing
to know just catch my eye
and ask
perceive for real the complexity

(Inspired by "Jennifer's Badges and Banners" in *Bi Community News*, Issue 47)

Born in the sixties in the UK of coal-mining stock, Bobbie spent her teens lurking in the far left,
in tears at the Rocky Horror Show, *listening to Lou Reed and feeling invisible as bisexual*
amid the separatism of the eighties. Now married with three children and working as a therapist,
she realizes how important it was for her mental health to discover and "come in" to the internet
bisexual community in the nineties. She'd love to live in a world where labels for sexuality are
redundant, but in order to avoid falling into the shadowed chasm between the gay/straight
binary, for now she chooses to call herself bisexual.

VICTOR J. RAYMOND
IOWA, USA

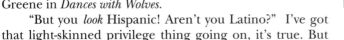

Remember what they say about making assumptions? People do that with me all the time.

"Oh, you're Native American! What was it like growing up on the reservation?" I don't know, having grown up in the inner city of a midwestern American metropolis. The libraries—public, high school and university—were all nearby; so were grocery stores, theatres and restaurants. Being a tribal member doesn't mean I dress like Graham Greene in *Dances with Wolves*.

"But you *look* Hispanic! Aren't you Latino?" I've got that light-skinned privilege thing going on, it's true. But my background isn't *hidalgo* (though possibly *mestizo* if you stretch it). Besides Rosebud Sioux, my other peoples of origin include the Scots and the English. And yes, I sometimes wear a kilt. My parents want to get me a beaded sporran. Bring it on, I say.

"Oh, so you must be one of those *berdaches!*" "Berdache" isn't even a Native American term, and I would not want to use it to identify myself. I sometimes say I am *two-spirited*, but I just as often say I am a bisexual man.

"You're bisexual? I thought you had a partner?" I am, and I do. These things are not mutually incompatible, despite public belief to the contrary.

"But I thought you were married!" Yes, my partner is of a different gender than myself and yes, we did let the State recognize our relationship, mostly because we had seen what had happened with Sharon Kowalski and Karen Thompson. (If you live in the United States and don't recognize these names, you need to do some research and make a contribution to either MassEquality or the Alternatives to Marriage Project.)

"But you mentioned a boyfriend…?" I am indeed polyamorous, and I've certainly been in other relationships in the past. However, my torrid affair with academia has been the only major "secondary relationship" in my life of late.

"So aren't you doing this just to get attention?" No, I'm "doing this" because it is *who I am*. Don't invalidate who I am or what that means just because I don't fit your stereotypes. I refuse to get cut on the edges of the pigeonholes that other people assume I should be stuffed into. I'm "doing this" because I strongly believe that all people deserve to have their identities recognized and respected, no matter their race, creed, gender, or sexual orientation. Not everybody fits neatly into a box.

So don't make assumptions about who I am. Listen first; that way we can have a conversation.

GLOSSARY: Hidalgo: A member of the minor nobility in Spain; *Mestizo:* A person of mixed racial ancestry, especially of mixed European and Native American ancestry. *Sporran:* A pouch worn at the front of the kilt in traditional

Scottish Highlands men's dress. *Two-spirit:* A person, especially a Native American man, who assumes the sexual identity and is granted the social status of the opposite sex. *Berdache:* French word used to describe a two-spirited person.

Bi activist Elise Matthesen once described Victor as "the only Russian-speaking bisexual Native American bagpiper" she knew. All of the questions and comments in quotation marks above are taken from question-and-answer sessions from Victor's participation in speakers' bureau presentations on behalf of either OutFront Minnesota or the Iowa State University LGBT Student Services Office.

ESTHER SAXEY
ENGLAND, UK

Your body is like a blog; everybody bloody reads it.

Do people read me as straight or gay? *Can* people read me as bisexual? And am I a girl or a boy—or have I achieved something in between? I'm dying to know how I'm read. But at the same moment, I don't think I *can* know. There are only ever partial partisan answers, an array of interpretative contexts, no objective assessment. There are public readings: "When you walk down the road with your boyfriend, you look straight." Does that road really go on forever? Does it wind from the town centre off into political activism, plough through my bookshelves and bedroom, while my family picnic on the verge? Am I always walking down it, always holding hands with my boyfriend? It's a bit like the Wizard of Oz.

The road I actually walk down is in Brighton, an English queer/alternative/ student enclave. There's a lot of female masculinity in this city; the inhabitants are genderfuck literate. I would look more butch in Bath or in Bristol. When I walk down this specific road, alone in my grandfather's navy greatcoat, am I read as a student, a queer, a boy, a skinhead?

There are family readings from my mother: "That suit—it looks like you're making a statement." A very confident reading. But I had to come out first; only after that do my clothes make the "statement" that she says she can read there. Mother happily altered my first suit for me, and around the same time she failed to read my crewcut as a declaration. A year later I came out to her; now my skinny limbs twitching in a three-piece are as clear as a slogan T-shirt.

There are friendly readings: When I ask, could I pass as a boy? "Yes," he says. I say, I could wear a baseball cap, it makes one look more masculine. "No," he laughs. Because I'm not a street-savvy, fashionable cap-wearing kind of youth. In the eyes of my friend it would be easier for me to rejig my gender then change my class and culture.

Last week I visited the local museum, for an exhibition on "the dandy." Claude Cahun, Stephen Tennant, Radclyffe Hall faced me with impeccable genderfucked masculinity. My heart pitched. The mirror at the end of the exhibition presented me with myself again. *This is the only place I'll be read in the right context. I should stand in this gallery forever.*

How would I like to be read? A lanky unphysical anachronist fop, effete and dandified and out-of-touch, a bookish boyish bi-ish English librarian. I suspect that nobody will read me that way, and that I am similarly illiterate in reading the careful, nuanced multi-adjectival presentation of others.

In fact, these days, now my hair has grown, I get read as Harry Potter. People point at me in the road and shout my new name. A woman in a pub presses my hand and says "You'll always be Harry to me." He's boyish, bookish, odd and aloof if not queerish. He has his own slash following, that queerest of queer reading practices where straight male characters are rewritten into homoerotic acts. He'll do. I am therefore the bestselling bisexual of the new millennia. And if a bisexual woman approaching 30 can be read as a twelve-year-old fictional wizard, there is hope yet for queer reading.

Esther lives in Right-on (Brighton) by Sea, England; she is writing the Great Bisexual Novel, which she expects you all to purchase.

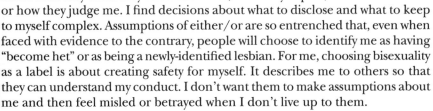

MARY HEATH
S. AUSTRALIA, AUSTRALIA

Some of the students I teach think I'm straight because they have encountered me with a former partner in activist or social environments. Some think I'm a lesbian because they've seen me with my current partner, or in "lesbian" contexts, or because I teach about how the law constructs families to exclude same-sex partnerships.

Bisexuality could be a metaphor for my life. Internally, it all looks fine. I don't struggle too much to put the pieces together. But externally, people constantly mistake the part for the whole. It isn't a straightforward process for me to assess what they think they know about me, what they expect, or how they judge me. I find decisions about what to disclose and what to keep to myself complex. Assumptions of either/or are so entrenched that, even when faced with evidence to the contrary, people will choose to identify me as having "become het" or as being a newly-identified lesbian. For me, choosing bisexuality as a label is about creating safety for myself. It describes me to others so that they can understand my conduct. I don't want them to make assumptions about me and then feel misled or betrayed when I don't live up to them.

Many non-bisexual people think of bisexuality as a split experience of the self. They think of a bisexual as sometimes gay or lesbian (with a side serve of heterosexism) and sometimes straight (with a side serve of heterosexual privilege) by turns. They imagine her sense of herself is split into two pieces.

Sometimes she plays for one team, and sometimes on the other. Sometimes she's on the right side, sometimes she's a traitor. But either way, she is not to be trusted. In popular culture, lesbians claim women who engage in sex with people of both sexes as lesbian if they are well behaved. If they are badly behaved, they are identified as evil bisexual women. Definitely not lesbians.

But the life writings of bisexual people do not reflect this picture of an unavoidably fractured identity. Bisexual people often experience the decision to adopt identity as naming the entirety of their experience as a unified whole. Many of us experience choosing bisexual identity as a homecoming. It allows us to name feelings, experiences, and self-understandings as part of a whole, rather than demanding that we attempt to understand ourselves or explain ourselves to others as sometimes one thing and sometimes another. **In a sense, it is a choice in the direction of unification, exactly the opposite of being split.**

Of course, choosing bisexual identity is not the end of every struggle, but merely a new stage in working out an ethics and politics of self and of community. Perhaps this process has particular pertinence for bisexual women, who claim this identity while being labelled as traitorous, unethical and indiscriminate.

I understand bisexuality as a metaphor for the rest of my life. Other people find my combining activism and a job in a law school strange and contradictory. They imagine that I spend part of my time upholding the law, and part of my time breaking it. Personally, I don't find the consequence of these different aspects of my life particularly contradictory. I experience them as distinct but related components of my life. I don't think of myself as one person at work and someone completely different when I'm facilitating a meeting, running nonviolent direct action training or singing at a community picket.

My life is more about weaving than about splitting apart: bringing together different strands into an overall shape, a changing shape, not readily identified as a simple whole.

Mary teaches law in Adelaide. She trains groups in meeting facilitation, inclusive group process and nonviolent direct action. Her current activism focuses on ending rape and eliminating violence against GLBTTIQ people.

JAMIE PHILLIPS
PENNSYLVANIA, USA

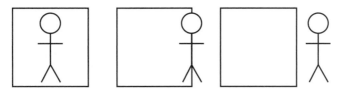

In college, an anthropologist came to talk to our class about thinking outside of the box. He drew three boxes and three stick figures on the board. Like this:

He said that we have a choice. We can either live in the world, outside of the world, or with one foot in and one foot out of the world. He also said it was helpful to be able to shift between all three boxes. I remember that class vividly. The chalkboard was green. The boxes were drawn with white chalk, and the anthropologist was happy. He sounded enthusiastic about these choices.

Today I asked my therapist about my sexuality. She said I could probably be happy in a number of different situations—either dating women or men. I often struggle with the choices. It seems that there are too many of them and I like each one separately. Women are soft, caring, beautiful, smart and strong. Men are bold, beautiful, sensitive and strong. They each have bodies that are nice to touch, whether by hand, mouth, or both arms embraced. When I press my body against theirs, I feel the electricity—tingling, surges and once, both. This inspires me to love them each, body mind and soul regardless of their gender identity.

I guess I want to be with one foot in and one foot outside of the box. My therapist says that's one understanding of bisexuality. I asked her to draw it, but she said it was too complex. She then said I would have to draw it myself, even though I had never seen it before. So I went in search of colors.

Maybe my box would be labeled gay or maybe straight, or maybe dyke or byke, which is the new word for bisexual dykes! But I don't like labels.

So maybe my box is not a box after all. Maybe I will only draw shaded areas of gray, blue or green, maybe watercolors. Smooth like sky—where I am not outside of the box because there is no box.

I told this to my therapist and she said congratulations. I'm me now. No more boxes to step outside of, or into, or to straddle.

Jamie lives in Pittsburgh and is in love with the sky, earth, trees and water. She was a bike messenger for a few months, but tired of the exhaust fumes and now works in the field of adult literacy. She enjoys experimenting with food and dreaming.

Chapter VI:

Relationships

Some bi-identified people are in relationships; others are not. In this chapter, monogamous, polyamorous and single people talk about their relationships in the context of their bi identities, and their bi identities in the context of their relationships.

Contributors discuss desire, coming out to partners and changes in their lives over time. Some have always been monogamous, others polyamorous, and yet others have been both at different points in their lives.

Those who have chosen monogamy discuss issues of visibility and the challenge of maintaining a bi identity while in a monogamous relationship. When in a "lesbian" relationship, does a bi woman become a lesbian? When in a "straight" relationship, does a bi person become straight? The writers in this chapter answer with a resounding "No!" They are themselves, self-identifying as bi, regardless of the biological sex or gender or their current partner(s), if they are even partnered at all.

Those who choose polyamory discuss how they maintain balance in their lives and deal with jealousy, freedom of choice, communication, integrity and maintaining trust and commitment in relationships.

Single writers discuss what they are looking for in a relationship, and the challenges and joys of dating.

Some contributors discuss how their own internal process of self-discovery has affected their relationships; others describe how their partners supported or resisted their coming out. Some discuss the particular experiences and advantages of being in bi-on-bi relationships. We also hear from the gay partner of a bi-identified man.

Contributors from eight countries—Austria, Belgium, Bulgaria, Cuba, Denmark, Ireland, the Netherlands, New Zealand and the United States—share their vulnerabilities and their strengths, their challenges and their successes, their histories and their hopes for the future.

—Robyn

PEGGY SEEGER
NORTH CAROLINA, USA

Being a Gemini, I suppose it was pre-ordained that I would have two life-partners by the time I reached 69, my present age. Ewan MacColl was a dynamic man, as different as night and day from myself in every possible way. I loved and liked him; we worked together, lived together for thirty years and had three children. Twenty years older than I, he died at 74. During that time of grief I grew closer to my friend Irene Pyper-Scott, whom I had known and worked with for 25 years. Twelve years younger than me, Irene is also as different from me as could possibly be. I love and like her. Our passionate love affair rocked any boats that I thought I had moored safe and sound in the conventional harbor.

My children took it well, albeit my daughter less well than my sons, one of whom occasionally refers sympathetically to my "coming out" as if I had always been a closet lesbian and was at last showing my true colors. Not true. I was as heterosexual as a woman could be. I just happened to fall in love with another woman at a crucial time in my life. Neither Irene nor I look on ourselves as bona-fide lesbians even though our relationship is in its 15th year now. We both have the same deep-down conviction that were we to part we might conceivably each enter into a love relationship with a man as likely as with a woman.

Two true loves. Love is love. The lovemaking is of a different nature of course and that quality gives rise to different power structures within each relationship. Each has its constructive and potentially destructive aspects, its expansion and occasional contraction of the ongoing human experience. I will say that having had both types of relationship has given me more tolerance and understanding of those power structures. I certainly now have a deeper understanding of how heterosexism underpins and controls our entire social, economic, cultural, religious and moral world. Because of that I understand why so many heterosexuals are terrified of same-sex relationships and why the establishment finds them so threatening.

I have no more a preference for associating chiefly with lesbians because I have a lesbian relationship than I had a preference for associating mainly with heterosexuals when I was a heterosexual. I understand fully why gays and lesbians need to come out, why "we" need recognition and self-esteem as full citizens but I don't participate fully in Pride events or issues. Why? Certainly not because of cowardice. I do not hide my relationship with Irene. I casually acknowledge it on stage and when media events present an opportunity. I am suspicious of labels, especially those which marginalize and, in the end, disenfranchise the bearer. I did not define myself as a capital H back then and don't feel that I need to declare myself a capital L now.

I've had it relatively easy. I am lucky to have lived in tolerant locations (London, UK and Asheville, North Carolina, USA). I am a singer, thence an "artiste," thence by definition non-conformist. Oddity is expected of artists—it is part of the charisma, the pseudo-glamour. Homosexuality, lesbianism, drugs, drink, multiple marriages, outrageous behavior—folks in the worlds of music, drama, film and various arts get away with departures from "normal" behavior more easily than other people. Being in the arts has been part of my luck. Incidentally, I don't feel "different"—I feel natural.

Peggy is a singer/songwriter whose songs have been recorded on numerous records, most of them made with her first life-partner, Ewan MacColl. She has made 19 solo albums. Her best-known songs are "Gonna Be an Engineer" (a feminist anthem) and "The Ballad of Springhill" (about the 1958 Nova Scotian mining disaster). She lived in England for 35 years and has three children and seven grandchildren. She now lives in North Carolina and tours regularly worldwide.

C.S. GILBERT
FLORIDA, USA

I call myself bisexual because that's what I am. I never had a choice, no more than heterosexuals or homosexuals have a choice; we're born that way.

It's been tempting, of course, to identify my sexuality according to the gender of my partner—until I was over 50, I only had one partner at a time, in turn one man (the father of my children) for over twelve years and one woman for almost eight years. When conventionally "married," it would have been so easy to identify with heterosexual privilege, and present myself as straight. Those were the early years of the modern women's liberation movement, the 70s and early 80s. Lesbian feminist separatists didn't trust straight women much—but they trusted bisexuals even less. Years of absolute loyalty and exhaustive labor won me the respect of my lesbian colleagues in the National Organization for Women (NOW), if not the sort of affection I occasionally yearned for, but I'm ruefully amused that even today my bisexuality is off-putting in certain lesbian circles.

Then came the 80s. Exit Doug, enter Jan. Neither of us brought a U-Haul to the second date, but eventually we shared a home, a life, a household bank account and (uneasily) my children. It would have been comfortable then to call myself a lesbian, especially in NOW. But it would have been a lie. During the Jan years, I usually tried to keep my mouth shut and let people assume what they would, except in conference workshops on bisexuality.

Abracadabra, suddenly it was almost the 90s. Jan departed, announcing that she'd found herself "a real butch." Rather stunned in my eternal naïve androgyny, I looked around and saw my dear, straight friend and drinking buddy of 17 years standing by, always there for me and the children. It took some months, but eventually we developed a sexual relationship. We could have celebrated a 15th anniversary on Valentine's Day 2004, if he believed in such things. Barry (as I well knew) is polyamorous. He taught me a lot. The two heterosexual secondary relationships in which he was involved when we finally got together have ended; I am the one who twice—from 1994-96 and from 2000 to the present—has had relationships with dear and wonderful women even as Barry was primary in my life. I fervently wish my current female love would choose to be co-primary, or would entertain the notion of a triad—she and Barry are very good friends. But no. She is a fiercely independent soul, and I love her even as she is.

I've learned two major lessons from the past 15 years. First, I tend to be monogamous within gender, taking only one partner in each gender with which I'm involved. Second, while I am perfectly capable of monogamy—as 20 years of my history shows—I am in fact completed, balanced, and calmed by the combination of male and female energies in my life.

While my life no doubt would have been smoother, less difficult—less *interesting*—had I been born heterosexual or even homosexual, being bisexual has allowed me to have it all. Even as we age and appetites diverge, loyalty and commitment live. I love strongly, and I believe myself to be among the most blessed of beings.

C.S., 65, is a partner, lover, mom, recovering college teacher and political public relations consultant, barely-retired journalist, feminist/gay rights activist, role model, crone and published short story writer and poet—not necessarily in that order. She lives happily in Key West, loves visitors, and is presently most involved with the national White Ribbon Equality campaign she helped originate, supporting the right to same-sex civil marriage.

V.R. PANFIL
OHIO, USA

"I'm looking for someone like me: charming, romantic, intelligent. Can also be aggressive, gorgeous, and witty," I said. Overdone, but exactly what I want. I used to think that I was such a catch. Anyone would be lucky to have me, to have me love them. Those whom I've loved have told me that, yet all of my relationships so far have ended in the complete loss of civility and contact. Being "just friends" is just too hard. I can admit to seeing red, and anticipating the ballistics report, and laughing in the middle of fights. And I can admit to crying over her at night sometimes. I miss her the most. While we're on the subject of admitting, I can admit that I don't fit into clean little categories. I don't represent butches or femmes or straight chicks or lesbians or bisexuals or drag kings or skaters or Liberals or gluttons or bookworms. Classifying myself is difficult. Life and love isn't a big dichotomy for me; and yet I like things to be black and white. The grey scale is not for me. Instead, I choose the whole spectrum. I want to be loved in every shade of blue. I want to be called on my bullshit and love someone in every shade of their favorite color. I do know what I want. Someone like me: Such a catch.

V.R. is a teenager living in Columbus who has always wanted to grow up faster, but only if she could be an astronaut. She is growing up, but she still manages to love roller coasters, fireworks, the Smashing Pumpkins, candy and dreaming. She enjoys learning as she goes.

ADRI VAN DEN BERG
NETHERLANDS

I came to bisexuality through my polyamorous feelings, rather than the other way round. About 23 years ago, I was in the midst of a loving relationship with my then boyfriend. I felt so much love for and from him that I felt I could love other people as well. So I became involved in love affairs with other people, men and women. Unfortunately that boyfriend—whom I continued to love—could not cope, so after a few years he left me. I then re-encountered my first lover, Luc, who has become my partner for life. Together we have developed a polyamorous and bisexual relationship, in which there is room for love and sex with others, separately or together in triads.

Six years ago we married in silence. At the alternative marriage ceremony in the gay S/M bar which we frequent, **we promised to be as slutty as we like, and remain faithful to each other**. To us, this is the basis of polyamory. I feel sexually and emotionally attracted to both men and women, or rather, to people regardless of their gender. In sexual relationships I prefer bisexual people, as they are usually more tolerant and understanding of my bisexual life. I sometimes jokingly call heteros, gays and lesbians *gender-fetishists*, as their sexual preference is based on a specific gender.

A board member of the Dutch Bisexual Network, I aim to encourage the visibility and acceptance of bisexuals in society. Too many people think bisexuals are unreliable and unfaithful, or cannot choose. Too many gays only accept the same-sex aspect of bisexuals and neglect or disdain the other-sex part; and too many heteros do the reverse. I think that many more people are bisexual but are afraid to say so, and I hope I can stimulate their coming out and help create a safe environment in which they can do so.

Monosexual monogamy is still the default lifestyle in Western society. At the edge of my 50s, I feel more happily deviant than ever.

Kiss me twice, I'm bisexual!

Adri lives in Den Haag (The Hague). She is a 50-year-old social anthopologist interested in African and gender studies.

TSVETOMIR MARIO DELIYSKI
BULGARIA

The term bisexual constantly annoys me, especially when I hear it applied to myself! I do sleep with both men and women, yet not at the same time. The first time I went to bed with a boy was in 1998. He was my best friend and we are still friends today. Then, in 1999, I fell madly in love with a girl and had my first sexual experience with the opposite sex. When we made love our bodies would prevail over rationality; for hours we were unable to tear away from each other. I felt free with her. I had the most ferocious orgasms that ever passed through my nervous system, and after each one we would fall in stitches. Our relationship lasted for exactly one year; then we parted as she wished. She had found a more well-to-do man with whom she could spend more money. I was at university at the time and trying hard to make ends meet. I had a hard time getting over her, but my love for her never ceased. I turned to men and male sex, though.

In the beginning I was not selective of my partners. If the guy had a penis between his legs it seemed enough. The sex, however, was neither satisfying nor relaxing and I was always searching for new experiences and new emotions. Of all the men I was with in that period, only one is worth mentioning. I met him via the internet—he was my first date arranged in this way. I was very nervous, but I did my best not to let it show. After our first night together we started seeing a lot of each other and for the best part of 2000 I was happy. I started to miss sex with women. I caught myself eyeing couples hugging and kissing in the street. I gaped at love scenes on TV and in movie theaters. I cast myself in the man's place and was eager to experience that feeling again. Women increasingly filled my fantasies and my daily life.

So I gradually withdrew from sex with men and set out on another relationship with a girl, which lasted for two and a half years. I felt I had been given wings. I could have all and feel all that I had been dreaming about for months before. This happiness lasted for only two years before I began fantasizing about men again. I would look at them in the street; in the gym I stared at those that I liked and would bump into the apparatuses and drop my weights. I got erections in the bathrooms and locker rooms of gyms seeing men in the nude and showering. I could not control myself and often masturbated over gay porn on the telly. I started to neglect my girlfriend and even treated her badly. I realized I was on the verge of another gay phase and decided to plunge into it. I broke up with my girlfriend and posted my profile in several gay websites. Once again I started having sex with men only.

Gradually it dawned on me that I was attracted to muscular and hairy males—with them I felt best and felt the most sexual pleasure. I liked their bodies, the muscles intertwined beneath their skin, the strength and toughness in their every move, their desire to conquer and overpower. Simultaneously

I found out that the road to bed with men of that description is rather hard and fraught with hurdles. But this did not stop me; it only enhanced my desire and ambition. Yet the complexity of communication did not allow me to stay with any of those men long enough to call the thing between us a relationship. Meanwhile I was gaining experience and impressions, and came to realize that I preferred being active ("top") with men who were weaker and more feminine-looking than me, while with older and physically stronger men I assumed the passive ("bottom") role. I was now able to anticipate the shift in my sexual desires and with it the ebb and flow of those "male-gay" and "female-straight" periods in my life. I now seem to be coming to the end of my male gay period, because a girl has been flirting with me. As she actively makes her desires and intentions clear to me, she is a catalyst for the change in my orientation. We are often together, and she does not leave me alone until she gets into my bed, if only to sleep. I can gradually feel my desire for her getting stronger and more lucid. I think of her more and more and often miss her presence. Nonetheless, I keep seeing men.

I believe that a person's life in general can be called bisexual. But I wouldn't apply the word to the person, or refer to a particular period of their life. Speaking of a given time span, we could term it either a gay or a straight phase, but not as a bisexual one. This is why I get so shirty about the use of this word to generalize, and most of all, when they try and identify me with it.

Born in 1973 in Sofia, Tsvetomir graduated in Pharmacy at the Medical University of Sofia and is currently employed at the Bulgarian Drug Agency. Since 2003 he has served as an executive director of the Queer Bulgaria Foundation.

JORGE LUIS PUENTES
HAVANA, CUBA

Jorge, a 42-year-old Cuban divorcé and father of a four-year-old girl, had his first homosexual encounter with Luis. Bored and lonely on a Saturday night, when he was working as a guard, Jorge let 30-year-old Luis please and caress him. It was 12 o'clock at night.

"I never thought this would happen," a nervous Jorge told Luis.

Luis continued to visit Jorge for several days, until the divorcé convinced himself that he enjoyed this new relationship. Jorge had been feeling lonely. His wife had left him, and he anxiously awaited Luis's phone calls and the nights they spent together. Luis helps him unwind.

"We need to be discreet. Let's not see each other for a couple of days," Jorge told Luis one night.

That same night, he told Pedro: "We should be cautious. Make sure you only come here very late at night."

Thanks to Luis, Jorge began to live as a bisexual. "I have always liked women," he claims, "but now that I'm alone, I can experiment. I like this."

For Jorge to maintain a relationship with a man, his partners must be respectful and discreet. At the end of a night full of tropical bliss, Jorge declares: "I don't like sissies. If I'm going to have a relationship, it needs to be discreet."

Jorge was born in 1973 in San Antonio de los Baños, a suburb of Havana. In 1990, he completed a course in journalism and writing at the Instituto Internacional de Periodismo José Martí in Havana.

KLAUS SCHWEINZER
AUSTRIA

It took me a long time to acknowledge my bisexuality, and even longer to accept this part of myself.

For me, bisexuality is the ability to have a relationship (not just sex) with a woman or a man. These relationships need not take place at the same time—though they may. But that is more a question of fidelity than of bisexuality. Many people in relationships have dreams about sex with others, but don't act on these feelings.

As I remember, I fell in love with both females and males. When I first realized that I have sexual dreams about both girls and boys, I thought, "I'm gay!" This was a shock. I thought my family and my friends would hate me or wouldn't love me anymore. So I talked to nobody about it. I tried to have sexual contact with one of my friends from school. But I was too shy to really show him my desire, and he was too. I put a wall around my soul, my thoughts and my feelings. My life—especially my sexual life—took place in my dreams. During this time (which was before the internet), I tried to find information about my difference from others. I read a lot of books about being gay, coming out, and so on. I learned that there are a lot of gay people out there and I learned to accept my same-sex attractions. I tried to contact gay people, but I never completely fit into the gay community because I had still sexual feelings for women too. Most gay people do not have sexual feeling for both genders, and some in the gay community are even angry at bisexual people.

I had a long relationship with a man followed by one with a woman. After it ended, I recognized that I enjoy sex with a woman or a man, that I can fall in love with a woman or a man, and that I can have a relationship with either. My good friends take me as I am. Most of them know that I have been attracted to men too. I started researching again using the keyword "bisexuality." This time, getting information was easier. The Internet allowed me to find material quickly and *privately* at home. I discovered I'm not the only one in the world who is bi! This was important for me, but has not solved all of my problems.

Currently I live in a relationship with a woman. The first day we met, I told her about my bisexuality. At the beginning, she had no problem with this. We had a lot of fun sitting in a park watching men and talking about the ones that attracted us. Later, she started to have trouble with my "second" sexuality. In her mind she could never compare with a man and will never fulfill all my sexual wishes. This might be true, but in any heterosexual relationship one or both partners dreams of things they can't do with their partners, or would prefer to do with others. Once again "faithful" is the key word for a relationship—very important, too, in both senses of the word. The partners in a relationship have to find their own way to live together. Whether to be faithful, and what this means for daily life, is their decision. In my experience a bisexual person is no more interested in other sexual contacts than a heterosexual person, especially when in a long-time relationship.

In the future, maybe I will fall in love with a man again. This would not be so easy in daily life: if a business partner invited me and my "wife," what would I say? She's a man? There is still a lot of homophobia out there and maybe more biphobia, because the bisexual community is still more closeted today in Austria. There is still much work left to do before homosexual or bisexual people are accepted as they are, and not as interesting freaks. This is another reason for me to start being a part of the bisexual world out there.

Facing the fact that I'm bisexual, and finding a way of life for me and my partners in a relationship, gives me the chance to become a happy and satisfied man who enjoys living his own life.

Klaus is a 43-year-old male born and still living in Austria. He owns an information technology company.

MATILDE BERGENHOLTZ MANSA
DENMARK

Can a bisexual woman be married to a man and still have female lovers without turning her life into a total mess? Many of my friends don't understand our marriage and way of life, but my husband and I agree that I should have my cake and eat it too, without guilt.

I met my husband four and a half years ago, and we married last year. When we met I wasn't aware of my bisexuality—that came later. Before I came out, I would look into the mirror and wonder whether the person in there was me or somebody else. Sometimes I felt that I might not exist as a real being, only a mirror image. I had a long period where I felt lost and everything seemed wrong. My husband and I talked a lot and he suggested that I might be bisexual. I could almost hear the sound of things snapping into place, like Alice realizing that she might be able to go through the looking glass.

In the past two and a half years, I've had some female lovers and found a very important part of myself, a part that was missing before. When I was with a woman for the first time, I recognized the person in the mirror. My two worlds aren't separated but mingled; I'm not two different people. My reflection and I depend on each other.

My husband respects my bisexuality. He says he loves me for who I am, and I wouldn't be the same person if I weren't bisexual. His acceptance of me is not about fulfilling his fantasies—we've never had threesomes—and so far I've kept my relationships with women separate from my life with my husband.

I love my husband deeply. He is, so to speak, the love of my life and my foundation. Until now my relationships with women have mainly been about sex, though two of these partners have become close friends. But sometimes I wonder. If it's possible to share your love, why shouldn't it be possible to love more than one person? I've made an effort not to fall in love with a woman while with my husband, but a day may come when I meet a woman and fall for her. But I hope that I'll go on loving my husband no matter what. Maybe I'll find that it's possible to love both a man and a woman.

So far, jealousy hasn't been a major problem, perhaps because my husband helped a lot in the process of realizing my bisexuality. I've told him everything I've done with my female lovers to avoid jealousy, because I don't want to hurt him. My biggest problem has been wondering whether I should feel guilty or not. But he supports me and helps me when I feel guilty or when I'm feeling down because I'm having problems with women.

You might think I'm having the time of my life, getting sex in abundance, but in fact it's often quite hard to meet women who just want to have sex. I don't feel very comfortable in the gay subculture that, like straight culture, doesn't understand the concept of having your cake and eating it too. I don't want to lie to these women, so I always have to explain for hours on end who I am, how my relationship to my husband works, why I don't feel a lot of guilt, and why I don't characterize this as being unfaithful. Dating sites on the web don't work either; the women there only want to try sex with another woman, and the last line is quite often, "and then I would really like to have my boyfriend watch us because it would really turn him on." I don't want to be the guinea pig of some wannabe-bisexual, I just want to meet women who are aware of who they are and who enjoy the intimacy and pleasure of cuddling and sex with another woman. Ideally I will find a bisexual woman, who, like me, has a relationship with a man and doesn't want all my love, which I can't give.

About half a year ago my husband and I joined a fetish society that includes some bisexuals, and there I hope to find what I'm looking for. This community is Wonderland to me—where I pass through the looking glass and become Alice. If I'm lucky, that's where I'll find my Cheshire Cat.

Matilde was born in Denmark in 1981. She studied theology for two years and is now changing her focus to art history. She married Stefan in 2003. Two of her passions are photography and the designing of fetish outfits.

FRANK AND MIRJAM
NETHERLANDS

Mirjam and Frank

We are bisexual and polyamorous. For us it is not complex at all. It feels very natural—the way we are and live. We don't see why we should be so selfish to give all the love we have to just one man or woman. And why should we keep our beautiful partner only for ourselves? In 2003 we married, because we wanted to make a statement that we are the most important persons in each other's lives, but we told the people at the wedding that we also love many other people around us, men and women. We seem to have stimulated several people at the wedding party to start thinking about their own life and relationships. We respect it, of course, when people are really and comfortably hetero and/or monogamous. We only want to show people that are not happy in their relationships that there are more possibilities than they can imagine. **We don't care what people choose; what counts for us is that people make a choice rather than simply follow the dictates of their church, political party or social environment.** Lots of people would be much happier if they could freely choose their own relationships, and there are actually many more bi and/or polyamorous people than are apparent. It is a pity that most bi and/or poly people don't dare to act on their feelings. In the future we would like to see more people dare to choose the kind of relationship(s) that they really want!

Frank (43, information analyst and publisher) and Mirjam (40, dental assistant) live in Leerdam.

KOEN BRAND
NETHERLANDS

My name is Koen. I'm a bisexual man from the Netherlands. I have been married for almost 30 years. My wife Annette and I have two sons, 27 and 26 years old, and two grandchildren.

In February 1999, I stayed home from work because I wasn't feeling well. At first, I thought I had the flu, but I remained tired far too long. Finally, my wife said that she didn't think there was anything physically wrong with me. Some weeks earlier she had told me about a man who had come in for a medical check-up to the place where she works as a physician's assistant. That man had told her that he had been a wreck a year earlier, but that his health had improved considerably after he realized that he was gay. Over the years I have occasionally felt sexual tension or attraction toward other men. I never acted on it. My wife knew about it, because I had told her. So it was my wife who gave voice to my same-sex attractions, which I had denied even to myself until that moment. After talking with Annette I decided that I had to integrate that side of myself into our lives. I love my wife dearly for bringing up a subject that brought into her life a lot of uncertainty about the future.

I began to seek out information on bisexuality, reading about it in books and on the internet, meeting more experienced people at a bisexual support group, and joining a mailing list.

We have told our children, siblings, parents, and several friends that I am bisexual and have gotten supportive reactions from most. Ignoring my bisexuality had been hard on me. Accepting this change was a challenge. We have worked hard to find a way to integrate my bisexuality into our lives, through communication, through openness and mutual respect, and by going slowly and being considerate of each other's feelings.

In the past five years we have opened our marriage. My first boyfriend was another married bisexual man, and we dated with the consent of our wives. I have some boyfriends now, with whom I spend an evening two or three times a month. This amount of time is acceptable for both my wife and myself.

To us monogamy was not the most important issue. Staying married was far more important because we have such a good life together. We laugh together, share ideas and feelings. We respect and stimulate each other. We share good and bad days. We have raised our children together and enjoy being grandparents together. We have helped each other grow. We have a strong emotional and sexual bond that we want to preserve.

Our road is not the conventional one. But for us it works. From the beginning we have stated that we chose to go on together and handle this change in our relationship as something to integrate in our marriage and not as a reason to split up. I must say that I did not get negative reactions on that, although my wife still hears from others that they don't understand her agreement to my having male friends.

When I look at the situations of other people I have met in the past years, it seems we have been able to make a quick and relatively smooth transition. Annette is comfortable with my bisexuality, and the past five years have brought us even closer then before.

A prerequisite for us was communicating, communicating, communicating. We have—and still do—talked a lot about our feelings and the changes that happen in our lives. In openness and mutual love we work on continuing our marriage.

I do not know where we will be in ten years, but I feel confident that we will still be together.

Since coming out in 1999, Koen has become an active member of the Dutch Bisexual Network. He helped organize the first European Bisexual Conference (EBC1) in Rotterdam June 22-24, 2001.

PAUL GORRY
IRELAND

Lar and Paul

Most people find a certain security in knowing that their partner fancies only about 50 percent of the population, believing that the opportunity for sexual encounters falls to the gender that the person fancies. For your partner to come out as bisexual cuts that security blanket down to a small facecloth.

To be told by your partner of seven years (it's twelve now) that he now fancies women as well and would like to explore his sexuality, have kids, and have a family is not easy. Looking for an open relationship is a big step. Fine, I love children and would like to have some of my own too, but are we not a family? Unfortunately I was not blessed with child-bearing hips. What could we do?

It is hard to make adjustments, but what comes across for me is: a guy that I love and need in my life is being honest with me. For Lar it is very hard to talk about his sexuality. Avoidance is the name of the game and he often needs real deep emotional arguments, tears and comforting in order to discuss the subject.

For a person who has had various abusive relationships in my life it is hard not to fall back into self-doubt. On reflection, if Lar is honest with me, who he fancies has not changed the feelings I have for him. After all if Matthew Broderick turns me on, then why not Kate Moss for Lar and Brad Pitt too? What makes our relationship work, and makes it special, is the fact that we are there for each other in all aspects of our life. We have decided on joint parenting and are currently meeting women interested in the same. We intend to share fatherhood...

Paul is a 30-year-old gay-identified man living in Dublin. He has been going out with Lar for twelve years in total now.

GARY NORTH
CALIFORNIA, USA

My wife doesn't really feel all that comfortable with it, but she loves me and more than tolerates my sexuality. My late husband couldn't understand it, but he loved me, too (or at least appreciated me). It's often less than fulfilling, but a heck of lot better than some alternatives.

Gary is a journalist and bi activist living in Southern California who currently serves as BiNet USA's secretary. Previously he was a regional editor for the Bisexual Resource Guide.

IONA WOODWARD
NEW ZEALAND

I'm sitting in a café with my boyfriend waiting to order breakfast. Tonight we're going to the housewarming party of my ex-girlfriend and her partner. This is how my life is. This is normal.

Some people say, "If you're in a relationship with a man, why don't you just call yourself straight?" But that would be saying I never loved her. I am my history as well as my present.

Perhaps if I was a different person—someone who, on breaking up, disengaged entirely and never saw him or her again—maybe then I could change my identity with my partner. If the past was dead and gone, would it matter what I called myself?

But we are all friends, see each other often. My now-boyfriend is also my ex, and he used to work with my ex-girlfriend's girlfriend's ex-girlfriend. It's a tangled web of relationships and caring. We're family.

Some people say, "If you're in a relationship with a man, why don't you just call yourself straight?" But **I am my future as well as my present.**

I came out as bi before I'd loved a woman, because I knew I could. Years passed. I forgot.

Then one evening the young lesbian I'd been flirting with leaned over and kissed me, and soon after I came out all over again, went round my social group and told them the news: I'm in love with C. Thankfully my friends accepted this as good gossip, not a shocking or frightening revelation.

When I was with her, I couldn't imagine ever going out with a man again. It turned out that was nothing more than a failure of imagination.

My now-boyfriend is also my ex. (When I joked that I'm practicing circular monogamy, my ex-girlfriend's partner raised her eyebrows in mock threat.) This is the second, even better time around. I've learnt a lot about life and love in the intervening years, thanks to her, thanks to another him.

Now and then I'm asked, "What's the difference between going out with men and women?" I say, "I don't know: my samples aren't statistically significant." What I mean is each relationship is different. How can I tell which variations are related to sex and not to culture or age or personality or or or?

Of the people I'm attracted to, some are men and some are women, but my type isn't about gender. The people I'm attracted to are analytical, creative, kind, trustworthy, articulate, thoughtful, funny, and interested in me.

And now I'm happy, carving out a new path for this different-sex relationship. We live separately and like it that way. I don't want what everyone else seems to want. I don't know whether this is a cause or effect of being bi, or something else entirely.

Iona Woodward is a bi New Zealand maid. A writer and editor who invests far too much time in her weblog, she has also dabbled in film-making, poetry and art. She likes cake.

CARLA IMPERIAL
MASSACHUSETTS, USA

Carla and Megan

My partner and I met at a lesbian pick-up touch-football game. She introduced herself and said, "Have we met before?" I shook my head, certain she was just feeding me a line. However, she was convinced that she had seen me before, and we listed groups and friends, trying to find a common thread. We discovered immediately that we shared a love for travel, having both recently visited Scotland. I joked, "Maybe you spotted me at some pub in Edinburgh nursing a pint of Guinness."

We didn't figure out where she had seen me, but a connection was nevertheless there. We started going out almost immediately. During one of our more serious discussions, I told Megan that there was something on my mind. She was expecting the worst of news. **With a bit of reluctance I told her that I did not identify as a lesbian, but in fact, as a bisexual.** I was ready to launch into a line of reasoning to explain why it was important for me that she understand, but was halted by her laughter and loud sigh of relief. She proceeded to tell me that she, too, identified as bi!

No further words were needed. We hugged in relief. I had been hesitant to share that part of my life, and assumed that Megan was a lesbian given where we had met. Many of my friends did not understand bisexuality. They assumed that because I was with women, I should not feel the need to uphold the bisexual label. Megan and I understood, however, and our new knowledge nourished our bond even more. Later that day, Megan exclaimed, "I remember where we met!" Within moments we pieced together that we had both been at the Pride March just six months prior. We had been the two newcomers recruited to hold the banner of the Boston Bisexual Women's Network. Imagine! We had marched side by side, ten feet away from each other, but it hadn't been our time to connect.

A few weeks ago, Megan and I celebrated our tenth anniversary. Throughout our relationship, we have hiked through the Canyonlands of Utah, the Andes of Ecuador, and the foothills of the Himalayas. We have sailed down the Nile, and walked through the jungles of Uganda. We volunteered for a year at an orphanage for children with AIDS in Kenya, and this year we are heading to the Philippines, back to the village where I volunteered years before meeting Megan. Our passion for traveling and helping children around the world feeds our relationship, and throughout all of our experiences, we continue to hold the Bi Banner high.

Carla is a Filipina-American writer/artist/musician and student of life.

GAIL AND ANGELA
PENNSYLVANIA, USA

We, Gail and Angela, are bisexual women who just celebrated our eighth anniversary as a committed couple. I, Gail, am a lesbian-identified bisexual. It took me a while to embrace the bisexual part of myself. I, Angela, am a bisexual lesbian. I find it hard to identify myself as bisexual without attaching the lesbian part; it feels inauthentic. Neither of us talks about it much to anyone. In fact, when a friend of ours who used to identify as lesbian ended a relationship with a woman and found herself attracted to a man, she was surprised to discover that we both identify as bisexual.

Gail and Angela

Gail: I first came out as lesbian because in my community you couldn't get much play if you told people that you were bisexual. I guess it was a trust issue. I heard people say things like, "Bisexual people just need to get over it and come out as gay" or, "She'll end up with some man." The attitude was that bisexual people were cowards—as if being bisexual were a way to play it safe and be half way out if you weren't sure you wanted to be gay. I was in a budding relationship with a woman whom I was crazy about. When I told her I was attracted to men as well as women, she dropped me like a hot potato. Well, I never did that again. I ran into the bisexual closet and slammed the door.

Angela: I came out as bisexual through a bisexual support group at the Cambridge (MA) Women's Center. It was a very supportive environment, but I was mainly interested in meeting other women like me and potential female partners. For a long time, though, I primarily hung out with lesbians and identified that way. I didn't really start identifying as a "bisexual lesbian" until more recently when I began to really assess who I was through teaching about counseling GLBT clients in my cross-cultural counseling course. I had to admit to myself that I am attracted to both, though I prefer women in relationships.

Gail: I am attracted to both men and women and have had wonderful, sexual, loving relationships with both. In fact, I've had more male lovers than female. I would have to deny so many of my past experiences in order to identify as solely lesbian. I am a woman who is in love with a woman with whom I expect to spend the rest of my life. Simply that.

Angela: For me, being in a bi-bi relationship enhances our connection because it adds to what we share in common. The couple that lusts together stays together. Do I find myself attracted to men? Yes, occasionally. For me, though, the attraction is clearly not as emotional as the attraction to women. Only one of my past relationships with men was sexually and emotionally satisfying. Most were neither. I can sexually fantasize about men and become aroused by my fantasies, but I find women emotionally and intellectually much more complex, interesting and satisfying. So, for me, there's a fuller relationship package with women.

Gail is a documentary filmmaker and an instructor in video production at a university in Philadelphia. Angela is a professor at the same university and has also begun dabbling in film production. They live with their two cats, Diva and Niecie, a mother-daughter pair who are both lesbians. Both cats are very tolerant of Gail and Angie's bisexuality although they perked up their ears and blinked a little when they read the essay.

KATHY HESTER
LOUISIANA, USA

I am a lesbian-identified bisexual. I've been an out bisexual since I was 16. A combination of the naughty scene in *The Diary of Anne Frank* and the stories in *Cosmo* made me aware of my attraction to women and there was simply no turning back. I am still a bisexual even when I am in a monogamous long-term relationship. For me, being bisexual doesn't entail dating multiple partners, only thinking both leads are sexy in a movie. And if I am single and meet a nice man, I just might go out with him. But what I really want is to meet a great woman.

It's hard enough trying to date at all these days, much less with all the bi stereotypes scattered in front of me like shards of broken glass. My lesbian friends don't challenge my commitment to the queer community. I've lived more in the lesbian realm than in any other. I march in the dyke march every year, support lesbian businesses, go to lesbian poetry readings, get crushes on girls, read queer magazines, go on lesbian retreats, belong to lesbian and queer groups. Where it gets tough is in the dating realm, as I am immediately pegged as an over-sexed dating machine. Ironically, I'm celibate and not dating very much at all, just waiting for my girl—wherever she is.

I have always been out to my straight friends and co-workers, but lately on a few occasions I have let a new lesbian friend assume I was a lesbian too. Though I'm only looking for a girlfriend, I simply don't feel comfortable lying about myself. However, I do grow tired of the lesbians who think they already *know my kind*, so they don't need to try to get to know me.

This year I found myself liking a cute boyish girl and decided to come out to her. She asked me if a friend of mine was bi and said, "All the bi girls come out to me. You wouldn't believe how many bi women there are around here." I thought this was a safe time to come out to her as bi. But as in many things obvious, I was wrong. I got the same list of irrational questions that I have grown to expect from most lesbians I try to date. Now don't get me wrong: some lesbians are secure with themselves and have no problem with my identity. I just wish I could find more of them!

Maybe I should start carrying around a laminated card that I can hand a potential date. Maybe then we could jump over the inevitable awkward conversation of *just how queer am I anyhow*, and actually plan to meet for dinner.

Perhaps it could read:
- Monogamous by nature, but capable of being in an open relationship if it's important to you
- Has never left a girlfriend for a man—or a woman, for that matter
- If I wake up in the morning feeling the need to be penetrated, I'm sure you are capable enough to get the job done (which could be why I'm handing you this card in the first place!)
- I'm 90/10 (leaning toward the gals).

Maybe on the back I can get reviews from lesbians who know and trust me:
- She acts lesbian to me. –Liz
- I had so much fun, I didn't care what she was –Barb
- She talks about girls more than some lesbians I know. –Marla
- Good to the last bite. –Bobbie

Also add a few gay factoids about me:

- Lifetime subscriber to *On Our Backs*
- Cat-loving vegetarian who recycles
- Loves Melissa Ferrick, Indigo Girls, and other folksy girl music
- Knows all the online sex toy stores and is not afraid to use them

Perhaps this could give me the credentials I need to live my life as I want. The lesbians could feel safe and I could get a date with some of them without repeating the same old thing over and over again. Just like all the other single women, I'm out here looking for Ms. Right. And I need all the help I can get.

Kathy is an out single 38-year-old Taurus living in New Orleans and—like many singletons—searching for love. She also identifies as a red-glasses wearing long-haired nelly computer geek who loves to tell stories.

Alison Bechdel

Chapter VII:

The Language of Desire

Bisexuality comes down to desire. After all the politics and the placement, most bi people ground their identity in their potential to feel attraction—fire in the blood, heat in the groin, the unspoken language of the body. But translating the trembling of a nerve into words can be a challenge.

Many people see bisexuality as a double desire. They use a twofold language to expand the possibilities of love, sex, attraction, longing. While some see bisexuality as excessive desire and bisexuals as oversexed, voices from within our community have sung, spoken, and shouted from their own twin experiences. These voices affirm the humanity that crosses gender lines by emphasizing the similarity between love for men and love for women. They speak of dancing at two weddings, having twice the power of love. These dual experiences do not always cleave cleanly along gender lines; more important may be the division between parts of a life, places, or cultures. The presumed doubleness of bisexuality becomes a metaphor for other things. Often these voices speak forthrightly of and attempt to heal a divide, or elide the need to do so with a stout refusal to take sides.

But these poetic images of doubling do not always capture our actual lived experience of desire. The human heart has more than two chambers; the world in which we live has unnumbered rooms. Bisexuals whose experiences with one gender do not mirror those with another, whose desires stir in more than two directions, or burn hottest at the blurry place on the gender map, speak a less symmetrical language. Even writers who use dual structures in their work describe a reality far more complicated than the mirror image supposes. Our actual lived experience is often messy. Nor is it entirely positive. As generations of bisexual, gay, and straight literature have shown, desire is often most powerful at its most obsessive, destructive, and doomed.

When bisexual people find language for desire, they speak in many voices. They may name their love for the rare, powerful force of beauty wherever it might be found, or offer a frank meditation on desire amid pain, or concentrate on a solitary soul, or thread many strands of desire through aggressive and hostile voices. Many bisexuals return to desire and their own potential to feel it, whether or not they act on it, as a site of self-affirmation. In this they affirm that language itself is malleable, that words are not only tied to their roots. In this language of plurality number remains unspecified. Plural may mean many more. It may also still mean two.

We all walk individual paths; we confront not only desire but its absence. The desire, and desires, that bring us to bisexuality take different forms, and our experiences are complex, often mingled with regret, joy, confusion, satisfaction and longing. Desire is expressed through words, through actions and through silences. It is not always acted on. Often poetry gives it voice. Always, we hear it in translation from the body, its source.

It is then fitting that this section contains many pieces in translation from other languages, which themselves (like English) divide into different dialects. These pieces from Brazil, Canada, China, India, Mexico, the Philippines, South Africa and the United States speak the language of desire.

—Sarah

HUANG LIN
CHINA

My desire longs for beauty.

I love milky skin, bright and long-lashed eyes, an active and healthy body and a soul that is my equal and can communicate with me.

The people I love include both men and women. Usually my love objects of the other sex appear more feminine than average. Men I love are beautiful in terms of their skin and appearance. Their skin is silky and their faces feminine. They all look a lot like the famous character Jia Baoyu in *The Dream of the Red Chamber*, a classic in Chinese literature. My ideal man must have a sweet heart and honey mouth. When watching falling leaves and withered flowers, he can be as sentimental as I am. He has an artistic temperament. When we are together, we talk in the language of honey, which only we can understand. Oh, I like the type of man who is poetic, who has imagination, who can make the feeling of togetherness as wonderful as a beautiful poem.

I miss every man I loved in my life and I miss the beautiful time we have spent together. Our bodies were poetically connected, and we made love like writing poems. I miss even more the moments we were connected, soul to soul, and became one—his eyes tender with deep feelings. I prefer the atmosphere and expression of love between the different sexes, and the difference between the bodies is charming.

Now that I am out of the institution of marriage, I have a stronger desire for the aesthetic aspect of love. I do not need a man to take responsibility for me nor can I tolerate the ordinariness of married life. I am totally independent. My beautiful daughter and I live together, and our lives are aesthetically close to art. My daughter has inherited her father's jade-like skin. She has a natural sense of humor. Like sisters and friends, we talk about everything. We sometimes discuss the three levels of desire: desire of mind, desire of heart and desire of body. I believe the first two are at a higher level, but I also understand the elegance of the last one. I do not oppose erotic enjoyment. In fact, I like a man who can perfectly combine poetic feelings with erotic feelings, telling me that he wants to make love with me by saying, "Are your flowers blooming?" or "May I come into your river?"

The beautiful love affairs in my memory always wear the lovely clothes of language. The unpleasant experiences were often brought on by the violence of language. I remember the former but forget the latter. My past marriages have taught me that it is hard to sustain poetic feelings and avoid the hurt of violent language in a marriage.

I do not object to the tendency of men to have multiple loves. As long as he loves sincerely, one person or two, three or more people, in my view, it is fine. The principle of love is love. The more you love, the more you give. To control people is different than to love people. I think it is a totally different thing. Control destroys love, and love grows love as trees grow, naturally and lusciously.

I think love has a sense of sublimation because in love we discover life and appreciate life. In that sense, love is not that common.

I love the men with whom I fall in love, as well as the men who love me. On the other hand, I also love beautiful and intelligent women. They are my erotic ideal.

I love women who are the intelligent kind. What is the intelligent kind? It seems hard to describe in language. In my ex-husband's words, it is "beyond secularity." He thinks that I am that kind of person. A woman friend of mine describes me as "an Ariel."

Perhaps a person's desire can find a counterpart in an image. Maybe the men and women I love are the same kind of being as I am. We are the same kind of species. I think the pigeon has a symbolic relationship with my sexual desire. I love to call my man's sexual organ "my little pigeon." I live on the top floor of a building. There are a flock of pigeons living outside my windows. Some of them are like spirits. After a love affair, a pigeon always flies to my windows, singing to me, dancing elegantly.

I have had many chances to be with the woman I love. We are in the same room. She sits next to me. We flirt with each other with words. We touch each other in a joking and playful way. We stop at the boundary of politeness—we never cross the boundary of sexual contact.

What I really want and desire is beauty. The women I love are like flowers. The best way for flowers is to appreciate each other. I do not want to spoil the flowers. If violence occurred between my girl friends and me, the love between us is over. Actually, I am too shy and afraid that my soul would get hurt. I wrote many poems for the beautiful women I loved; even my first poem was written to a beautiful girl. My love for women is more fragile that than my love for men.

Nonetheless, the unforgettable men and women in my heart all have a poetic temperament. I always fall in love with them from mutual appreciation, from praise and by spending time discussing issues in depth with them. Perhaps it is more accurate to say that I miss and love the beautiful times the two of us would spend together. She or he reveals her or his beauty after we trust each other for a period. And suddenly, at a certain moment, one part of her or his body appears to be as perfect as it can be, and the brightness of her or his eyes stays in my heart like a bottle of well-aged wine; the longer it is stored, the better it tastes. After many years of separation, when I see that one again, I still love her or him. Yes, I still love them. I wish I could live in the reemergence of love and beauty every moment. I am a woman who loves beauty.

Lin is Professor of Chinese Literature at Beijing Capital Normal University and editor-in-chief for the journal Feminism in China.

JESSICA DAY
NEW HAMPSHIRE, USA

Who I want: The boy at the grocery store who zags his hand through his hair while he gives me my total. He is young, vulnerable, only a little gay. Jim, who teaches a tango class, dancing so precisely. And he never minds wearing those tight shirts because they show his muscles, how well they are thrown into relief under stage lights. The girl who lives in the next apartment—pink-haired, a pixie who made me chai tea once and who cries for a poet boy with glasses. Or the girl from the Post Office with one rippling sheet of long, daylight hair. She may want me too. I'm not sure. I met her at the gym once and she helped me stretch out. She put her hand on my thigh. Sometimes even my best friend Larry, who is quiet, brooding and very, very skinny. When I'm in that sort of mood.

It's only been four years since I gave myself to Ralph and four years every night after that. But because I can't stop thinking about them, and because I cannot enjoy them on my own, they tiptoe into my room at night and watch me with Ralph. They whisper to each other, howl when I'm finished. I turn my flushed, exhausted face toward them while Ralph grunts beside me, a snuffle of love into my chest. I smile at them over his shoulder as they crowd around me, hug Ralph a little tighter, and wait for them to leave.

Jessica, a bisexual undergraduate, studies Creative Writing at Allegheny College in Meadville, Pennsylvania and calls New Hampshire home.

JANE BARNES
NEW YORK, USA

I THOUGHT YOU LOVED ONLY WOMEN

why because curly hair Rosie
was on my arm? She's my ex

Charlie here's my new love doesn't
he have cool sideburns? funny

how they're back "in" again

THOUGHT YOU LOVED ONLY MEN

Where's Charlie? oh we
broke up seeing Rosie now

had a rag doll with that name
mother stole her washed her

ruined her this Rosie I'm
going to ruin another way

WHICH DO YOU LIKE BETTER
either

HOW DO MEN SEEM
DIFFERENT FROM WOMEN?

Rosie's allergic
to cheese

Jane lives in Manhattan and has taught English at NYU and CUNY. She knew she was bi at twelve; reading Colette at 23 confirmed it, as did real life and reading Woolf. She has published poetry in 50 magazines and a dozen anthologies, mostly lesbian. Someone was going to publish her autobiography but wouldn't because she was bi. Likewise, the lesbians wouldn't take boy poems, and straights got nervous about lesbian and bi poems. A novel decorated with lesbians, bis and some straights seeks an agent. She is currently working on another novel set in New York.

CAROLE E. TRAINOR
NOVA SCOTIA, CANADA

Perhaps I was in India when they gave instruction as to how to be the heterosexual kind. Perhaps I was asleep in the hot sun during a warm Caribbean wind storm when the word was put out. (Could I have been wearing ear muffs?) Did the call come in on that day I was wrapped in a large, heavy quilt? Whatever the reason, I missed the invitation to Heterosexuality. That's as much as I know.

Did you know that Dandelions come in green? Well, they do. I was born knowing that. Somewhere there are lone fields of yellow grass full of dandelions in various shapes and in various shades from light to lime rickey greens. They grow there for those of us who need freedom more than we need butter for our bread. They grow there for those of us who know that twelve dead, red roses wrapped in cheap paper simply can not ever convey the worth of something that is absolutely and undeniably living—like the gold flecks in the grass in autumn.

For much of my childhood I dreamed of laying down in the soft yellow grass of the world without my clothes on. I would imagine the thrill of the wet, cool ground against the warmth of my back. I would dream of a girl friend or a boy friend laying naked beside me, each of us undeniably connected to, and in love with the other. Each sucking on a strand of the others hair, or on the thumb or the finger of the other. Each exploring the face, body, mind and moods of the other. Each with fire in the bosom. Each with queer-knowing, queer-penetrating, kaleidoscope eyes.

Carole is the editor of the Canadian feminist compilation, And I Will Paint the Sky. Her works have been published in various newspapers, magazines and journals throughout Canada, the USA and the UK.

JULIE EBIN
MASSACHUSETTS, USA

"Nobody can dance at two weddings at the same time."
—Raymond Bergler

My life is no less
ordinary than most people's except
that I would reschedule the weddings or have them be in
the same place
so I could dance with joy at both. I get
to date a cute boy, look for
my American Dream—a nice Jewish girl
to settle down with. No less
ordinary, except from where others stand.

Julie runs the BiHealth program at Fenway Community Health in Boston. She is a Contact Improv dancer, poet and bi activist who has a lifelong interest in learning to talk about sex.

MARK ANGELES
LUZON, PHILIPPINES

The Red Room

The lights flicker in silence
I grow patience inside me.
I learn to wait. When I'm alone
I write his name beautifully
only in my mind where his tears
are mine, his eyes arrests me.
The room is red in darkness,

as he speaks to me. I bleed.
We celebrate an interlude
   of thought, the swift
and sweeping feeling around us
in solitude, the stars scattered
around us. I begin to shatter.
Later, when I remember him not
with me, he only rests in my blood.

Mark, 24, became the vice president for Luzon of the College Editors Guild of the Philippines, the only progressive national alliance of campus publications in his country. He is a published poet and short story writer.

MUSA
BRAZIL

Angel

I want to be free and independent
To love immensely
Intensely
Freely
And, always, for eternity

It does not matter that you avoid me
That you undermine, condemn or criticize me
That you label, ignore or insult me

When you're finally capable of not inhibiting my pleasure
Nor repressing my way of living
Nor censoring my way of being
You'll understand how pure,
And sincere
Is the love that I offer you

Musa (1952-2004) was born in Recife. She began identifying as bisexual in 1974, and continued doing so for the rest of her life.

GABRIELA GRANADOS
MEXICO CITY, MEXICO

confession

i am one of those women who stares distractedly at the
moon
until melancholy arrives
and begins to notice its contours and colors

i am one of those women who asks themselves who am i
seeing herself in his fingers
in her fingers

Gabriela makes her living as a journalist, and likes all kind of diversity: musical, religious, sexual. She loves world dance and cats.

RACHEL BOLDEN-KRAMER
MASSACHUSETTS, USA

I like legs... creamy close-freshly-shaven-soft legs in the bath
last night around eleven o'clock waiting for his call.

I stepped into the tub as hot passioned steam curled up
my legs my thighs and further. Heat embraced my body
as I relaxed into a moment of dreaming calm and fantasy.
Bubbles abundant swallowed my breasts and tickled my
earlobes. Thoughts of bubbles becoming his lips invaded
my mind.

I begged the phone to ring (him on the line). What are you
doing? he asks innocently and I contemplate how to draw the image of my
nudity in a steamy enclosure in a way that would arouse him, even a tickle of
pleasure, as he envisions me, anxious as I am to feel this body.

When his call interrupts my prayers I begin to float, all I imagine, him me,
intimacy pleasure excitement (words can do a lot).

Yet tangled in my driftings enters she...of spirituality, longing and deep-seated
emotion. Lust and love and the intense love-making, enters a picture of the
last time we touched (that evening of fine food before indulgence in each
other).

Smooth... mmm...and jazzy hip-hop beats, hips beating lips and fingertips,
tension (tongue drum rhythms). Her heart sings poetry into my mouth.
But this flow is cut short, abbreviated and lost. Stopped, dropped, shut down,

and tossed (like a mosquito too close to the ear, I cannot decide what not to hear) cause they say if you have long hair you aren't really queer.
And why are you like that? What a waste.
And girl, with your waist you could get a man.
And from a man: Baby you only need me.

And a woman: I can't mess with someone who likes dick

And my mother: Honey, you don't look like a lesbian
Cause I said, mama, I ain't a lesbian!

Gay is white, lesbians shave their heads
You're confused, you're young, you don't know, you won't know
Don't have sex
Fucking or making love?

Male or female/ top or bottom/ in or out/ up and down/ round and round/ over and over

When does it end?

This is a flow from one to the other, one day to the next, not necessarily belonging to a certain context.   I'm pretty sure it never will.

Rachel is a poet, dancer and filmmaker born and raised in San Francisco, California.

BERNEDETTE MUTHIEN
SOUTH AFRICA

neutron?

i am an infinite ravine
engorged rivers erode my scar tissue
lickmarbling the craters
on all sides
nations inhabit my being
as i moisten for his mastery
and fingertip her open-legged vulnerability
all the while aware
of all our innocence
made of nothing but
air
+/- i am charged
with no sides

Bernedette is an independent activist-scholar based in Cape Town.

water earth fire

i.

killer whale she is... soft & large & sleek & elegant but with jaws that can kill... the sitting-under power, the hiding power, muscle under blubber... she towers above me short hair broad shoulders harassed on buses... & i am looking up into long-lashed pretty-pretty girl eyes...

clench... the fist in my heart, a small knife turning... small pain, babies, this (s)exquisite yearning, this delicious desire... too long since this clench has entrenched me quenchable clench drinkable sinkable...

& in spite of my previous transgresssions, she runs her fingers through my hair... & in spite of my shortcomings i am beside her now...playing...a hand on a belly, a tongue in an earhole...she is not ready for more...& i am not available...

when it is time for her to go, she comes to the kitchen to say goodbye...i show her my tattoo & she grasps my arm like a water snake...turning...soft-soft stroking of the inside of my arm...

& then she twirls me around like a ballerina femme... & then she smiling swims away...

ii

the temple dust settles at my feet
my soles color red
like a temple dancer

leaning forward, my
salwar blouse
opens slightly
a small rustle of wind
through a many–leaved tree

my man,
you look upon me
shadow on my breasts
& then into my eyes

this eroticism between us
is rustling too

you place a handmade brush
into my palm

we mix our paints
from rocks & tree gum
& water in coconut shells
with our fingers

sometimes you wet your fingers
& let it drip
into my shell

sometimes your hands
too big for my body
hurting without meaning hurt
in our act of love

but
so gentle is our art
as gentle as your eyes
caressing me

      iii.

the incredible sinking woman, how long can she go on??
look at her, with a row of rain-filled goblets, balanced upon
her eagle-stretched arms

when a tumbler tumbles, water turns to vodka, & the earth
gets drunk

& now she is riding a unicycle along the edge
of a wall made of dung
& there she is turning no-handed cartwheels
like a gymnast on a balance beam

& here she maintains a mango on her head,
waiting for the divine archer to set it free

like a cracked glass globe, filled with liquid
& still not bursting

how to explain
the extremes
in which she finds harmony??

"Devaki Menon" is one of the many pseudonyms and identities of a 36-year-old diasporic South Asian queer activist and artistic dabbler. "Devaki" returned in 1999 to the South Indian state of her grandmothers, where she continues to make love and make trouble.

MARGARET ROBINSON
NOVA SCOTIA, CANADA

February

She was round and soft
and moved like she knew she was beautiful
Her hair was a dark, false red
And she wore blues and greens and whites
The colors of the ocean

At a lecture on Women's History
she leaned over and whispered to me
The great thing about this top, she said,
is that it has so few buttons.
Later, drinking burnt coffee out of Styrofoam
I revealed myself in layers like a striptease
bisexual, polyamorous, sm dyke
Waiting for the light behind those green eyes to flicker and fade
What about you?
She licked her lips and tucked a red curl behind a seashell ear
"I choose not to label my sexuality."
She leaned forward and placed a hand on my arm
"Is that going to be a problem?"

Later, lying naked like a piece of wood tossed ashore,
Covered in her wetness and my wetness
With fingers waterlogged and wrinkled
I finally understood what people meant
when they said sexuality is fluid.

Margaret is a biracial bisexual activist and writer from Nova Scotia. She currently lives in Toronto where she is completing her PhD in theology.

Roberta Gregory

Chapter VIII:

Community

Both during the coming out process and afterward, many bisexuals experience a great deal of isolation. We may face criticism or rejection from our heterosexual and homosexual friends and be pressured to "pick a side." Being unable to find or connect with other bisexuals can exacerbate the strain. Sadly, lack of community is a critical element in the experience of many bisexual people. Some are amazed to discover that a bisexual community even exists. For those who discover or take part in the rewarding work of creating one, the benefits can be great.

Community comes in many forms, including friendship networks, organizations, conferences, and venues in cyberspace. The internet has made it easier for people to find communities of common interests, and increasingly people turn to it first for information and support. In the physical world, conferences on bisexuality provide important venues for thousands of individuals, bringing together experienced activists and newcomers to bi identity for brief but intense doses of community and support.

One distinctive feature of the bisexual community is its forthright acknowledgment that identifying as bisexual can be a temporary or transitional period for *some* people. The community extends its welcome to anyone willing to embrace the bisexual label, and also to those who may not. (Likewise, for many others, identifying as gay or lesbian may be a temporary stop on the road to bisexuality, but other communities are rarely as welcoming.)

The bisexual community also characteristically brings together a diverse array of voices that do not easily coalesce. Young, old and in-between; monogamous, polyamorous and celibate; single and partnered; out and closeted; seasoned bi activists and the newly-out; world-changers and the apolitical; people looking for political discussions, for dates, or for both—all make bi community a challenging and exciting place.

But we must also remember that there are many bisexual communities, each different. The bi community of a given city or region may be small or large, predominantly female or male, monogamous or polyamorous, oriented toward people in same-sex or different-sex couples. In some places, such as Mexico and parts of the USA and Canada, existing bi communities are likely to be strongly allied to the transgender community; in others they remain largely separate. Likewise, in some places the bi community is more distinct from or more subsumed into the larger LGBT community. The diversity among bi communities echoes the diversity among us as bi-identified people.

The following pieces from 13 countries—Australia, Brazil, Canada, China, France, Germany, Italy, Mexico, Paraguay, Poland, Spain, the United Kingdom and the United States—provide varied perspectives on bisexual community: its existence or lack, its problems and benefits. In most places the bisexual community is just beginning, and you can help write its next chapter.

—Robyn and Sarah

TOM ROBINSON
ENGLAND, UK

Some are born bisexual, some achieve bisexuality, and some have it thrust upon them. **Until it happened to me, I always thought "bi" was a cop out—a kind of maimed, halfhearted version of "gay," desperately clutching at a small shred of respectability.** But to hell with respectability: the real point about being bisexual, a friend pointed out, is that you're asking something other than "What sex is this person?"

Gay liberation (we early campaigners always maintained) was everyone's liberation: the universal freedom to love and be whoever we wanted. It offered a sense of connecting to a wider world of fun, passion, discovery, sexual adrenaline and possibilities. Today the term gay has been shackled to the narrow, rigid, stiflingly dull definition of male-on-male monosexuality. And woe betide any members of that congregation who deviate or stray from that One True Path of Righteousness.

For years—as gays and lesbians—we urged our het brethren to get in touch with the bisexual side of their nature and not feel threatened by it. It never occurred to us that this particular mantra could equally apply the other way.

Nowadays I get mail from gay men and lesbians who—like me—have become involved with someone of the "wrong" sex. People who enjoy having gay friends and a gay lifestyle—and who don't want to lose their queer identity. If these people consider themselves still queer, how dare any outsider presume to know better?

These aren't isolated cases. To make sense of them we need a new emotional space to inhabit that's as wide and inclusive as "gay" once was. A space where everyone's welcome and anything goes: straights, dykes, males, females, drag kings, families, transsexuals, skinheads, the androgynous and the very, very gay...a space where people can define themselves any way they want, or not at all.

And if we want a name for that space, bi is as good a name as any.

The first openly gay singer to reach the UK Top 20 (with his 1978 hit "Glad To Be Gay"), Tom spotted the boyfriend of his dreams four years later across a crowded room at a Gay Switchboard benefit. On closer acquaintance he inconveniently turned out to be female. Over the years they became friends and eventually lovers—resulting in a brief period of tabloid hell ("BRITAIN'S NO 1 GAY IN LOVE WITH GIRL BIKER" screamed the Sunday People). Robinson now has to his credit 24 albums, including a mid-90s album cheerfully titled Having It Both Ways, *and two children. In 1998 the bisexual epic "Blood Brother" won him Best Song and Best Male Artist at the Gay and Lesbian American Music Awards in New York.*

JORGE PÉREZ CASTIÑEIRA
SPAIN

Being bisexual entails a culture and a community, which involve ways of thinking, feeling, living and desiring. Our culture and our community are unique and at the same time a mixture of an infinite number of other cultures and communities, and we are aware of this. This allows us to love each other regardless of our gender, race, etc.; to know each other; to learn from one another; to understand each other without fear; to dream together; to respect those who don't belong; I could go on. I believe this is what makes me bisexual. To me, being able to identify with people to this degree is essential in the world. I feel more complete.

Jorge, 23, lives in Vigo, and is Coordinator of Bi-Legais, the bi group of LEGAIS, the Lesbian & Gay Collective of Vigo. One constant in his life is not fitting into preset categories: he has dual citizenship and is ambidextrous, bilingual, bisexual, etc.—experiences which have broadened his political awareness. He also identifies as a pro-European, feminist, antiracist, ecological, far-left, atheistic, Galician independentista.

BETH FIRESTEIN
COLORADO, USA

Sometimes my bisexuality makes me feel like a permanent outsider. At other times, I feel it provides me with a 360-degree view of love, sex, gender and relationships. I get to see these important aspects of life from many possible angles and live them from more than one perspective.

Recently, I have been exploring the natural affinity between bisexual and transgender perspectives. Bisexual people and transgender folk both transgress binaries and rules about who you can be and who you can love, albeit in differing ways. It takes a special kind of courage to choose authentic self-expression at the risk of social ostracism, ridicule and the potential to be the object of hate-motivated violence. I am out to my family, my friends, my colleagues and in a large portion of my professional work as a psychologist, author and artist. **I have always been afraid to come out, but every time I have chosen to take that risk, I have been rewarded with an increased sense of connection, acceptance and community.**

It's hard to blame anyone for choosing to pass, but I reserve a special place in my heart for every person who has the passion and commitment to be out and proud about the ways they are uniquely themselves. I find a particular sense of acceptance and completion in the company of other bisexuals, and the days (and nights!) I have spent at national and international bisexual gatherings have been among the most fulfilling experiences of my life. My bisexuality informs every aspect of my life: my work as a therapist, my relationships, my sexuality and my creative artistic expression through visual art, poetry and photography.

Beth is currently editing a book on counseling bisexual clients, pursuing her interest in photography and beginning work on a documentary film about her 79-year-old horse trainer, with whom she shares a very special friendship. She is the editor of Bisexuality: The Psychology and Politics of an Invisible Minority *(Sage, 1996). She lives with her cat Beau and her horse P.J.*

ESTRELA
POLAND

Being bi in Poland is not easy. First, we don't fight. People think there is nothing to fight for. We are comfortably hidden behind the heterosexual part of ourselves. If we don't show our bisexuality, we don't have to fight against injustices and biphobia.

But, on the other hand, we need—we *really* need—to know other bisexuals. We would like to have a bi association, not to fight, but to meet other people like us. We want to have bi friends to talk about this side of our lives, which can be so rarely discussed with other people. And we don't want to feel like some sort of monster! **If we had other similar people around us, we would know we are normal and not alone!** This is important for everybody (bi or not bi).

But the *real* problem is that we are uninformed. We have no information about bisexuality. There are no books, no articles, no TV programs—nothing. So how can we know who we are? How can we know how to act, how to live as bisexuals?

It goes without saying that there is nobody to tell us, "It is so normal and so beautiful to be bi!"

And that brings us full circle. Uninformed, we think we are strange, abnormal, so we are afraid to reveal ourselves, especially when it is possible to hide our sexuality. But can we hide our problems from ourselves? Clearly, we can not. And we would not have to, if we knew more about bisexuality. If we could only know...

Estrela lives in Poland and is hungry for bi community.

ALEX DALL'ASTA
LOMBARDIA, ITALY

Drawing a picture of bi Italy is no easy task, for bisexuals mostly lurk in the shadows here. Most bisexual men pretend to be straight, although not enough to avoid looking for toilet sex every now and then. The easiest way to realize how many there are is to spend a few hours chatting on the internet. You'll spot lots of "bsx 27" and the like in the chatrooms. Guys mostly, some of whom will never publicly admit to being bisexual. They have girlfriends, and are looking for a "no-strings-attached" thing. When you meet them, they look nervous, patently embarrassed, complex-ridden. They can't handle their bisexuality. Most—though not all—of those I've met were totally closed to discussion on the subject. Despite the existence of a strong and very active gay movement in Italy, the concept of bisexuality is still very little known.

The idea of a bisexual culture is far from the Italian mind, a luxury perhaps "enlightened" northern European societies can afford, as some here would point out. The Catholic influence is still very strong; the Pope is on television almost every day, and the Church demands its say on every aspect of political and social life. Growing up in Italy means growing up with religion and its legacy. I remember going to the priest in my early teenage years to confess my sins. He invariably asked me whether I masturbated. I couldn't look him in the eyes. I muttered, "Yes," and hoped the thing would be over quickly. Some of my friends bragged they'd lied to him, but I was too terrified to lie in a confession. Many bi people in this country are still unable to look others in the eyes when it comes to their sexuality, as if continuously watched by stern priests.

Sex and sexuality are still an off-limits topic in many places in Italy (especially in the South). Some will discuss sex pretending not to be embarrassed, but that's often fake. Why otherwise would it be so difficult (and it is) to convince people to get together for meetings on sexual orientation issues? One funny thing is that Italy is overloaded with sex images and talk in the media. That too is just garbage—part of the national habit of speaking a lot but acting little. Despite all this sex fuss in magazines and advertising, when it comes to education about sexuality in schools, faces turn stern, and bigotry once more sets in.

Things are changing rapidly, though. New generations are much less easily convinced of anything on traditionally moral or religious grounds. There's a lot of curiosity. Those who are 16 to 18 years old today are growing up in an age dominated by communication—TV, the internet and other media. They flock to Britain, France or the USA every summer to learn languages, and meet foreign friends from all over the world. This is creating a new culture that's a lot more open. As always, the ability to make comparisons provides the strongest tools for pick-axing old prejudices.

Yet for Italians, coming to terms with a bisexual identity seems to be a hurdle harder to overcome than others. It's hard to tell why. Gay people have done a lot to improve their social acceptance in this country; they're active in politics, they have a large network of associations. Bis don't. Being an Italian myself I understand my fellow countrypeople. They're clear-cut, never something in between: Mediterranean extremism. You're either straight or gay, in Italy.

Why, some would argue, should bisexuals get together as different? They can always side with gays for social activism, while adapting to a more "acceptable" straight lifestyle, if they want to. You know all too well what my answer is.

Alex was born in Piacenza in 1973 and holds a degree in musicology from Parma and York University. He has travelled extensively, has lived in Japan and currently works as a journalist in Milan.

VENKATESAN CHAKRAPANI &
L. RAMKI RAMAKRISHNAN
INDIA

While bisexual orientation and behavior occur across cultures and through history, bisexual identity is relatively uncommon in India, mainly because here, even people with alternative sexualities do not think in terms of sexual orientation and identity. Also, even among well-educated persons the word "bisexual" is unfamiliar, though this is changing. Doctors often mistakenly apply this term to intersexed individuals.

Conventional heterosexist pressures cause most people to opt for marriage with other-sex partners. Bisexually-oriented individuals generally treat their same-sex aspect of their attractions as incidental and supplemental, not to the exclusion of marriage and relationships with the other sex. These heterosexist pressures also force those who primarily are attracted to members of the same sex to prioritize conventional (straight) marriage and family. Men who feel different from the mainstream because of inadequate attraction to members of the other sex sometimes adopt identities such as "kothi" or "gay" depending on their socioeconomic background and self-perception of their gender.

"Kothi" is an identity found among people of lower socioeconomic—predominantly non-English-speaking—strata in this highly class-conscious society. Kothis think of themselves in stereotypically feminine terms and identify themselves in opposition to "panthis," constructed as "real men" or "masculine men" who are predominantly attracted to women. Nevertheless kothis also get married and raise children. Kothis seek out panthis for sexual and/or romantic relationships. Typically, panthis are predominantly attracted to women, but occasionally have sex with men. Whether they do so out of desire or are merely seeking sexual release is debatable. Some panthis establish semi-permanent relationships with kothis, usually supplemental to their marriage and children.

The term "gay" is associated mostly with urban middle and upper class Anglophones. Many such individuals in cities like Bangalore, Kolkatta (formerly Calcutta) and Mumbai (formerly Bombay) have organized social/support groups. These groups associate the word "bisexual" more with men who are married than with men attracted both to men and women. They use the terms bisexual, married gay men or married MSM (men who have sex with men) interchangeably, even though this population likely includes both homosexuals and bisexuals. Similarly, the word bisexual is often applied to married women with occasional or exclusive same-sex attractions, thus reflecting marital status rather than dual attraction.

Within the HIV/AIDS medical establishment and social service agencies in India, bisexual connotes behavior rather than identity or orientation. As a result, these groups often vilify bisexuality as the conduit for HIV from homosexual to heterosexual populations.

Thus far a behavior-centered definition of bisexuality predominates in India. Nevertheless, the urban middle and upper class has a growing awareness of bisexual orientation and identity, as articles discussing bisexuality in magazines and recent anthologies show. The mailing list biindia on the popular host service yahoogroups.com has about 140 members, mostly men. While discussion on this list is minimal, some members organize bi gatherings in their respective cities, primarily Bangalore and Delhi. The city-specific list "bimumbai" began in 2001. Support group meetings for bisexuals, including panthis, meet on alternate Sunday afternoons.

Many metropolitan cities also have active swinger communities, with their own mailing lists and private social events. In contrast to North American swinger circles, which tend to encourage only female bisexual behavior and frown upon male-male sexual activity, these Indian swinger circles seem to be equally open to male and female bisexual activity, as posts on their mailing lists show.

Recently, many organizations working for empowerment of sexual minorities have adopted the "LGBT" label to refer to their constituencies. Whether this will translate into inclusionary policies or remain confined to mastheads and mission statements remains to be seen.

Bisexual folks of South Asian origin are somewhat more visible and vocal among diaspora communities. DesiQ 2000, an international queer South Asian conference organized by Trikone in San Francisco, included a workshop and caucuses for bisexuals. One of us (L. Ramki Ramakrishnan) co-organized that workshop and was pleasantly surprised by the number of presumed gay and lesbian people who attended and outed themselves as bisexual!

Dr. Venkatesan Chakrapani is an independent researcher working on MSM (men who have sex with men) issues with financial support of a MacArthur Fellowship. Dr. L. Ramki Ramakrishnan is Country Director (Programs and Research) of Solidarity and Action Against the HIV Infection in India (SAATHII). He has been active in South Asian queer activism and bi-specific organizing since 1996.

CHRISTIAN
CIUDAD DEL ESTE, PARAGUAY

I call myself bisexual. For me, a bisexual is someone who has simultaneou:
sexual relationships with people of the other sex and of his own. I see bisexuality
as more a sexual practice than an affective one. But I have fallen in love with
people of both sexes.

In Paraguayan society, almost all men are bisexual. In women, bisexuality
almost doesn't happen—women who to some degree feel attracted to other
women remain heterosexual in order to avoid discrimination as lesbians. Within
Paraguay there are several societies, some more conservative than others. Your
freedom to express your sexuality depends upon where you are. For me it wa:
very easy and a bit more acceptable to publicly declare myself gay, and even then
I was the brunt of jokes. Bisexuality is much more common among the lower
social classes than what we call the middle class. Middle class tradition doe:
not allow relationships between people of the same sex—they are condemnec
or simply seen as sinful. Nevertheless bisexuality also happens in higher socia
classes, where traditions and the behavioral models are very similar to those
of the lower classes. But the upper classes, unlike the lower ones, take into
consideration the affective side of same-sex relationships. Bisexuality is closely
associated with men who look for sex in the streets with prostitutes and "tax:
boys." Many men look for younger men in order to have a relationship.

Bisexuality is rarely mentioned. When scientists or people who work with
gays and lesbians mention bisexuality, it is seen as a sin. When the mass media
talks about bisexuality, people are scandalized. Many people think that bisexual:
are promiscuous, thinking only about sex. I don't believe that bisexuality ha:
ever been seen as something positive, with advantages. But being bisexual ha:
allowed me to understand the interior world of both sexes.

In our culture, people tolerate a man who penetrates another man, but no:
a man who is penetrated. Many people believe that bisexuals take the "active"
[activo] role, and see gay men as passive [pasivo], as a replacement for women
In prisons, for example, it is well known that men look for intimacy with other
men because they lack access to women. In Paraguay this acceptance has deep
roots in the culture. It is considered an instinctual matter: men who canno:
penetrate women will penetrate men when there is nothing else available. This
magical thinking holds that if the bisexuals were allowed to choose, they would
pick a women as a partner first, and a man second. The truth is that there are
different kinds of bisexuals, including those who practice receptivity [pasivos]
in sexual relationships.

I believe that two bisexual men can have a relationship, but generally wil
not make an emotional commitment, unlike gays, who maintain long-term
relationships with their partners. I believe we all pass through a period in our
lives in which we experience moments of bisexuality but later we adopt our true
identity, which could be any identity. Most people deny their homosexuality
because it's socially unacceptable. In our society there are only two acceptable

options: to love men or to love women. Bisexuality is not seen as an option, but as a desire.

As a bisexual man, I fear for my work, my family, my son. In the rest of the world bisexuals are freer than here. Socially I feel oppressed, not so much within my circle of friends who are lesbians or gays, but when I go to a pub or restaurant, I face a lot of restrictions. I find it very interesting that a group of intellectuals are starting a movement considering how far from open our society and our culture are. I am very happy that these organizations and their leaders are working for our rights in this country because they represent us and provide a face for us—something that most of us have not been able to achieve because we fear discrimination. **I believe there are no exclusively bisexual movements in Paraguay because bisexuality is considered a much lower subculture than is homosexuality**. In relationship to our legal system, we haven't made much progress. We will need to redouble our efforts in order to achieve policies that will protect the rights of our peers and we should unite to support them.

Christian works as an accountant for a popular supermarket in Paraguay.

[From a lengthy telephone interview conducted on 12/20/2003 by Fabian Gamarra, translated by José Falconi, and condensed and modified by the Editors.]

ELIZABETH M. HAGOVSKY
MARYLAND, USA

I have reached the point where I need to know other people whose skin is set on fire by multiple genders and sexes. 26 years of disconnect is long enough. I NEED IT. NOW. I am bisexual.

Come friend draw from my strength…provide me with a tender shoulder to rest my head from the weight of the day. Share the uncertainty, the rage, the yearning I feel when I am too submerged in "straight" or "queer" spaces. Years of football players and dyke marches, boxes my round body does not quite fit into.

"Queer is taking over the movement…We bisexuals are invisible," says the strained voice on the other end of the telephone line.

"I am here. I am bisexual. What is your name, friend?"

Elizabeth is a Ph.D. candidate in the American Studies Department at the University of Maryland as well as the LGBTQI graduate advisor for Student Involvement & Community Advocacy. Her graduate work focuses on public policy and long-term care as it relates to family/informal caregivers.

JOE DECKER
CALIFORNIA, USA

About ten years ago, I walked, frightened, into the Billy de Frank center i San Jose, California. I was in my early thirties, and while I'd identified as bisexua since my mid-teens, I was out to no one (except my partners), and was frightene of how people would react. Nervous, arms tingling from the adrenaline, opened the door, walked to the middle lobby, found the Bi Discussion Grou and walked in. So began my association with the diverse groups and peop that form the greater Bay Area bisexual community.

Over the next couple years, fear gave way to excitement, and excitemen gave way to a balanced sense of comfort and self-acceptance. In each phase, th existence and visibility of role models—folks who were comfortable with thei relationships and sexuality—acted as a firmament for me to stand on.

Of course, my experience isn't universal. More and more people are ab to come to their bisexual identity without dealing with the sorts of fears I dea with—some, but not yet all.

Some of my friends have recently started questioning the need fo a specifically bisexual community. To them, I give this answer—maybe t community *per se* isn't something you personally need. But beyond serving pur social needs, a social community of bisexual and bi-friendly folks provides **path to help more people escape the damage done by the bisexual closet**—an helps promote bisexual visibility as well.

I'm hardly the shy one anymore. I was a facilitator for a bisexual discussio group for a few years, a host for the bi coffee social for over five years, and hav developed a reputation as being one of the more out and flamboyant member of my community. And for that, I will always be grateful to the folks of the Ba Area bisexual community. Thank you, one and all.

Joe is a bisexual activist, a polyamorist and the owner of Rock Slide Photography, a natu photography business.

STEVE KADAR
VIRGINIA, USA

In February of 1993, I discovered I was bisexual. I wa sitting at my computer at work writing some kind of repor when the idea popped in my head that I could have the sam emotions, feelings, and love for a man as I do for a woman. didn't have a clue what to do next, since up until that momen I had been a very straight 33-year-old male.

I suspect, as for many of us, the seeds were planted long time ago, suppressed in anxiety and social shame. had never desired a same-sex relationship before, and th ruth is it wasn't about the sex, but the emotional bonds I could build. This accidental discovery left me excited and somewhat nervous because...well...I didn't know any bisexuals!

Within a few days, I visited the only BGLT bookstore in Richmond, and found little on bisexuality. What they lacked in reading materials the owners offered in moral support and social networking via a Monday night get-together of BGLT folks called Black Cat Cafe.

In April of 1993 I attended and took part in the March on Washington for Gay, Lesbian and Bi Equal Rights and Liberation with a group from my Unitarian Church. Being with so many others, I felt a new sense of beginning and hope, and soon found myself more at home with non-straight people than with straight people.

In the summer of 1993 I heard that a bisexual support group would start in my city. In October eight of us held our first meeting at the bookstore. We chose the non-threatening name ROBIN (a.k.a. Richmond Bisexual Network) because the word bisexual was not obvious. Richmond is a pretty conservative place, and we felt a name that would scare people off or make us an obvious target of all the stereotypical remarks made about bisexuals even within the gay and lesbian community would not be helpful.

For the next five years, **I spent almost all of my free time, energy and resources promoting bisexuality** as part of Richmond's GLBT community. Much to my amazement it actually worked. Sadly, I ended up doing the one thing I did not want—living two lives—since I could not be out at my job or within my profession.

In January of 1994 I became the first chair of ROBIN and served for four years. The group has ebbed and flowed ever since. *Bi Lines* (our paper newsletter) ceased publication after several years and then was reactivated as Bi Lines On Line, an electronic newsletter with an even larger readership. ROBIN continues to attract new members via brochures, our newsletter, our web page and voice mail.

How different would my life be if I hadn't come out? I would never trade the experiences I have had with BiNet USA and meeting other bisexuals and our transgender allies. My own coming out has influenced how I make decisions about other aspects of my life. Being bi (and part of the larger BGLT community) influences where I attend church, what non-profit causes or groups or politicians I support, and even my decisions about where to shop, as I boycott businesses that openly discriminate. And I hope to find a relationship that allows me to share all that I have.

By education and professional experience Steve is an architectural designer and urban planner living in Richmond. He is the editor of Bi Lines.

ALEXANDRA MARTINS COSTA & ALEXANDRE TOLEDO
BRASILIA, BRAZIL

We created Núcleo de Bissexuai shortly after an incident at the 11th Brazilia Conference of gay, lesbian and transgende people, which took place in Manaos, Amazona in 2003. Attendees at this conference decide to remove the letter "B" (referring to bisexuals from the acronym EBGLTB (Brazilia Association of Gays, Lesbians, Transgende People and Bisexuals), because of allegations that no representatives from this category were present. This was followed by discussion on the interne and, in response, the two of us founded Núcleo de Bissexuais, the first grou of bisexuals organized in Brazil, in October 2004. To our knowledge, the onl other space for bisexuals is an open discussion forum in São Paulo.

Núcleo de Bissexuais is the bi interest group of Estruturação [Expansivity]—Brasilia's citywide homosexual organization, which also has interest groups fo lesbians and for transgender people. We initiate conversations about bisexua issues. As the group is still very new, we have only a small number of participant and have trouble keeping our attendance at meetings high. To address thi problem, we created the BIS journal—a monthly four-page bulletin, distributed in Brasilia and also scanned and posted on-line. This bulletin is our springboar for communicating with the public and provides outreach for the various grou meetings. More men than women attend our meetings, and a coordinator o the trans group also identifies as bisexual. Within the Núcleo we support sexua education and the use of condoms to prevent AIDS and other STDs.

Our politics are not directed toward bisexuality as much as towar sexual rights, and we consider the discussion of bisexual concerns part of the movement as a whole. Núcleo de Bissexuais works for comprehensive human rights, including sexual liberation and freedom from the myths and conception taught to us by our hetero-normative society. We are constantly confronted with ignorance about homosexuality and heterosexuality as well as about bisexuality We did not intend to found an exclusionary bisexual group, which woul further fragment our movement. On the contrary, by remaining open to all, we have created a space for open discussion, we are strengthening ourselves and we are making possible the expression and recognition of our socio-politica identities and positions. Our objective is to look for commonalities betweer people who identify as bisexual and those of other sexual orientations, with the aim of working together toward our common goals. Together with those around us, we hope to create a world in which there is room for all worlds and further education about sexual plurality.

Alexandra is a journalism student, an anarchist and a social activist particularly interested in gender and sexual orientation. On her birthday in 2002 she became an activist for sexual diversity rights by joining Estruturaçao. As a bisexual, she has felt welcome in this group and over time has built strong ties with other activists in this group. She came out publicly as bi in 2003. Alexandre believes that he has always been bisexual and has never had any issues with his sexual orientation. In his youthful self-exploration and search for pleasure, he had relationships with both sexes. He became a sexual diversity rights activist in Rio in 1993. He always tells his partners about his bisexuality and has noticed that men have a certain curiosity about it and, unfortunately, women feel insecure. He believes that if everyone were to act naturally on their sexuality, it would be much easier to confront our prejudices because those around us would learn to treat us with respect. Both Alexes live in Brasilia, the capital city of Brazil, are coordinators of Núcleo de Bissexuais and write for the BIS journal.

ANGÉLICA RAMÍREZ-ROA
MEXICO CITY, MEXICO

Our group, the Bisexual Women's Discussion Group (Taller Reflexivo de Mujeres Bisexuales—TREMUB) emerged as much out of difference as of similarity. We met in 1995, and one year later formed the group that has provided us with such an enriching experience, both at the individual and community levels.

Each of us had been searching insistently for a women's group. We wanted to know, or at least confirm, that women were an important part of our lives and that we were not just like our heterosexual friends, but also had inclinations toward women; we not only perceived women as friends, we could relate affectively and sexually to them. This search had taken us, individually, to join one of the (surprisingly) few organized lesbian groups that exist in Mexico City, one of the largest cities in the world. There we found many women with whom we shared identities, affiliations, and experiences. We made friends and found partners. Our common ground was an undeniable attraction toward women; we now felt, for the first time in our lives, part of a larger group.

Nevertheless, over time we started to feel that certain parts of our sexual and affective predilections were different from those of other group members. When, in informal conversation, one of us would mention that men were not outside of our orbit of interest, our friends' expressions changed suddenly from hospitality and flirtation to open rejection. We were the objects of derision. Some women even stopped talking to us. They called us insultingly "bi-cycles"; some who considered themselves radical told us that we were sleeping with the enemy. They stopped trusting us.

This difference motivated us to seek information about bisexuality. For a long time we had heard that it was just a mask, that people like us did not want to own up to their lesbianism and, due to cowardice, preferred to call themselves bisexual. Some said that this identity was a transitional phase on the way to the real definition, which was exclusive homosexuality or heterosexuality. No other identity—including the one that we were pondering and then discussing—was valid. It was not easy to find information and even more difficult to construct a coherent discourse about our preference. Finally, starting from our common personal experiences, we obtained a broader perspective and were able to name ourselves bisexual, with all of the pride, security and happiness that this path of discovery and growth brought us. We came out as bisexuals within the lesbian group and then we tried to open ourselves up to incorporate larger spaces. That is how our group was born. It was March of 1996.

Angélica was born and raised in Mexico City. She is currently a Ph.D. student in Cultural Studies at the University of Alberta, Canada.

CAMILA
MEXICO CITY, MEXICO

My name is Camila. I live in Mexico City. I first came out as a lesbian eleven years ago and only began recognizing myself as a bisexual three years ago.

After finishing my Licenciatura (bachelor's degree) in International Relations in Mexico City, I went to England to pursue a master's degree in Sexual Dissidence and Cultural Change at the University of Sussex at Brighton. While at Sussex I participated in my first march, Brighton Pride.

While at Sussex I also began to question my lesbianism, as I found myself attracted to a man. Nevertheless I was very reluctant to accept my bisexuality. I saw bisexual identity as very indefinite, unlike gay and lesbian identities, which have been more clearly defined. I also knew that while there was a somewhat structured gay and lesbian community, that was not the case with the bisexual community, and that made me feel unprotected.

In March 2003 there was a lesbian march in Mexico City. I was the only bi woman on the organizing committee. **After some discussion the committee agreed that bi women could march "as lesbian women." That meant having to be closeted in the march, but I really wanted to participate, so I agreed to the conditions.** When I announced my bisexuality to the committee, one of the members told me that we (bisexuals) had to build our own identity as bisexuals and organize our own community. Back then that seemed like a daunting task, but a year later I can see that we have made good progress towards building a bi community in Mexico.

The first time I marched as a bisexual was at the Mexico City LGBT march in 2003. I carried the bi flag. It was the first time the bi flag was present at the Pride march. The other two other bisexuals I met at the march had never heard of the bi flag. In the 2004 LGBT march in Mexico City, as I was walking through the floats I saw a van with a huge bi flag. This is how I came to meet the members of Opción Bi, a coed group which meets once a month to discuss bisexuality.

Another area where I have participated in bi activism is the internet. I found several groups on yahoogroups.com for both lesbian and bi women, but I noticed there were no groups specifically for Mexican bi women. So I decided to create a group, called "Chicas Bisexuales México." For some of the women, this group is their only contact with a bi community.

I think a lot still needs to be done to build a bi community in Mexico, but Opción Bi and the internet group for bi women are good steps in that direction. For myself, it feels nice to be a part of this nascent Mexican bi community.

Camila is a bi activist in Mexico City.

NANCY LECLERC
QUEBEC, CANADA

For the past year and a half, I have been involved with a not-for-profit group in Montreal called Bi Unité Montréal (BUM). This group offers support to local bisexuals and educational workshops to groups wanting to learn about bisexuality. We hold monthly discussion groups and social events as well as an annual Bi Camp. We also participate in the yearly Pride Celebrations.

Since I have become involved with this group, I have noticed a lack of participation in most events that require public identification as a bisexual. It is always difficult to get people to speak in conferences and workshops, even when the audience is bi-friendly. We also have difficulty getting people to participate in the two Pride events in which we participate: namely, Community Day and the parade.

For a while, I thought it was apathy. I felt that many people wanted to take advantage of the services offered by BUM but did not want to pitch in to help the organization grow and flourish as a solid entity in the larger bi and queer communities. Then I started really listening to what people said during our discussion groups and on our online discussion list. **I realized that in many cases people do not participate because they are scared.** They are afraid to identify as bisexual in both the straight "mainstream" society and the queer community. They are afraid that they will lose their jobs, their spouses, their friends and their well-being.

In a city such as Montreal, which is reputed to be queer-friendly and which attracts many queer tourists every year, there is no reason for this unease to persist. Its very existence strengthens my resolve to promote bi awareness in every corner of society through writing, talking and whatever other means are at our disposal. We owe it to the people for whom being out would compromise their well-being and to our children who have the possibility—if we persist in our efforts—of growing up in tolerant society.

Nancy is a 30-year-old French Canadian woman from Montreal who is married to an understanding man and is the mother of a 4-year-old boy. She has a master's degree in social anthropology and an interest in the evolution of sexuality, gender relations and identity, as well as cross-cultural relations.

YOU YUN
CHINA

Bisexual identity seems to carry somewhat different meanings in China than in the West. To a large extent, the gay or lesbian community does not exclude bisexual people. The absence of the so-called "biphobia" that exists in the West seems obvious, although such an absence is apparently not complete. Indeed, because in China the general public still strongly disapproves of same-sex love, some bisexual people see their being able to form heterosexual marriages as a real advantage. Although not every bisexual person in China may think that way, it's extremely rare for bis to be accused by gays or lesbians for being "not brave enough to admit it." Practically, the prevailing heterosexism puts all people who have same-sex romantic passion in the same boat.

In addition, the Chinese LGBT people (not only in Mainland China, but also in Hong Kong, Taiwan, and some other Asian countries) conceptualize their sexual identity with the term "tongzhi" (meaning "comrade"). "Tong" means "homo," and the Chinese term homosexuality, "tongxinglian," also starts with the character. In some senses "tongzhi" is similar but not totally equivalent to the English term "queer." In the LGBT context, tongzhi means people who are not traditionally heterosexual, therefore including gays, lesbians, bisexuals, transgenders and transsexuals, cross-dressings, even S/M, even heterosexual people who are willing to accept sexual minorities. In other words, the tongzhi community includes bisexual people.

Yun was born and raised in China. She was a regional editor for the 2000 Bisexual Resource Guide.

SARA PONCET
FRANCE

In France, I know of only one bisexual association for the whole country, called BiCause, located in Paris. I've never been to their meetings because I live in the south of the country. They appear to be quite active, but one group is not enough. I don't know of any bisexual events in France apart from the LGBT Prides where bisexuals are invisible amidst lesbians and gays. Once, in 2001, a weekend-long bisexual seminar was organized at a university in Toulouse (where I am from) by the bisexual francophone network InfoBi (linking France, Switzerland and Belgium). It was interesting but short—so you can imagine how happy I was to spend a year in London and find all those bi groups and meet so many bis at the annual BiCon in August, 2004.

Sara is a 24-year-old French physiotherapist who spent a year in London volunteering in a Jewish old people's home. There she met her husband. They are now back in France.

THOMAS LEAVITT
CALIFORNIA, USA

I tried writing a bisexual manifesto at one point because I do think that we are truly different, that in the mode of Harry Hay's conception that gays and lesbians have something truly unique to offer our culture, we do as well.

I see it when bi people come together, a vision of a world where we can be comfortable expressing love and affection for each other, regardless of gender, on a physical and emotional plane...connections across barriers both within genders and between them, that are otherwise left unbreached.

When I am in "bi space," I know it. I can feel the difference. It is as though a weight has been removed from my shoulders, as though a barrier that stands between me and the world during the ordinary course of my existence—even in the safest spaces, an instinctive level of caution and wariness—is no longer there. It is like a sudden burst of oxygen. I step into it, and immediately think, "Wow... now I remember what this is like; how could I have waited so long to feel this way again?"

I truly believe that we have a reason to be here: we can help bridge the chasm between the genders. As bisexual men, we can take some of the insight we gain from the experience of loving and being attracted to other men, and use that to be more effective lovers, partners, companions to women. We can take some of what we learn in loving and being with women, and use that to construct relationships with men that are more conscious and less driven by "masculine" culture.

I see "bi space" as a place where the commodification of bodies is less prevalent, where people are loved for themselves...where "masculine" and "feminine" can be celebrated in both genders. I love our diversity, the casual affections we bestow on each other. **I do think, however tentatively, that there is a bi culture, a bi way of being.**

The most bi people I've ever seen at once is 70 or 80 people marching at San Francisco Pride a few years ago. My experiences at FLIRT, at Bi Coffee, at our booth at Pride and during the march, leave me hungry for more.

Thomas has served on the Executive Board of South Bay Bisexual Organizers and Activists (SOBOA) for the past several years, has co-hosted Bi-Friendly Santa Cruz since 1999, founded the

Poly Greens in 2002, was elected Secretary of the National Lavender Greens Caucus in 2003 and recently became co-chair of the Santa Cruz GLBT Alliance. He lives with his bisexual wife (who serves as President of SOBOA) and two daughters from her first marriage in Santa Cruz.

ELLYN RUTHSTROM
MASSACHUSETTS, USA

I have loved and been loved by men and by women and I hope that pattern will continue in my life. I am a very woman-focused person because even before I defined my sexuality I defined myself as a feminist. Some people may misinterpret my sexuality because of that focus, but I know who gets me hot, and I know who has found their way into my heart. Bi community is a wonderful place to come out in. I have found the bi community to be **one of the most accepting spaces for anyone to spend time in.** I don't think we are given credit for providing an incredibly safe space for lesbians and gays to come out within. We don't really care if you define yourself as other than bisexual; if you're happy, so are we. I love that.

Ellyn is in her 40s and lives in Somerville. She is the editor of the BiWomen *newsletter and has served on the board of the Bisexual Resource Center in Boston.*

KAELIN BOWERS
OREGON, USA

Until 1996, I lived life as a straight woman. Today I live my life as a man who is more often attracted to men than women.

I started to seriously consider changing from female to male a few years ago. It has been a fascinating journey and I have yet to regret any of it. After having been on testosterone for almost two years, I have strong secondary male physical characteristics. The result of still having some primary female characteristics and secondary male characteristics is that people perceive me as a butch lesbian. Being a mostly gay man, this makes finding a date almost impossible. Gender identity and sexual orientation are different in many ways, but as a trans man the subtle connection between gender expression and sexual orientation has taken on a whole different meaning for me.

My sexual orientation, like everything else, has changed a few times. Before taking testosterone, I considered myself bisexual. Two months into taking testosterone, I identified as gay. Now, two years into taking testosterone, I identify as gay—most of the time. Occasionally I go through periods where I find women attractive, but I cannot see myself in a long-term relationship with one.

I used to belong to a group for bisexual women. After starting my transition, I stopped attending because I felt I was intruding. Essentially, I was a man in the midst of women talking about women stuff. Leaving the group felt like a natural outcome of becoming a man. People I had known long-term in the group felt they should make me an honorary member. I declined because it seemed illogical.

Occasionally, I miss the fellowship shared by bisexual women. However, I enjoy feeling at home in my body and I hope that at some point I can find a similar fellowship with a group of mostly gay men.

Kaelin was a political activist and educator on gender identity and civil rights issues who lived in Portland. He passed away in the fall of 2004.

ANDREW MILNES
VICTORIA, AUSTRALIA

My sexuality has morphed over the years, both in identity and attractions. I've had attractions to both women and men, although the intensity and focus has been in flux; I've had a more pronounced attraction to other men, but my sexuality also has a distinct heterosexual (for want of a better term) component.

After spending my youth believing I was straight, although knowing at some level I was not, when I was 20 I identified as bisexual, then came out as gay to family and friends at 23. I'm now 32, and the label I feel most comfortable with (if I feel comfortable with one at all) is queer. There are things I still don't like about it (the implications of deviance when my sexuality feels natural to me), but it probably is the closest fit, for the moment anyway.

My partners in the recent past have all been men, but I'm reconsidering this as my attractions for women have increased noticeably in the last few years. I'm still grappling with how I go about exploring these feelings and what I want from them, given that dating women—and its ramifications—is quite a different experience from dating men.

Recent involvement and connection with the organized bisexual community in Australia has left me with mixed feelings. While I have found many of the people involved in bi activism or social groups to be lovely, interesting and intelligent (and some very cute!), I haven't often felt a connection of being in similar headspace about relationships and sexuality. But **having never really fully fitted into straight suburbia or gay mainstream culture and its values, I suppose I'm not surprised by not fitting into yet another group!**

This may be partly due to the fact that I've come from a "gay" background (rather than a "straight" one like many bis I've met) which has colored my worldview. For better or worse, my involvement with the gay community has been one of the most formative influences on my life. I am also very strongly drawn towards monogamy, at least emotionally, which puts me in somewhat of a minority position in some bi circles.

But most of all, I have a deep ambivalence about the identity politics, that—although embryonic—I sense in much bi political activism. Having found the stereotypes around straight malehood and gay male culture problematic, I am wary of investing too much in what could end up just another box. Though I come from a fairly left-wing background, I'm starting to believe that identity politics (particularly around something as fluid and complex as sexuality) are a dead-end in terms of left activism and certainly liberation.

Yet I am aware of both systematic homophobia in our culture and entrenched biphobia. I think it's important to work to overcome those obstacles and I get angry with apathetic queers who do nothing—particularly bis in opposite-sex partnerships (with the societal privileges those arrangements receive) who don't do anything to work either against biphobia or to support same-sex partnerships.

I guess in the end I believe any bi community will be so diverse—ranging from queer-identified bis like myself to polyamourous pagans, pansexual s/m advocates, radical feminists and bi-curious swingers—that its strongest links would be political activism around shared issues of tackling biphobia (and homophobia), and building alternatives to the dichotomous views of sexuality in our culture. That's where I could see bi activism heading, but I don't know where that activism and community, as well as the possibility or reality of relationships with both genders, fits into my life. I'll just have to wait and see how it develops.

Andrew is a queer journalist, writer, musician and poet from a Catholic lower middle-class background. He has worked in community radio, overseas development and disability work, and his interests include left politics, radical Christian spirituality, songwriting, travel and languages. His writing has appeared in Melbourne's MCV *newspaper, the online journal* Word is Out, *the HIV periodical* Lifeblood *and is included in the forthcoming anthologies* The Burning Pillow *and* Lost in Thought.

FABIAN DOLES
NORTH RHINE, GERMANY

For lack of a better word, I call myself bisexual. I have come to learn that this word means many different things to many different people. Before attending my first International Bi-Symposium in Berlin in 1996, I naïvely believed that there I would encounter people like myself. There **I met bisexuals from all over the world and I was shocked to realize the diversity that exists under this banner.** There were the free spirited esoterics who seemed not to be able to have sex without making it into some kind of spiritual experience; the fetish-orientated leather and S&M groups (some of them looked really scary); the usual loud exhibitionists and eccentric types (who would do or wear anything to get attention); and many academic book worm types—not to mention the hippies (trust me, they still exist) with their 1960s ideology of make love (with everyone), not war. There were the Kinsey 1s and there were the Kinsey 5s.

Later I met people that I would classify as bisexuals who did not classify themselves as such and vice-versa. I was asked to be politically correct and accept their self-definitions; I was not given the right to define and order the world the way I saw and understood it. It is very common—at least here in Germany—for people to resist labels or categorization. I know people who, because they do not like the word bi say they are not (though they sleep with both sexes). Political activists tell me everyone has a right to define themselves. I disagree here. We have to agree on some definitions, otherwise we cannot communicate. If I say white and for you the color is grey or beige, we will have problems speaking with each other. Defining bisexuality is difficult—are you bisexual if you dream or fantasize about same-sex experiences? Not necessarily. Can a virgin be bi? Yes. Can a person who regularly engaged in same-sex experiences—in prison, for example—be hetero? Yes. Is a lesbian who lived ten years with a woman, but then marries a man and has children, hetero? Maybe, maybe not. Bisexuality, like an emotion, is not always fixed. Bi-emotionality can swing toward people of one sex or the other (the swing can last for years!), but the lesbian in the example above knows she is capable of loving another woman, even if she now defines herself as heterosexual.

I realized that there are many facets to bisexuality and in fact I see myself as a conglomerate of all of the above at a given time. I can be camp, I can be professional and cool, I can be nasty and I can be gentle, but to say that I am only one of these things would be wrong. I am bisexual because bisexuality is multifaceted. I am complex, I am bisexual.

Fabian lives in Köln (Cologne). Born in the USA in 1963, he has a B.A. in Art History from the American University of Paris, France. He is Chairman of the Bi-Group, "Uferlos e.V." in Köln and is webmaster of their site. He is lead singer of the Blue Sun Band in Köln.

AMY ANDRE
CALIFORNIA, USA

When I discovered that the North American Conference on Bisexuality was going to be in my state of California, I jumped at the chance to attend. The conference nourished me in many ways, but one incident there threatened to mar my experience. In a workshop on social research on bisexuality, someone mentioned a study in which white and black men who have sex with both men and women were asked their sexual orientations. Black men were more likely to identify as bi. White men were more likely to identify as gay. These results seem pretty straightforward to me; they indicate that, for some reason, white men resist a bi label in the face of bi behavior, while black men do not.

Imagine my surprise when a workshop attendee expressed surprise about the behavior of the *black* men! "Do you think that's because black men don't like to call themselves gay?" he said. "[The gay label] is pretty stigmatized in their community."

I was stressed. There were black people in the room, my mixed-race self included. "Their" community is really our community. Some black people are bisexual. This use of the word "their" made me feel separated, silenced, as though I was there only to observe, not to fully participate.

Research shows that no group, apart from IV drug users, is more stigmatized than bisexuals. Therefore the attendee's implication—that blacks choose a bi label because it's so much harder to be gay—doesn't make much sense. Moreover, the implication is racist, because it marginalizes the experience of black men making choices in identity. It presumes that no black man would choose "bi" were it not for the strength of homophobia in the black community. These are stereotypes and assumptions; it's not easy to be bi, regardless of one's racial community.

The comments implied that black men who have sex with men and women *would* call themselves gay—i.e., would do what the white men do—were it not for some community-based hindrance. It's as though the choices white men make are the norm against which we should be comparing men of other races. But doesn't what the white men are doing—calling themselves gay and having sex with both men and women—seem illogical? Granted, people call themselves bi for a variety of reasons, both because of and in spite of their own sexual behaviors. But, from a purely "A" plus "B" equals "C" perspective, I would have to agree with what the black men are doing: having sex with men and women and referencing their identities accordingly.

I went to the Bi Conference excited to immerse myself in community. I saw workshops on defining bisexuality, bi health issues, bi relationships, love, sex, science, art and so much more. I put it all together and thought, "These are my people, my fellow bisexuals, my lovers and friends, my advocates and allies, whom I fight for and with every day that I out myself and speak my truth." Wouldn't you know it, just like out there in the monosexual-centric world that I butt heads with every time I give myself permission to love and breathe, **here too we have those among us those who would internalize biphobia, give voice to racist notions, and marginalize *me*?**

I'm glad the conference happened, and will happen again, that the bi community exists, and will continue to do so. But I came away sadder and wiser, realizing that we are made up of the same people who challenge my race politics and my bi politics across the board. Nevertheless, I'm still glad I came to the conference because the experience strengthened my resolve to keep fighting racism and biphobia, wherever I find them.

Amy is an African-American Jew who just completed a master's degree in sexuality studies at San Francisco State University. She works as a sex educator and currently lives and loves in San Francisco.

FAUNE
NEW YORK, USA

I've known I was bi since junior high school, and I have been more or less out since freshman year of college. At first my sexuality was manifested as a "divided self" with straight and gay expressions that were separate and distinct. Over time I have been able to integrate these and other aspects of my self to create a bi identity that celebrates all that I treasure in my sexuality and my self.

Bi conferences and other bi events have had a huge role in my personal growth. Through formal seminars and informal conversations, I have questioned my own assumptions and considered new options, exploring polyamory, BDSM, gender identity, etc. Many of the individuals I have met on this journey have become very dear to me, but an even greater gift has been a sense of community that transcends geography or ethnicity or demographics and yet at times feels almost tribal.

I have seen so much growth in the community (with accompanying growing pains), and there is still so much work to do. I've been a bi activist for some time, although the extent of my involvement has waxed and waned. Nevertheless I am inspired and encouraged by those I hold dear, our "bi tribe" and our allies.

As Rita MaeBrown once wrote, "An army of lovers cannot fail."

Faune lives in Brooklyn.

PETE CHVANY
MASSACHUSETTS, USA

I desire men regularly, women sporadically. I *love* women and men all the time.

Genitalia are fabulous. All of them. Traditional sexes and gender roles are nice. So are untraditional ones. I can tell the differences, and I don't believe "anything" goes ... but I've been drawn to more than one kind of person, and I won't be surprised if I am again. And this is something good about me.

Am I gay? If that means "Do I love people of my own sex a lot?" then yes, very. You can think of me as gay. That's fine.

But if you think of me as "not bisexual," you miss some of the best of me Dreams, hopes, fantasies, real people in my life, real events that happen because of who I am. Including sex. And more than that. Things that make up my self my history, and my future.

Why would you want less than the best of me?

It isn't the gay community, wonderful as it is, that has helped me be my best self. Not primarily. It was, and is, bisexuals and other people who believe that we should each have the sexuality that's right for us.

People like us are worth treasuring. And listening to, even if our experience is different from someone else's. And even if it sounds "the same" as a gay or straight person's experience and we insist it's still bisexual to us.

Bisexuality isn't better than other sexualities. But it sure isn't worse. It just is. Simple.

If you're bi, I hope you will be yourself, honestly and openly. If you're not bi, I hope you will be yourself, honestly and openly. Easier said than done? Keep at it. Everything gets easier with practice.

I want a world where all this is taken for granted, and I don't have to explain it. But I'll explain again, if it helps us all get there.

Sure I "want it all." But not just for myself. For everyone. Why settle for less?

Pete is a bisexual activist and organizer from the Boston area, and also a computer system administrator, writer, musician and photographer. He is co-editing an anthology of writings on bisexual men, "Bi Men: Coming Out Every Which Way," to be published jointly by The Haworth Press *and the* Journal of Bisexuality *in 2005. Happily partnered, he learns more about life all the time.*

Alison Bechdel

Chapter IX:
Bisexual Politics

What are bisexual politics and what is bisexual activism? The diverse voices in this chapter speak for themselves. They include leaders of various bi movements—some long-established, others new—and "bisexuals on the street." Because not only bisexuals have bisexual politics, we also include one straight man who, like many others in this chapter, is grappling with what bisexual politics mean to him.

Although each contributor answers these questions differently, recognition and visibility of bisexuality and bisexual people are recurring themes. Contributors from Argentina, Australia, Canada, China, Denmark, India, Israel, Italy, Japan, the United Kingdom and the United States meet the challenges of their specific contexts. Some speak of engagement with the world and resistance to external limitations. Some actively build a bisexual movement within their countries, while others bring their bisexual voice and perspective into other social justice movements. As bisexual people, they combat domestic violence, advocate for elders, speak out as people of color, and conduct disability activism and human rights work. They do important work within the larger LGBT community, insisting on bisexual visibility and an inclusive movement for all. Not surprisingly, many bisexual activists describe a bisexual politic that encompasses more than sexual orientation, seeing the world through what one contributor calls "bisexual-colored glasses."

Although only this chapter acknowledges the fact in its title, in truth much of this book is concerned with politics. The essays in "Crossing Lines," "Bis in Community" and "Coming out as Bisexual" are also deeply political. It is not a coincidence that they are also deeply personal.

—Robyn and Sarah

BISEXUAL MANIFESTO
AUTHOR UNKNOWN

Because we are not real AND our attraction to the same sex is only a phase AND we'll just leave for a member of the opposite sex any day AND our way of loving is only a period of confusion AND when we haven't changed in 5 or 10 or 15 or 20 years we are still just confused AND we see personal ads that say "no bisexuals" AND when we date members of the opposite sex we are holding onto "straight privilege" AND when we dare to suggest that we have our own identity we are being ungrateful or difficult or radical AND if we don't no one will know who we really are AND every historical figure or celebrity who has ever had a same-sex affair was really gay or lesbian no matter how they may have felt about any husband or wife or lover of the opposite sex AND the government does not acknowledge our existence by labeling us as something that fits their definition of who we are even through it doesn't fit our own AND we're told we can't make up our minds AND when we make a long-term commitment to a member of the same sex we've "come all the way out" AND when we make a long-term commitment to a member of the opposite sex we're really just straight AND when we don't choose to make a commitment to anyone at all it's because we aren't capable of it AND for lots and lots of other reasons, WE ARE PART OF THE BISEXUAL PRIDE MOVEMENT.

LORAINE HUTCHINS
WASHINGTON DC, USA

To me, bisexual politics is nothing less than sexual liberation and social justice for all. None of us are free until all of us are free. And we only achieve freedom by creating a world where everyone lives together in peace. We build this new world of caring relationships step by step, and being out bisexuals is a powerful part of it. But there's nothing binary about bisexuals. Bi is just a provisional term reminding us, however awkwardly, that when it comes to loving, family and tribe, margins and middle intertwine.

Author and activist Loraine co-edited Bi Any Other Name: Bisexual People Speak Out *and has contributed to many other anthologies, textbooks and journals on sexuality and spirituality-related topics. She has a sex-coaching practice.*

MEG BARKER
ENGLAND, UK

What do bisexuals really want? From the titles of UK BiCon workshops it seems that we want to have lots of sex, some sex, kinky sex or no sex, just as long as everyone has safe sex. We want multiple relationships. We want one person to love. We want to be alone. We want to embrace our masculinity, or femininity, or both. We want to fuck with gender or we don't think it's important at all. We want a political voice. We want to play silly games. We want to explore our spirituality. We want to escape religion. We want to sing and dance. We want recognition of the diversity of experiences that fall under the category bisexual.

Meg is a lecturer and researcher. She identifies as bi, poly and SM and researches all these areas as well as lives them. In her spare time she writes fiction.

JANE BARTON
NEW SOUTH WALES, AUSTRALIA

When I was 17 I fell asleep in my Fine Arts lecture and had a dream. Perhaps it was influenced by the "cunt art" we were looking at in this lecture, or perhaps it was the boy sitting next to me. But suddenly there it all was, in vivid color—him, me and it. All objectified, all there.

I woke up when people started filing out of the huge hall. Below, the lecturer packed up his slides. I thought people must see my dream written all over me. They'd know. It took effort to stuff it back into my subconscious, but I did. Of course, in subsequent weeks, months and years it leaked out, appearing sometimes in hot dream sequences, but most often in a confusion that blanketed my life like a fog.

What the hell was I?

The word bi, when I finally got around to trying it out, was kinda cool. But it wasn't a public label I wanted to wear. I could use it to justify my desires in private, to myself, but I didn't want to stand up and own it. I still feel that way. If I were part of the straight majority, I wouldn't have to label myself. I'm a private person and find being defined by a label shaming.

I LOVE my sexuality. It suits me down to the ground. But I don't want to have to spend my life acting in a certain way, being seen and labeled as representative of my minority group, or being put under surveillance for my sexual choices. I just want to do it and be free to do it without having to justify or demean the exquisite balance with a label.

This is a difficult thing. The political activist in me, the ratbag, says I have to identify, stand up and be counted. But the sensualist, the individual, refuses.

Perhaps I can afford the luxury. I'm not persecuted, I have a relative degree of freedom and I take my political, sexual and other rights for granted. But then why not? I've lived through the confusion of a postmodern revolution—and I feel I should make a conscious effort to enjoy its fruits, picking and choosing which bits of the cultural norm fit best.

For two years I screwed myself up into knots daily as I went to meetings, attended conferences and introduced myself as "the Lesbian Community Health Worker." I never came out in that fearful, tight environment as bisexual. The struggle nearly killed me. I was suffocated by the feminist clique, the stale separatist ideas, smothering and maternalistic, controlling and controlled by a dominant ethos.

Suddenly I realized my sexuality was a political thing. It was conscious reaction to the fixed, intransigent positions of the radical separatist camps and the ignorance of the heterosexual world. So I discovered and am still discovering my stance. I will not decide. I cannot decide. I don't want to decide. When I have tried to deny one side or the other of my desires I've become unwell. The practicalities are difficult, but not insurmountable. Bisexuality is about communicating honestly, staying in the moment and being honest with myself. I love men's minds—not all men. I love their rigor. And I love some women—their emotions, their sophistication, their subtlety and wisdom. I am proud these days that I can be so open to both. This is a gift, a wisdom, a knowing.

Jane is a writer/political activist in Sydney. She currently works as a therapist in a drug and alcohol clinic, but has been a community worker, full-time writer, festival coordinator, traveler and graffiti activist.

LIN MU
CHINA

Everyone—not only bisexuals—can go through a process of struggling to understand bisexuality. The following essay is written by a heterosexual man. —Editors

A friend asked me about my attitude toward bisexuality. After she learned that I do not object to bisexuals, she asked me to write my view. I agreed without much consideration.

Yes, I oppose neither homosexuals nor bisexuals. Why should I? That is other people's freedom of choice! I am not like most people, who think that bisexuality is disgusting. The world is as various as it can be; each person has their own reason to exist. The world is full of diversity but not queerness—this word "queerness" is derogatory and discriminatory. I was secretively quite self-satisfied that my mind is not so narrow that I can not think about bisexuality in a balanced way.

Then, when I began to write this article, I realized that I did not know what to write. I started to doubt my own position. Do I really not discriminate against homosexuals or bisexuals? Is my attitude built on a false premise that, like a building in the air, can be blown away or caused to sway at any moment? The last few days I have been trying to avoid thinking about the whole issue and have made excuses to avoid writing this article. I tried to repress my doubts.

However, avoidance cannot solve the problem, and I have to face up to this issue again. "Why do I doubt my own attitude?" I ask myself. I have only one answer: homosexuality and bisexuality are too far away from my life, from my private life, and even from my family. This answer leads me to another thought: a woman friend of my wife is a lesbian. Many times she tried to express her love to my wife, but my wife refused her absolutely. My wife could accept love from a person of a different sex, but not from someone of her own sex. She does not accept bisexuality either. Whenever we talk about homosexuality or bisexuality, she shows her disgust with her facial expressions, gestures and language. Based on observation, I know most people here share her attitude. I discussed our attitude toward homosexuality and bisexuality with various men and women. Most of them do not accept either.

At that moment I was proud of myself being righteous and just. How tolerant I am! Yet today, I began to reflect about whether my standpoint is firm enough, because, after all, I do not have gay or bisexual friends. Moreover, no friend has expressed his love for me. If one of my friends were to say to me, "Lin Mu, I love you," even if his expression was subtle, what would I do? Can I still treat him calmly? Will my attitude be intense? Could I still calmly speak to him? Would I run away immediately? Perhaps my attitude would be worse than my wife's, because she feels disgusted but still treats that woman as a friend and still hangs out with her. But me? What would I do?

I realize there is no answer to my question. I have not had this kind of experience and cannot know my true inner feeling. Right now, I only can express my verbal support toward homosexuals and bisexuals. I somehow only can say but not do. Maybe this kind of attitude is enough.

Mu, poet and editor for Chinese Women's Daily News, *lives in Beijing.*

RIFKA REICHLER
TEXAS, USA

My bi identity is *not* about who I am having sex with; it is *not* about the genitals of my past, current or future lovers; it is *not* about choosing potential partners or excluding partners based on what is between their legs.

It is about potential—the potential to love, to be attracted to, to be intimate with, to share a life with a person because of who they are. I see a person, not a gender.

I want my personal identity to be based on who I am as a person, not only my sexuality or my sexual identity. I demand to be free to legally marry anyone without regard to their gender. I demand the right to speak openly about my same-gendered partner at work. I insist that my parenting skills be evaluated solely on my performance as a parent, and my qualifications as a foster or adoptive parent be decided by the same guidelines used for heterosexuals. I demand the right to kiss whomever I want in public without fear of attack. **I am a full person and will not be defined only by my sexual orientation.**

But until that day comes, one of the lenses through which I see the world is bisexual-colored: my sexual orientation colors the email lists I belong to, the way I look at people, the comments I make and the consciousness-raising I do as I live my life.

Rifka is a native New Yorker living in Austin with her sweetie. She is Jewish and a mom. Her hobbies are talking to family and friends about life; and laughing. She came out as bisexual in 1986 and since then has been a committed bisexual political activist. She wears purple at 39 and plans to continue doing so forever.

ALEJANDRA SARDA
BUENOS AIRES, ARGENTINA

For me, just saying I'm bi is a political act. For me, politics is the refusal to be indifferent to the world around us, the act of engaging, in body, mind and soul, with transforming (or doing one's best to transform) the world around us. A world that hurts, because it is unfair, unequal, ruthless. A world that impoverishes itself by forcing people to be miserly on some issues (declaring that you can belong to one sex/gender only, or love one sex/gender only) and spendthrifts in others (you never will be able to have enough money in the bank, enough clothes, enough appliances...).

I believe that anything one does or says that resists that logic is a political act. To say that one is bi, to hold open the doors to whatever life might bring, to refuse to pretend to be in control of one's sex, gender, love, lust, affection, while at the same time choosing to be in control of what one reads, buys, sells, refuses to buy, refuses to sell...these are, for now and for now only, my bi politics.

Alejandra lives in Buenos Aires and works as Latin America and Caribbean Program Coordinator for the International Gay and Lesbian Human Rights Commission. In spite of being a dedicated and passionate activist for sexual rights and social justice, she wishes to retire one day and devote herself to her other passion, writing fiction.

RUKMINI
DELHI, INDIA

Ever since I first heard the word *bisexual* I knew that was me...and quite comfortably. Maybe this was because initially it meant I could continue living a straight life. That's what I did. I lived a "rather straight life" until I was 25 years old: I fell in love only with people of the opposite sex, dated them, married one of them, then divorced. I had slept with girls and loved them as very close friends, but viewed those experiences merely as schoolgirl games or explorations.

But when my ex-husband and I decided to take a break and look at our relationship I explored the world of same-sex love. Although the exploration began as professional research, I believe now somewhere within I was trying to figure myself out. Not even a few weeks into meeting lesbians I was deeply attracted to a woman. A few months more and I was in love.

I have been rather open about my sexuality when needed, and always with my partners. But I don't consider it my duty to shout and scream about my orientation for the benefit of homophobic people. My sexuality is as personal a subject to me as for any straight normative woman. Privacy is my right too. That said, my co-workers and most bosses know about my sexual orientation, as do my brother, my cousins and my present boyfriend.

Watching closely, I have noticed that I am extremely different in different kind of spaces. In other words, my feelings and actions in a straight homophobic space are different from those in a straight but open space and different again in a gay-friendly space. I may be out in all three spaces but my level of confidence differs. Contrary to popular belief I feel very empowered in straight open space. As a journalist—well-versed in discourses of rights—I am rather belligerent when I see any form of discrimination. I love being whatever I am. In fact, I only understand being like this...loving a person and not a gender...attracted to people and not a sex...

My sexuality deeply influences my work in TV journalism and my personal relationships. Once—when I was first beginning to understand how organizations working with sexually marginalized people operate and relate with authorities—I chanced upon a television report that said a gay club was busted in Uttar Pradesh. After a few calls I realized my fear was true: the "club" was a non-governmental organization addressing HIV and issues of sexuality. The outreach workers were caught distributing condoms. The Lucknow Police declared the dildo used for safe sex workshops the ultimate sex toy. We exposed the falsity of the police version, helped by their homophobic sound bytes.

In my very small way—because it affects my life and the lives of my loved ones—I intervene in reports that have anything to do with sexuality. Most reports in Indian media are on Hijras and sex workers. It has been quite an uphill battle to convince people to use empowering language. Sometimes I fail miserably but I do see that the alternative discourses are heard.

I create space for discussion, acceptance, deconstruction and understanding of sexualities amongst my family members, friends and co-workers. As a bisexual woman I question and challenge stereotypes. Being a happy woman divorcée in the small town where my parents live is rather unusual. Being a self-sufficient woman and "still choosing to be with a man" (I have a boyfriend) has concerned some lesbian friends in the big cities where I work. Lastly, some close friends and family wonder why I still call myself bi when I am with my boyfriend. I refuse to live by stereotypes of any kind. **Belief in egalitarian values is meaningless if we confuse equality with sameness**. We are all different from each other. We can be responsible while being different. This is my politics, my personal life and me at work.

Rukmini is a feminist, bisexual woman journalist. She grew up in India and works in Delhi, India's capital. As a journalist she has worked on issues of women and sexuality.

JEN COLLINS
CALIFORNIA, USA

I cannot claim for myself one label or another without lots of interesting modifiers. This fact reminds me that no one issue exists on its own, an island untouched by other matters. Through a bisexual identity, I live and love into collaboration, coalition, union, the space that occupies the void between one pole and the other (i.e., the infinite varieties of bisexuality that fall between Kinsey 0 and Kinsey 6). No one lives at one point on the spectrum all of the time.

As an anti-domestic violence activist, I first joined a movement that clarified for me the connection between sexism, the effect of our upbringing in our sexist society and domestic violence. As I did the work of reaching out to battered (mostly) heterosexual woman, I realized that these women were not just battling sexism. They were also struggling against racism, classism, an oppressive capitalist system and many, many other forms of oppression. It would be useless for the domestic violence movement to focus only on eradicating sexism; sexism is inexorably linked to other forms of oppression, all of which work together to keep some on top of the heap, while the majority are trapped at the bottom.

Activists need an awareness of how various forms of oppression work against all people to create a movement that is comprehensive and collaborative. For instance, **I will show up at your march to raise my voice against violence against women, but I will ask that you include in your program information about women who are battered by other women, not all of whom are necessarily lesbian** and to talk about how homophobia, biphobia, and transphobia tie to sexism.

My lived experience of bisexuality has opened my mind and made it easier for me to see the reality of these connections. I do not focus my desire in a single location, could not even if I tried—and believe me, I've tried. So, too, have I tried to focus my activism in a single direction. But other issues kept popping up. I kept hearing these few voices around the edges of our anti-domestic violence movement—sort of like those voices of bi activists who keep calling out to gay and lesbian "leadership." These voices said, "If we are not working to end all oppression, if we are not looking at how all the forms of oppression are intertwined, then likely we are actively participating in the oppression we say we're working against."

My complex experience of bisexuality brought me out of the box that society put around sexuality and desire, the box called "one or the other only." Stepping out of that box not only allowed a wider experience of desire, it gave me a better understanding of the spectrum of interconnections between "your" issue and "mine," and all of the various possibilities for collaboration. And only through collaboration, through relationships, can we—you and I and he and she together—change the world.

Jen is a freelance writer whose work can be found in Set In Stone: Butch on Butch Erotica, Young Wives' Tales, Best Bi Women's Erotica, Tough Girls, Best Fetish Erotica, *and* Bare Your Soul: The Thinking Girl's Guide to Enlightenment. *Now living in San Francisco, she can often be found engaging in the transformative work of smut-writing at any of a hundred cafes around the city.*

BOB ALBA
CALIFORNIA, USA

My bi politics encompasses the intersectionalities that affect my everyday life. I have had to overcome and continue to face struggles that affect me and others as well.

I am Mexicano-Chicano born in the US; I specify Mexicano because the term Chicano no longer refers only to Mexican-Americans and while I am not anti-American I chose not to include the word American in my label for its misusage and for other political reasons. Because of my Chicanismo, I have been subject to racism, especially in the public school system. So, I have chosen to acknowledge, learn, and celebrate my Chicano culture, and I plan to keep giving back to the community that has brought me thus far.

"Crip" is the term I use to describe my disability activism. I have reclaimed this word from the term "cripple" and made it self-empowering.

Likewise, I prefer to call myself queer rather than bi or gay because the term is self-empowering too, reminding me of where I have been and where I need to go. I also find queer more inclusive of transgenders, bisexuals, lesbians, and gays, gender non-conformers and allies, although I acknowledge that the older generations might take it with a grain of salt.

I consider myself a feminist because I have long felt strongly about women's right to make choices about their own bodies and to have an active voice in their own communities and the larger society. We all have a sister or a mother who deserves these rights and the respect of all. I have strong reservations against war and imposing our corporate will on other unwilling nations and am able to address this through my involvement with the San Diego Chapter of the Peace and Freedom Party and other community groups.

Bob is a 24-year-old Chicano Queer Crip Feminist anti-war Activist and a student at San Diego State University with a double major in Classics (language emphasis) and Chicana/o Studies.

BOBBI KEPPEL
MAINE, USA

"Gray Haired and Above Suspicion," my chapter in the now famous book *Bi Any Other Name*, started my official career as a senior bisexual even though technically, at that time, it was my lover, not me, that was gray haired. That was in 1988; I was only 55. Others wrote of their bi parents or their bi kids, but only Cornelius Utts and I wrote from our own experience as older bis. Soon, I was being introduced with "This is BobBI Keppel. You know her: 'Gray Haired and Above Suspicion.'" And they did know, because *BAON* was being read all over the English-speaking world.

As part of the Maine and Boston bi communities, and as a clinical social worker, I was focusing my bi activism on improving mental health services for bis, knowing bisexuality is an area of great professional ignorance. I frequently appeared before social workers, counselors, domestic violence workers, teachers, students, parents and others using the scales I had developed to explain how bisexuals fit into the larger picture of sexual orientation and urging my audiences to recognize and support bi identity.

Now, I had a new career: elder bi activist. **I call it mandatory activism because in some ways I don't seem to have a choice. If not me, who?** Those of us who are out must do as much as we can to support other bis who can't be out, to find allies for the work, to educate others, and to fight against bi oppression by lesbians and gay men as well as heterosexuals.

I've heard many sad stories. Bi identity for elders is even harder than for bis in general. In a culture that already marginalizes elders and marginalizes aging sex even more, there's no place for older people to work out attractions and behaviors with more than one sex and gender. Older people fear they will be misunderstood and isolated if they live (or even give voice to) their attractions and fantasies. Older people who come out into the lesbian and gay communities, and later discover they are still attracted to another sex and gender, are in danger of losing their newly found same-sex/same-gender community, usually without a replacement bi community. Elders may be unable to publicly cherish their past of marriage/partnerships, with or without kids, when their current choices take them into same sex/gender communities. It is no wonder so many elders remain closeted.

In the late 1990s, I added safer sex for seniors to my activism role by joining the Bi Health Project at Boston's Fenway Community Health Center. Our teams of outreach workers teach everybody how to be safe with everyone else. In the trainings, I call attention to specific elder issues like language, lube, and lack of recent new partner experience; plus, my presence confronts the stereotype that safer sex is only for boomers and younger.

So, here I am, 71 and still looking for a way to retire. I love the work. I love the changes that bi folks have brought about. I rankle at the injustices inflicted on bis everywhere. I know that if we stick together, young and old, we'll have a bigger voice and we shall overcome.

Bobbi is a 71-year-old bisexual activist and educator. She is a sexual orientation consultant and educator—and a fiber artist in her spare time.

KUWAZA IMARA
CALIFORNIA, USA

I am an African-American man. I am also a bisexual man. The first of my identities is very obvious. The second is not. And while there has been much effort to understand ethnicity and race, we rarely address sexual behaviors or identities that are neither heterosexual nor homosexual.

That is why I choose to speak up.

As a visible bi person, I can help destroy some of the confusion and myths about sexual identity and behavior that exist in our communities. While popular culture and the media sexualize nearly everything, there is little discussion or understanding of the array of sexual expression and being that exists in our communities. The scarcity of persons who do claim a bi identity—especially in communities of color and of non-European and/or mixed ethnicity—results in distorted perceptions of sexual identity and behavior.

Although identity politics may reinforce stereotypes and limit understanding of the complexities of an individual, to self-identify as bi gives visibility and positive validation to other bi people, helping them be more comfortable with their (bi)sexuality even if they are not out to anyone but themselves.

It is important for everyone to see people of color who are comfortable claiming their sexual identity.

As an out bi man and a "baby boomer" now moving fully into middle age, I give visibility and draw attention to a larger overlooked group—men over 50 years of age who are just starting to explore their sexuality. Some of these men may choose to be sexually active with members of both sexes, some with the same sex. Either way, the phenomenon of men—or women—who may once have been heterosexually identified becoming bisexually active should not be ignored by either the larger society or the GLBTI community.

Finally, I feel that by being visible and out, by allowing my mental, emotional, spiritual and sexual dimensions to be recognized and present, I am able more fully to actualize and express my own humanity.

Kuwaza lives in the San Francisco Bay Area. He is an activist who has long worked for social and economic justice for all communities, a father of three and a grandfather. He currently works to ensure quality health access for all people.

ASTRID NEWENHOUSE
WISCONSIN, USA

For 22 years I have worked as an agricultural researcher, where I've noticed identity politics similar to those in the queer community. Within agriculture, you are somehow more valid a farmer if you were born near where you farm, or if you grow traditional crops such as grain, or if you drive a big tractor and talk the jargon of the three point hitch. The clincher for agricultural validity is if you "grew up on a farm." I grew up in a Chicago suburb and only spent weekends on a farm.

All this posturing reminds me of the queer community. You gain respect in certain groups if you are lesbian instead of bisexual, if you came out at an early age, or if you have never been with men. I know that I belong in the queer community. I feel isolated and can't breathe when I spend too much time in Hetland. Even though outwardly—living with husband and child—I may appear straight, I in no way ever feel het or feel part of het society. I maintain queer culture at home and recharge by periodic immersion in more queer culture. I continually out myself or I don't feel comfortable.

At work I sometimes name-drop the trivia of ag validity such as my experiences in 4-H or driving tractors. I tell myself that it helps my professional credibility. But I wonder whether instead I fell into the trap of validation by situation rather than validation by simply being.

Astrid lives in Madison and is a community activist who also raises oodles of fruit and vegetables.

AMANDA UDIS-KESSLER
COLORADO, USA

Given the variety of bisexual political approaches available today, I think we should jettison the words "monosexual," "monosexuality" and "monosexism." They may be technically accurate in a descriptive sense, but they are not very politically useful.

Consider the following:

- Virtually no heterosexuals, lesbians or gay men call themselves "monosexuals." We bisexuals have so much experience with having our sexuality rendered invisible or mislabeled; why should we visit that disrespect on anyone else?

- Joining heterosexuality and homosexuality under the term "monosexuality" ignores the different power of heterosexuals and lesbians/gay men in a heterosexist and homophobic society. Heterosexuals and lesbians/gay men do not have equal power to oppress bisexuals, though they do have equal power to exclude us and make us feel uncomfortable. Nonetheless, separatist lesbian-feminists did not make the laws that keep me from marrying my partner of seven years, and gay men don't bash us or kill us.

- Once the term "monosexual" exists, it is easy to make the leap to a bisexual-monosexual dualism in which bisexuality is considered better than exclusive heterosexuality and homosexuality—more liberated, more complete. (This leap should sound strangely reminiscent of the binary thinking that we have spent years trying to reject.) Some take this argument still further with the claim that monosexuality doesn't really exist, and that all "monosexuals" are really bisexuals who aren't yet in touch with their bisexual wholeness. In an ironic twist on biphobia as biphobic stereotypes, the "monosexual" becomes defined as either duped or nonexistent. This approach, needless to say, sets us against lesbians and gay men. In a heterosexist and homophobic society, we need all the allies we can get in order to work effectively for justice.

Even in a period of postmodern deconstructionism, there can be some value to identity politics coupled with coalition building. I hope that bisexual activists will stay focused on fighting sexism, heterosexism and homophobia, and that the poor misguided "monosexual" will be re-accorded dignity as a gay man, lesbian, or heterosexual ally.

Amanda has been writing about bisexuality, homophobia, feminism and religion since 1989. Her activism has largely focused on LGBT public education, though she does have a civil disobedience arrest record.

MARGARET ROBINSON
NOVA SCOTIA &
ONTARIO, CANADA

Remember musical chairs? There's a circle of chairs and the music starts and we all run around the circle. The music stops and everyone darts for a chair. But there are not enough chairs for everyone. Lately I'm feeling trapped in this game. There are only three seats, and gay and lesbian already have two of them. Trans and bi stand staring at each other and at that last empty chair...

There's just enough space (or so it's claimed) on banners, logos, and newspaper headings for three words: a holy trinity of sexual diversity. Increasingly, I've seen people use "gay, lesbian and trans." I admit: it makes me angry. But the appropriate target for those feelings isn't the trans community. It's the people who pretend there is only so much liberation to go around, and who would have us fight our trans allies for that last coveted spot.

As an acronym, GLBT is already problematic. Constituents are listed in some pre-determined order of importance. See what reaction you get when you change the order: "trans, bi, lesbian and gay." How does that make people feel? The oppression I've experienced as a bisexual is strikingly similar to what the transwomen I've met have reported. We are both sometimes labeled as "male-identified." Many lesbians assume bisexual women bring men with them wherever they go, and assume transwomen are men. The queer community frequently excludes us as pretenders or outsiders. We both know what it's like to be treated as a problem to be solved or an issue to be addressed rather than a person to be known. In light of this similarity, trans-identified people are natural allies of the bi community.

By agreeing to fight for third place we lose a lot. To begin with, we treat allies as competitors. Many transfolk support bi inclusion; many are also part of the bi community as activists, organizers and participants. Trans perspectives can help us define what we really mean by bisexuality in a multi-sexed and multi-gendered world. They challenge us to practice the inclusion we usually demand.

To return to the metaphor of musical chairs, treating liberation as a competition is a mistake in the long run. Every round they remove another chair, until there's just one kid left sitting.

Margaret is a biracial bisexual activist and writer from Nova Scotia. She currently lives in Toronto where she is completing her Ph.D. in theology.

CATHLEEN FINN
MASSACHUSETTS, USA

From 1992 to 1995 I was a member, plaintiff and media spokesperson for the Irish-American Gay, Lesbian and Bisexual Group of Boston (GLIB). During the course of our ongoing struggle to participate as a group in the Boston St. Patrick's Day Parade, I was interviewed by a variety of media reporters both mainstream and from the feminist and/or gay, lesbian, bisexual and transgender community. I was often misidentified as a lesbian although I always introduced myself as an Irish-American bisexual woman. This was a source of great frustration to me, as bisexuals are often negatively stereotyped as not being willing to stand up and fight discrimination based on sexual orientation, or as people who will choose to blend into the woodwork when the going gets tough.

In the years of our struggle for inclusion in the parade we faced a great deal of harassment and ignorance, including a death threat left on my home telephone answering machine. My family, including my parents to whom I had just come out, had an especially hard time with my visibility as a spokesperson for the group. The amount of time and energy my involvement required was also a huge source of stress to me personally. My partner, friends, the excellent people from Gay and Lesbian Advocates and Defenders, supporters from the local Greater Boston Parents and Friends of Lesbians and Gays (PFLAG) chapter, and kind strangers provided the support I needed to continue. Through our efforts, GLIB did a tremendous amount of good. Our actions and visibility educated the wider community. In 1992 and 1993 GLIB was able to march in the St. Patrick's Day Parade and experienced a broad range of spectator responses, from those who were supportive and welcoming to those who displayed unbelievable hatred—angry, yelling crowds throwing things at us, their faces contorted by hate and rage. These images were widely distributed by the media, including one sign along the parade route that read "God Hates Fags." Those who opposed our inclusion did so in such an ugly and extreme way that they unveiled the reality of anti-GLBT bias that lies just beneath the surface of our society. People who had not previously formed an opinion about GLBT people were moved by these images to take a more tolerant stance, since it reminded them of other times in our history when people seeking justice and inclusion in a nonviolent way were treated so badly. By marching with dignity we challenged the hatred our society directs toward people outside the mainstream. According to one public high school teacher, our visibility also provided a convenient "conversation starter"—a safe way for people to bring up and discuss the topic of sexual orientation—and an opportunity for dialogue.

Although we ultimately lost the case before the U.S. Supreme Court, I believe that we won in the court of public opinion and persuaded many that the battle for civil rights for all is an ongoing and evolving process. Speaking as an Irish-American bisexual woman, I would do it all again and hope to live long enough to serve as the grand marshal of the Boston St. Patrick's Day Parade one day.

Cathleen enjoys travel, politics and mediation. She works for IBM, and is married to Carey, her female partner of 11 years. They share a home in Boston with two cats.

ALEX DALL'ASTA
LOMBARDIA, ITALY

 Becoming aware of my bisexuality was a complicated process. It took me years to realize I had to stop wondering whether I was straight or gay, and live out my desires just as they were. I grew up in a little town in northwestern Italy, where there were no gay associations and the idea of bisexuality was—at least publicly—unheard of. This provincialism sent me running away from my hometown in my early twenties. I left Italy for long periods of time and traveled around the world, ending up in Tokyo, where my companion, a woman, lived and worked. In those years I experienced the full range of my sexuality. When my relationship ended in the summer of 2001, I decided it was time to come back home. I wanted to start working as a journalist, and began looking for opportunities in Italy.

Upon returning, I was determined to become an activist, in order to help other bisexuals understand and accept themselves. I wrote to several publishing houses and proposed to translate foreign books on the subject. The only books in Italian were two psychoanalytical studies, both of which labeled bisexuals as gays who did not accept their homosexuality. I also tried to set up a bisexual group. My idea was to create at least an "information portal," such as a website, to help younger bisexuals find a way to communicate. I knew that many of my teenage sexuality troubles might have been avoided if I had found help and advice from others.

In a few weeks, after sending dozens of emails, I received a reply from a young girl who with some friends had set up a bi website. She was eager to start something new, and we immediately began working on a new site. We agreed to make it bilingual in order to attract viewers from other countries. It would include a forum where visitors could communicate with one another, and a book section where we would publish reviews on new texts on bisexuality published around the world. The site took off a few weeks later. It was an immediate success. Through the mailing list we began gathering new members. We asked them to tell us their stories, and it was amazing to see how eager many were to write about themselves. Most of them had a desperate need to come out to others and share their feelings and experiences. Many concealed their sexuality to nearly everyone they loved for fear of being rejected.

The picture we got of bisexuality in Italy was not exactly encouraging: apart from a few, exceptionally broad-minded individuals, Italian bisexuals looked like a bunch of complex-ridden individuals who were unable to understand themselves. The group has had its ups and downs in these three years. I myself have at times been too busy to follow it, but it continues. And I have achieved at least one very important goal: I know that if a bisexual boy or girl out there is desperately wondering who he or she is, at least one convincing answer is within reach.

Alex was born in Piacenza in 1973 and holds a degree in musicology from Parma and York University. He has traveled extensively, has lived in Japan and currently works as a journalist in Milan.

DANA SHAW
ONTARIO, CANADA

Organizing bisexual community in Canada isn't easy. Think of it. We're the third largest country worldwide in land-mass, but for all that space we have a population of only just over 31 million people. The vast majority of those people are in urban centers as far south as possible so we don't freeze our Canadian butts off. These cities are so far apart that often the only way for one group to visit another is to book a flight.

I joined Bisexual Women of Toronto (a.k.a. BIWOT) in 1999. By then it had been around for five years, with waxing and waning membership over time, but an average of 25 people attending the meetings. BIWOT had appeared as an offshoot of the Toronto Bisexual Network, which had started in 1989. These groups had monthly meetings in a community center and occasional social events. A few people were doing bi-sensitivity workshops or writing articles to help educate people about bisexuality and combat biphobia where we found it. It all seemed rather well established and organized. A couple years later another offshoot was created in Bisexual Men of Toronto (BIMOT).

As I became more and more involved I started to want to reach out to other Canadian bi groups. I'd heard of BiNet USA and knew that there was an email list and web site for BiNet Canada. I joined the list and waited for the ideas to pass across the country, for the network to show its strength, to see the work people were doing across the country like we were.

There was an intense silence.

I later discovered that BiNetCanada was the brain-child of two dedicated folks. One was part of BiNetBC in Vancouver and the other in our local group in Toronto. They had thought of the idea of having a Canadian web site with bisexual group and resource listings across the country. They created the email list with the intention of working together with other groups to strengthen bi community. While membership in the email list grew to over 100 and the web site built its list of resources, nothing else happened. People didn't talk to each other about their work. No synergy was created.

In 2001 I joined these two intrepid originating organizers in trying to do the very first in-person meeting of BiNetCanada at the first-ever North American Conference on Bisexuality, Gender and Sexual Diversity in Vancouver. We were very excited. We created a Mission Statement, vision and values to bring with us. We wanted to find out if other people were prepared to put energy into this like we were. The answer? About a dozen people showed up to the meeting. Another five showed up via internet chat (Canadian bi folks could participate even if they weren't physically present). We offered a chance for people to volunteer to make things happen in BiNetCanada. We got maybe two nibbles. Follow-up after we got home went nowhere.

More resounding silence.

In Toronto we had an ever-stronger group of dedicated people. We were making a difference, educating people, appearing at Pride in various cities (Hamilton, London, Toronto, Montreal and Vancouver in 2001 alone). Our Toronto groups were becoming more and more diverse, with people across age, race, gender and label identification communities. We had three associated groups getting stronger and stronger. Another group for bi women started up and while we tried to create a linkage, they seemed to want to have sex parties and didn't care for politics, so we remained completely separate. All four groups continue to flourish, but groups in the rest of Ontario province were disappearing for lack of membership.

We knew there were thousands of closeted bi folks, but where were they? Why weren't they getting more organized instead of less? Why couldn't we organize across the country?

In the northeastern United States there is a cluster of strong groups with big membership numbers. It seems these groups constantly gain membership. One group's energy works with another and they can do more together than they could have done separately. Synergy happens because they feed off each other's energy and enthusiasm. They borrow each other's ideas and make them their own. They show up at each other's functions because they're close enough to do so.

I've come to understand the silence.

It's not that there aren't people in Canada who want things to happen here to make bi community stronger. There are. But the challenge of bridging the huge geographical divide is too great without a large enough number of us to make it happen, and getting us together to do that highlights a huge communications barrier. It's very hard to organize in email. People are more committed to doing things locally. We can't cross-pollinate across groups and cities like groups do in the northeastern United States. It's a five-hour drive from Toronto to Montreal, the two largest centers for bi community groups. The cost and time commitment for travel is enormous. We simply aren't able to get the necessary critical mass to move so few people over such a large area.

For now, we keep trying to figure out how to bring us all together and create that synergy with wide distances between us. Maybe it's dumb to keep trying. But that won't stop us from doing what we can to break the silence.

Dana identifies as a kinky, poly, ex-Jewish, pagan bi-dyke. She's been involved in organizing a vast number of groups in and around Toronto including Bisexual Women of Toronto, the Toronto Bisexual Network and BiNetCanada.

LARS NÆSBYE CHRISTENSEN ZEALAND, DENMARK

Phew! The past five months have been tough: a social support group for bisexuals in Copenhagen, a web page with a discussion forum, angry letters to bigoted newspapers that just don't get it. Two interviews in queer magazines and one due next week on the radio. Not bad, but it just isn't enough. **Bi-activism is an addictive drug once you see the results.**

Denmark may have been the first country to legalize pornography in 1969 and to establish the first same-sex partnership law in 1989, but things have grown increasingly difficult. The populist, nationalistic, anti-immigration and pro-nuclear family movements have been gaining ground.

The mass media in particular requires much work. A major Danish tabloid got my personal biphobia award for listing bisexuality alongside antisocial traits such as spontaneous violence, megalomania and lack of empathy when describing the then-presumed killer of late Swedish foreign minister Anna Lindh.

In addition, some people disrespect activism once they have gotten whatever they want out of it. "There is nothing left to fight for!" proclaimed an infamous Danish right-wing lesbian politician a few years ago. Sure, *she* has never been bashed and *she* is not personally interested in insemination or adoption. I wonder if she will ever realize the massive damage she did to queer politics with those seven words.

Denmark has no organized bi movement and the young and/or uncertain bisexual has very few opportunities to seek face-to-face advice, support and breathing space. And it is not always easy to establish that space, especially if you also plan to take your exams, make a living, strive to be a good loving boyfriend and a somewhat balanced and reflective social human being to boot.

But when things *do* work out exactly as planned, when I see people show interest in a support group I helped to found or when I get an e-mail telling me to keep up the good work, I feel proud.

Not proud of what I am, because it seems hollow to pride myself on my own desires. But of the things I choose to do and how they affect people in a positive way.

Lars was born and raised in Copenhagen. He is a 26-year-old student of musicology, amateur programmer and musician, office worker, bisexual activist and coffee drinker.

JONATHAN DANIEL HOFFMAN
ISRAEL

א בְּרֵאשִׁית, בָּרָא אֱלֹהִים, אֵת הַשָּׁמַיִם, וְאֵת הָאָרֶץ. ב וְהָאָרֶץ, הָיְתָה תֹהוּ וָבֹהוּ, וְחֹשֶׁךְ, עַל-פְּנֵי תְהוֹם; וְרוּחַ אֱלֹהִים, מְרַחֶפֶת עַל-פְּנֵי הַמָּיִם. ג וַיֹּאמֶר אֱלֹהִים, יְהִי אוֹר; וַיְהִי-אוֹר. (בְּרֵאשִׁית, פֶּרֶק א').

1 In the beginning God created the heaven and the earth. **2** Now the earth was unformed and void, and darkness was upon the face of the deep; and the spirit of God hovered over the face of the waters. **3** And God said: 'Let there **BI** light.' And there was light. (Genesis chapter 1)

I live in Jerusalem, Israel. Yes, you probably heard about it in the news. Let me just say—no, we don't ride camels anymore, we do have cable TV, we use fast internet connections, and yes! We are very hot: in terms of our politics, our weather, and well....you know....

However, we have no bi organization...well, we didn't used to have any...

In Israel, back in the "olden days" they established The Aguda, Israel's GLBT association. Other national organizations arose, among them The Other 10%, our GLBT student organization. Unfortunately, despite using the initials GLBT, the groups really have no bi content.

When I started "experimenting" with guys five years ago, I was exposed pretty quickly to the "other culture." Parties, books, trips, chat-rooms—I did it all. The only "problem" was that I was still attracted to and having relationships with girls. "Oh my god! You didn't." was a common reaction back then. "Yuck! Why did you bring a girl to 'our' gay party?" was another one. I was frustrated, longing for something to happen. I was searching like a lunatic for The One, the guy who would be so great and caring that he would make me a "complete and perfect gay." Looking back, I can honestly say that some of the main activists in the "GLBT" community really caused me mental damage while I was exploring my own identity. Bisexuality was just a word I knew, but never a reasonable, considerable, logical option. I had no one to turn to, no one to guide me through those "two roads diverged."

Then, one day my mother told me at lunchtime I needn't choose between pasta and rice and beans—I can have both. It came to me: Why should I choose? Why should I limit myself? Isn't being gay all about freedom of choice? Liberation? I browsed the internet, searched for "bisexuals" in Hebrew, and found nothing. I tried in Italian, and found some useful links. From there the road was open to finding American, European and Australian sites. I remember myself sitting at 23:00, still at work, reading about myself, exposed to what people had to say about me. Everyone online seemed to understand me, to be writing about my experience, my feelings. I was overloaded. Tears came to my eyes. With an immense sense of relief—completeness—finally I gained my identity.

I was so happy. Just as in all those coming out stories. I rushed to tell everyone... and got slapped in the face. The reactions were in a wide spectrum: "OK." "Well...good for you." "What the hell are you talking about?" "Since when?" "OK, what does it mean?" "Stop bullshiting me!" "Bisexual? Yehhh, right—there's no such animal."

Coming out of the bi closet in a country which doesn't entirely recognize the term bisexuality was really hard. No organization supported bis; no hotline, newspaper or internet site would talk about it. Bisexuality was only mentioned as a stage on your way to be a "true gay/lesbian," or as a trend!

I decided: No more! I stood up and told the organizations: you have the right to remain silent (as you did till today), but everything you say can and will be used against you in the court of sexuality. You have the right to appoint a bi proxy solicitor. If you can't afford one, don't worry, I'll raise the money myself!

I established "BIS" (Bisexuals in Israel); in Hebrew: "Bisexualim Be'Israel." We have created a mailing list of 157 people, and two discussion groups (in Jerusalem and in Tel Aviv), published two articles in major magazines, and are currently negotiating with a TV station that wants to do a cover story about us. We are also going to have an Israeli conference, and we're trying to raise enough money to publish a book of academic articles about bisexuality in Hebrew.

So, in a way, we just said in Israel: "Let there **BI** light. And there was light."

Of course, one small candle is not enough. Bringing the bi agenda to both straight and GLBT communities is hard. But the world's embrace and the loving support we are receiving from bi activists around the world, gives us the power to carry on.

Jonathan is a 26-year-old, LL.M student at the Hebrew University at Jerusalem. He was among six students selected as exemplars by Hillel's Charles Schusterman International Student Leaders Assembly for promoting social justice in the society.

MAKOTO HIBINO
JAPAN

A long time ago, I hesitated to assert my bisexual identity within the gay community in Japan. Unfortunately, there is discrimination against bisexuals in the gay and lesbian community in Japan. Japan has homophobia, though it differs from that in the United States. To struggle against homophobia is right, necessary, and important, not only for lesbians and gays but also for me. But some gay activists, especially those deep in the movement and those who see

themselves as the only victims of homophobia, find it hard to understand bisexuality and refuse to hear my voice.

A few years ago I learned of the bisexual movement in the United States. I was very empowered to hear of it. The news coincided with the start of my bi activism in Japan. On June 30, 1996 we put up a big placard reading "WE ARE PROUD OF BEING BISEXUAL" at the first LesBiGay pride march in Sapporo.

Through my activism I spoke with many people and I learned much from transgenders, genderqueers, feminists, asexuals and intersex activists. Recently I was criticized by asexual activists in Japan for my hidden assumption that all people are interested in romance or sex. Talking with them, I realized that the exclusion of asexual people may have parallels to the exclusion of bisexual people. I learned that even if we have no ill will, we tend to make mistakes. No one is perfectly innocent.

From my transgender friends I learned about non-trans privilege and about the binary gender system. Then my own gender transition started. Now I choose to identify as MTX transgender (or genderqueer or *okama*).

I see myself as an activist challenging the binary gender system itself, rather than as a bi activist or a trans activist, because the concept of the word bisexual ("two-sexual") is dependent on the binary gender system and my activism extends beyond that.

Today in Japan I know of no bi-specific activism. Rather, some bisexual people are working within a larger sexuality movement and/or other social movements.

Makoto lives in Kyoto and joined the International Solidarity Movement in Palestine in 2002.

LANI KA'AHUMANU
CALIFORNIA, USA

Bisexual politics is about love, liberation, the freedom to be whole human beings sharing the world with all living things. Bisexual politics is about justice, equality and peace in the universe. Bisexual politics is about coming out to your self, to someone else, and to someone else and so on and on. Bisexual politics is about personal integrity. Bisexual politics is about challenging yourself and others to go beyond what is familiar and safe. Bisexual politics is the art of listening and communicating as clearly as we know how. Bisexual politics is being accountable and trusting one another. Bisexual politics is about breaking down the either/or concepts of sex, race, gender, orientation, identity, age, ability, resources, relationships, etc. Bisexual politics need not indulge another horizontal finger-pointing dichotomy—

bisexual vs. monosexual—knowing the bottom line is heterosexism. Bisexual politics is about nature and nurture and choice. Bisexual politics is about feminism, about women's oppression being intimately related to homophobia and erotophobia (among other things). Bisexual politics is mindful of who is in our community and who is not present when important decisions are made. Bisexual politics pays attention to the silent and silenced among us. Bisexual politics speaks out, takes stands, works in coalition, makes alliances, and educates on issues of importance to bisexual people and our families that are not easily dealt with: immigration and the rights of immigrants; violence in all forms; homelessness; poverty; mental and physical abilities and access; healthcare; cancer; HIV/AIDS; veterans and the military; employment; and other issues. Bisexual politics refuses to maintain silence when our communities refuse to address injustice. Bisexual politics means sticking your neck out, making a big stink, facing hostility and ignorance, being a token, demanding respect whether we get it or not. Bisexual politics is educating each other about how race relations and economics and access to resources and anti-Jewish sentiment play out in our lives, our communities and movements and then doing the necessary work of challenging the status quo inside and outside our selves. Bisexual politics stands with the current scapegoat, understanding we must watch each other's back. Bisexual politics facilitates discussions of community concern. Bisexual politics works with and within all the various communities we call home. Bisexual politics lubricates the shifting paradigms by taking notes, making movies, writing letters to the editor, books, songs, poetry, prose, rapping, singing, slamming, performing, making music, dancing, playing, celebrating, organizing a support group, a gathering, a retreat, a conference, a fund raiser, a pot luck at your home. Bisexual politics embraces and celebrates the redefinition of family and personal relationships. Bisexual politics is about loving our selves, our bodies, our sensuality, our sexuality, our spirituality, our gender expression(s), our age, our aging and all that we resist. Bisexual politics is about the earth and our collective well-being. Bisexual politics is the joyful risk of self regardless of any of our identities.

Lani has been actively involved in social justice movements since the sixties when she was a full-time suburban housewife. She is co-editor of Bi Any Other Name: Bisexual People Speak Out, *which was listed on the Top 100 Queer Books of the 20th Century by Lambda Book Review and has sold close to 40,000 copies. Currently, Lani is working on her next two titles: "My Grassroots Are Showing: stories, speeches, and special affections" and "Passing For Other: primal creams and forbidden dreams – poetry, prose, and performance pieces."*

BILL BURLESON
MINNESOTA, USA

"You are too an activist," she said.

An activist? Hardly. I just do my thing. I facilitate support groups; I help with conferences; I speak about bisexuality at college campuses. I do it because I enjoy it. If it were activism, wouldn't I be doing it for some altruistic reason? And, come on, I hate meetings! Wouldn't a real activist like attending meetings, whereas I'd rather be getting a root canal?

I've spent an awful lot of my time in the last six or seven years working to raise awareness of bisexual issues and increase bi community visibility, and I've relished it. I've had the pleasure to work along side and become friends with many bi activists. I've enjoyed the fruit of seeds I've helped plant. I'm happy when people have told me I've made a difference in their lives. All along I've done it for selfish reasons: I get my support from speaking up, from being active, by working hard. Helping someone understand their sexuality helps me understand mine. Helping end another's isolation makes me feel more connected. Helping my community makes me feel a part of it. I've spoken out about bisexuality for my own reasons: by making my community stronger, by making fellow bisexuals stronger, I become stronger myself.

Perhaps this passion, regardless of its personal motivation, fuels all activism. I can't speak to that. I can say it fuels me; I get so much more out of my work than I put in.

"Activist?" I replied, "I'm just happy to help."

Bill is one of the founders of the Bisexual Organizing Project and the Bisexual Resource Center in Minneapolis, a past coordinator for BECAUSE: the Midwest Conference on Bisexuality, and produces the cable access show, BiCities! He is also the author of Bi America: Myths, Truths, and Struggles of an Invisible Community, from Harrington Press.

Roberta Gregory

ARTICLES
& RESOURCES

How to spell the word "Bisexual"

Tom Limoncelli

The word is spelled "bisexual." It's really quite simple. It has no hypen and the "s" is not caps. Unless it is at the beginning of a sentence, the first letter is lowercase.

RIGHT	WRONG
bisexual	bi-sexual
	BiSexual
	Bisexual (unless at the beginning of a sentence)

It's easy to remember the thing about the hyphen: It's not homo-sexual, it's not les-bian, it's not bi-sexual.

I see some people write it with the first letter in caps as in: Tom is a Bisexual.

I consider this to be bad form. Nationalities are first letter cap, but adjectives aren't. The word "bisexual" is an adjective, not a nationality. There is no Bisexualia from which we all come. Therefore this is correct: Tom is Italian. And this is correct also: Tom is bisexual.

On the other hand, some GLBT publications, like the *Philadelphia Gay News*, have an editorial guideline that dictates that they always capitalize Gay and Lesbian. Therefore they write: Johnson, a Gay activist, spoke at the conference.

In this case, we demand capitalization parity. Therefore in this case and in this case only the word should be capitalized. Therefore, *PGN* should write: Bob, a Gay man, and his partner Mike, who is Bisexual, also spoke at the conference.

However, we consider this a silly editorial standard since they don't capitalize the word "heterosexual."

I can't believe that I've been doing bisexual activism for more than ten years and this issue still comes up so often. Oh well. There are bigger fish to fry.

Bisexual Politics for Lesbians and Gay Men

Ramki Ramakrishnan

1. Unlearn binary thinking. To quote Alfred Kinsey, "The world is not divided into sheep and goats." Further, if you consider it homophobic when straight folks erase homosexuality and assume everyone around them is or should be heterosexual; then acknowledge that it is biphobic when you erase bisexuality and assume everyone around you is or should be gay or straight.

2. Do not assume "gay and lesbian" is a sufficient descriptor for the LGBT community any more than you would assume using the word "gay" is sufficient to make lesbians feel included, or that white queer cultures are a sufficient representation of queer cultures worldwide.

3. Just as some women use both "gay" and "lesbian" to describe themselves, yet others use both "lesbian" and "bisexual" to describe themselves. If in doubt about who identifies as what, assume there are bisexuals present in every group of queers. We often are.

4. The sexual orientation of people cannot be inferred by the sex/gender of their partner. Just as a person may be gay/lesbian and single, a person may be bisexual and in a same-sex relationship, bisexual and single, or bisexual and in an other-sex relationship. Thus a "lesbian relationship" may include women of whom one or both are bisexually identified and/or oriented.

5. As an addendum to the above point, the term "same-sex relationship" is preferable to "gay/lesbian relationship" because the latter has come to imply that both partners are gay/lesbian while in reality that may not be the case. Ditto for other-sex relationships, in which one or both partners may be bisexual.

6. Bisexuals are not the latest pesky addition to a bestiary of sexuality minorities clamoring for greater inclusion. We have been around as long as homosexuals, and have been part of queer culture whether or not we have chosen to identify ourselves as bi.

7. Naming and honoring bi and trans sexualities is not merely a matter of political correctness or minding one's P's and Q's. It is about us queers showing the same regard for diversity and complexity that we demand—and rightfully so—from our communities of origin, and from the world at large.

An earlier version of this work was previously published in *Trikone Magazine* (March 2003), and is reproduced here with permission.

Ramki is a biologist, musician, and queer community organizer. When living in Austin, Texas, he founded Trikone-Tejas, a pan-Asian student alliance dedicated to ending racism, sexism, and homophobia at UT Austin. He has since returned to India, where he continues his activism.

Alex Hirka

Bisexual Etiquette
10 Helpful Hints for Bisexuals Working with Lesbians & Gay Men

Robyn Ochs

I recently celebrated my 22nd anniversary as a bisexual activist. Much of my activism has taken place in the context of the Boston area GLBT community. In most of the lesbian and gay groups with which I have been involved, I have been one of two or three out bisexuals. During my decades of activism I have learned a great deal, both from my own mistakes, and other people's. I have said and done things which I have instantly and thoroughly regretted, and experienced moments of proud accomplishment. At times I have felt like a supplicant, a second-class citizen, a token, a nuisance, and at other times an equal, a leader, a decorated veteran, a sister.

What follows are a few suggestions I would like to pass along to other bisexual people who are involved in GLBT communities.

1. **RESPECT OTHER PEOPLE'S IDENTITIES**. Don't say, "Everyone's really bisexual." Don't say that bisexual people are somehow more evolved. Think of your frustration when someone tells you that there is no such thing as a bisexual, or that bisexuals are really lesbians or gay men in transition, or that we are really heterosexual tourists out for sexual adventure at the expense of lesbians and gay men. Avoid false absolutes: reality is delightfully, disturbingly complex.

2. **DON'T RAISE YOUR OWN SELF-IMAGE AT THE EXPENSE OF OTHER PEOPLE**. Examples of *bad* ideas taken from real life: a t-shirt that says "Monosexuals bore me." A button that says "Gay is good but bi is best." Please. As the expression goes, "Do unto others as you would have them do unto you."

3. **RESPECT OTHER PEOPLE'S IDENTITIES AND CHOICES**. It is our right to choose our own labels. Respect those who choose a label different from your own. Our goal should be not to create a space in which we are all alike, but rather to create a space in which our differences are recognized and valued.

4. Along the same lines, **REMEMBER ALL THE LETTERS**. Just as it is important for bisexuals that the word "bisexual" be included, so is it important to use "transgender," "lesbian," and, when appropriate, "queer," "intersex," and "ally." And so on.

5. **AVOID THE TRAP OF WEIGHING AND MEASURING OPPRESSION**.
Avoid thinking of oppression and liberation as a zero-sum game, with
a finite quantity of either to be parceled out. There is, unfortunately,
plenty of oppression to go around. Fortunately, there is also enough
liberation to go around. Don't say that bisexuals are more oppressed
than lesbians or gay men. We are *ALL* oppressed. Oppression sucks.
Each of us experiences oppression differently. A bisexual person who
has an other-sex partner experiences homophobia differently from a
bisexual in a same-sex relationship. Out people experience oppression
differently than closeted people. Butch women and femme men have a
different experience walking down the street than femme women and
butch men. Gay men experience oppression differently than do lesbians.
People who belong in more than one oppressed group, such as a disabled
Latina lesbian, have their own specific experiences. And bisexual men
have an experience that is different from bisexual women. It's OK that
we are not all the same. Even people within the same identity group
can have very different experiences. But oppression, homophobia, and
sexism, no matter how they manifest, still suck, and we have a common
interest in working together to end them.

6. **RESPECT SEPARATE SPACE**. There is a time for coalition building,
and a time to get together in our own identity groups to do our own
empowerment work. All members of oppressed groups have the right
to take space when they feel it necessary, and we need to respect that.
The difficulty, of course, lies in determining when separate space is
appropriate, and when it is not.

It is my belief that any event in which lesbians and gay men get
together is already by definition a coalition event. And I believe that
I, for example, as a woman-centered bisexual feminist woman, have
a lot more in common with most lesbians than do many gay men.
However, when an event is explictly a gay male- or lesbian-only event,
we need to respect other people's space. (I want to make a distinction
here between a lesbian event—an event produced by, or primarily for
lesbians—and a lesbian-*only* event. I am speaking of the latter.) This is a
bit more complicated than it may seem, but I have developed a personal
guideline, and I'll give a couple of examples of its application.

Boston used to have a group called Dyke Dialogue, which was organized
by Val Seabrook, a (wonderful) African-American lesbian activist. A
few lesbians regularly attending the group believed that it should
include lesbians only, and exclude bisexual and transgender women.
In this instance, to determine whether it was in fact appropriate for
me to attend, I asked Val, the group's founder and organizer. She told
me that the group was for all women, and she intended to welcome

bisexual and transgender women. In this situation I believe it totally appropriate for bisexual women to participate. Any lesbians unhappy with the group's composition were free to remove themselves and start their own exclusive group.

My second example came to me second-hand. A female-partnered bisexually-identified woman active in her local GLBT community was interested in joining a local mothers' group to get support as a queer parent. The only group listed in the local newspaper was a lesbian mothers' group. She called the contact person for the group and asked whether bisexual women were welcome, and was told that they were not. Disappointed, but respecting the organizers' wishes, she resolved to try to start a second group for lesbian and bisexual moms.

Of course, there are many gray areas: what about the bisexual woman in a monogamous same-sex relationship of ten years who considers herself a bisexual lesbian or a lesbian bisexual considering whether to attend an event advertised as being "for lesbians only"? Should her lover attend but not her? Should she go and keep her mouth shut about being bisexual? Should she go and be an out bisexual? Here the answer is less clear.

But one thing is certain: lesbians and gay men need to feel that there are places and times when their space will remain inviolate. There do need to be limits to inclusion, and inclusionary politics and separate space can exist simultaneously.

7. BE A GOOD CITIZEN. Don't insist on being included in a given group unless you are willing to put your energy into that group. While bisexual women and men have been active in the lesbian and gay community from the start, remember that few of us have been publicly identifiable as bisexual. Most of us have simply done the work, attended the events, and not corrected people's misassumptions about our identities. I can think of more than one political event or pride march I attended along with other bisexual activists, only to read that "thousands of lesbians and gay men rallied...," in the gay press. This oversight has allowed many lesbians and gay men to assume that there are few, if any, bisexual people in the movement. Just as *all* of us have been written out of the mainstream imagination, so have bisexuals and transgendered people been largely omitted from lesbian and gay awareness. Therefore, when we join a group as out bisexuals and begin asking for explicit recognition *as bisexuals*, many people believe that bisexuals have suddenly appeared out of nowhere and are now trying to muscle and whine our way into *their* movement, riding on the coattails of *their* hard-fought battles. Remember this when you enter a new group. Be a good citizen. If you

want to recognized as part of the community, don't just show up and tell *them* what to do. Join the group. Show your commitment as an out bisexual. Then express your concerns.

8. **CHOOSE YOUR BATTLES**. This has been a hard one for me personally. Is it *always* important to have every sentence end with "and bisexual"? Is it important to point this omission out every time? Sometimes it may be more constructive to just be your wonderful, out bisexual self. Choose your battles thoughtfully, and prepare in advance constructive ways to respond when you feel that the language used does not include everyone.

9. **LISTEN**. Rather than being always on the defensive, I have been trying hard to listen to the fears, concerns, and perspectives of my lesbian and gay male friends. I've been surprised at how much I learn when I stop defending myself long enough to listen well.

10. **REMEMBER,** underneath it all, we all want the same things. We want respect. We want understanding. We want to be listened to, and acknowledged. We want to feel safe. Accord others the same respect that you are demanding for yourself.

Margaret Robinson

Biphobia

Robyn Ochs

Bisexuals make people uncomfortable. Many people wish that we would just go away, or at least keep quiet about it, because they perceive our very existence as a threat to the social order. A declaration of bisexual identity often results in discrimination, hostility, and invalidation. Gay- and lesbian-identified individuals frequently view us as either confused or interlopers possessing a degree of privilege not available to them, and many heterosexuals see us as amoral, hedonistic spreaders of disease and disrupters of families. Why all the fuss?

To understand the dynamics of biphobia, it helps to understand the dynamics of oppression in general, in order to separate out what is actually about bisexuality itself, and how much of it is just about silly humans, and how we tend to behave as social creatures.

Sociology 101

First off, Western society likes to construct things in binaries: Male/Female, Good/Evil, and of course, Straight/Gay. In each of these binaries, one is given high status, the other lower.

Prejudiced behavior, or discrimination, is widespread. People in many categories and in many cultures have long been denied access to opportunities in employment, housing, and civil liberties. We are also denied the luxury of being able to see people who look and live like ourselves represented fairly on television, in the movies, in newspapers and in magazines.

Another example of discrimination is stereotyping: having a preconceived and oversimplified idea of the characteristics which typify a person. For example, bisexuals have been stereotyped as indecisive and promiscuous. Sexual orientation is what Gordon Allport called "a label of primary potency," one that is seen as so significant that "it magnifies one attribute out of all proportion to its true significance, and masks other important attributes of the individual" (p. 179). Attention is focused on this one aspect of ourselves, and all of our other qualities and characteristics get thrown into shadow. Bisexuality, once known, thus becomes foregrounded.

It is important to remember that despite this, each person has numerous simultaneous identities. I, for example, identify as bisexual, able-bodied, athletic, a dancer, left-handed, an activist, an academic, a student, a public speaker, a daughter, aunt, and sister, and as someone in a same-sex marriage. Many of us are members of more than one identity group within a given category: I, for example, identify as mixed-class, and my religious/ethnic heritage is mixed. I am Jewish but not religious, and one of my three parents was Christian. I have lived in Boston for 20 years but identify strongly as a New Yorker. Some of our identifications may be as members of the majority or in-group; others may be as members of the minority, or out-group. Few of us are in all respects privileged or in all respects oppressed.

Another factor directly affecting bisexuals' experiences of oppression is the invisibility of our particular minority population. We have to deal with the constant visibility of those of our identity categories that are visually identifiable by the fact of sitting in a wheelchair, or because of the hue of our skin). These characteristics do not give us the option of "passing" as a member of the dominant group in order to avoid discrimination. We experience identities that are not readily apparent, such as sexual orientation or religion, are experienced differently. While not constantly identifiable, which may in certain contexts protect us from discrimination, we suffer the disadvantage of not being able to identify others like ourselves, resulting in feelings of isolation and an underestimation of our large numbers by both members of our own group and members of the dominant group. In addition, the "privilege" of passing also carries as its counterweight the onus of needing to repeatedly announce ourselves in order to avoid being misidentified, as well as feelings of guilt or discomfort when we are silent. We carry the weight of constantly having to make the decision of how and when to come out and at what cost.

Homophobia

Biphobia cannot be understood in isolation. It shares many characteristics with other forms of oppression, especially homophobia. Audre Lorde (1984) defines homophobia as the belief in the inherent superiority of one pattern of loving, and thereby the right to dominance and the fear of feelings of love for a member of one's own sex, and the hatred of those feelings in others. The Campaign to End Homophobia, an organization dedicated to raising awareness among heterosexuals, divides homophobia into four distinct but interrelated types: personal, interpersonal, institutional, and cultural. Personal homophobia is an individual's own fears or feelings of discomfort toward homosexual people or homosexuality. Interpersonal homophobia is that same fear manifest in hurtful behaviors, such as name-calling, negative jokes, or the physical violence directed at bisexuals, gay men, and lesbians, known as "gay bashing." Institutional

 homophobia consists of a broad range of discriminatory practices toward lesbian, gay, or bisexual people, such as prohibiting same-sex couples from obtaining social benefits under their partners' policies or denial of legal protection against discrimination in employment, housing, or public accommodations. They define cultural homophobia as cultural standards and norms that pervade society, such as the assumption that all people are heterosexual or silence around issues of homosexuality (Thompson & Zoloth, 1990).

There is no doubt that homophobia and heterosexism exist. One need only look at the prevalence of bomb threats, murder, physical assaults, arson, vandalism, telephone harassment, and police abuse against GLBT people.

How does homophobia affect bisexuals, gays, and lesbians? Gordon Allport (1954) laid out multiple ways in which individuals respond negatively to stigmatization, including two of importance to the discussion of biphobia: aggression and blame directed at one's own group, and prejudice and discrimination directed against other minorities. Theoretically, this may assist us in understanding two phenomena frequently observed in sexual minority populations: (a) internalized homophobia and (b) the hostility directed at bisexuals and transgendered persons by some gay men and lesbians. Some act out feelings of victimization through anger at and rejection of those who are perceived as even less acceptable than themselves. They fear that these "marginal people" will give all gays and lesbians an even worse image than that which they already hold in the eyes the dominant culture, further impeding gays' and lesbians' struggle for acceptance.

Where Does Biphobia Overlap With Homophobia?

There is a considerable overlap between homophobia and biphobia, as well as specific ways in which each is unique. Furthermore, homophobia and biphobia affect men and women differently.

Visible bisexuals, like visible lesbians and gay men, may be targeted for discrimination. If theories of the "lesser oppression" of bisexuals were to hold true, the bisexual teacher whose sexual orientation has been disclosed would merely be reduced to half-time employment, and the bisexual individual being targeted by homophobic teens would get only half-gay bashed (punched and kicked half as many times, or perhaps half as hard?). Homophobia and biphobia inevitably intersect through the common experience of discrimination. To the bigot, we are all alike.

Another area of congruence between the experience of biphobia and the experience of homophobia may be with respect to "coming out" issues. A bisexual coming to terms with a same-sex attraction is likely to experience shame, ambivalence, and discomfort similar to that experienced by lesbians and gay men. Most world cultures deny both homosexuality and bisexuality, present distorted images of both homosexuals and bisexuals, and prevent the dissemination of accurate information about both groups to people in the general population.

In summary, we are all oppressed, and we can all be targeted. Whether the cause of this oppression is called homophobia or biphobia, it hurts everyone.

Biphobia

Most bi people I have met come laden with painful stories of rejection by both heterosexuals and lesbians and gay men.

A primary manifestation of biphobia is the denial of the very existence of bisexual people, attributable to the fact that many cultures think in binary categories, with each category having its mutually exclusive opposite. This is powerfully evident in the areas of sex and gender. Male and female, and heterosexuality and homosexuality are seen as "opposite categories." Those whose sexual orientation defies simple labeling or those whose sex or gender is ambiguous may make us profoundly uncomfortable.

Thus, bisexuals create discomfort and anxiety in others simply by the fact of our existence. We are pressured to remain silent, as our silence allows the dominant culture to exaggerate the differences between heterosexual and homosexual and to ignore the fact that human sexuality exists on a continuum. It is much less threatening to the dominant heterosexual culture to perpetuate the illusion that homosexuals are "that category, way over there," very different from heterosexuals. If "they" are extremely different, heterosexuals do not have to confront the possibility of acknowledging same-sex attractions within themselves and possibly becoming "like them." There is considerable anxiety in being forced to acknowledge that the "other" is not as different from you as you would like to pretend.

Because of our cultural erasure, bisexuality tends to be invisible except as a point of conflict. Given that studies reveal that only a small percentage of bisexuals are simultaneously involved with persons of both genders (Rust, 1991) and that we tend to assume that a person's sexual orientation corresponds to the sex of his or her current partner, it is difficult to make our bisexuality visible in daily life. As a result, most people usually "see" bisexuality only in the context of uncomfortable situations: a closeted married man contracts HIV from sex with another man and his wife contracts the virus; a woman leaves her lesbian relationship for a male lover. Often, when bisexuality is given attention, it is portrayed as a transitional category, an interim stage in an original or subsequent coming-out process, usually from heterosexual to homosexual. This has the effect of associating bisexuality in many people's minds with conflict and impermanence.

The word bisexual itself may be seen as a product of binary thinking and, therefore, problematic. Many people struggling to understand bisexuality can only imagine the concept as a 50-50 identity. In their minds, if a third category exists, then it must fall midway between the other two categories and have clearly defined, unchanging parameters. Using this measurement, they will find very few "true" bisexuals. Many people also assume that a bisexual must need a lover of each sex to be satisfied, raising the specter of non-monogamy, another hot button for many.

This association of bisexuality with non-monogamy is a source of biphobia within heterosexual communities, especially since the arrival of HIV and AIDS. In the minds of many, bisexuality has come to be strongly identified with images of married, closeted men bringing HIV to their wives and children through unsafe sex with other men, and these stereotypes are amply reinforced in the media. This has been a common theme since the second half of the 1980s and has most recently manifested itself in a frenzy of media attention about the "down low" – African American men who have sex with men and with women but who identify neither as bisexual nor as gay.

Biphobia directed at bisexuals by gay men and lesbians is complex. Its roots lie in the dynamics of oppression and the particular historical context affecting the growth and development of individual gay, lesbian, and bisexual communities. Coming out and living as gay can be very difficult. Many gay men and lesbians have experienced a great deal of hurt and rejection, and shared pain is one of the foundations on which many "lesbian and gay" communities have historically been based. External oppression may create a sense of not being safe and a strong need to maintain a clear boundary between "us" and "them." Bisexuals are by definition problematic in this regard, blurring the boundaries between insider and outsider. And further, bisexual visibility within the lesbian and gay community calls into question the inaccurate assumption that there is a monolithic lesbian and gay community with a single set of standards and values, composed of individuals who all behave similarly and predictably.

Lesbians and gay men may also fear that they are unable to compete with the benefits our culture accords to those in different-sex relationships, believing that those who have a choice will ultimately choose heterosexuality. Many lesbians and gay men believe that bisexuals have less commitment to "the community," and that whatever a lesbian or gay man might have to offer to their bisexual partner will not be enough to outweigh the external benefits offered to those who are in heterosexual relationships. There is some realistic basis for this fear: Heterosexual relationships are privileged, and many bisexuals, like many lesbians and gay men, adopt at least a public front of heterosexuality to avoid family censure, develop careers, and raise children with societal approval. However, I also believe that this line of reasoning shows some internalized homophobia. Many bisexuals, even with this perceived choice, still choose same-sex relationships. What gets lost in the fear is the fact that same-sex relationships also offer benefits not available in heterosexual relationships: the absence of scripted gender roles, freedom from unwanted pregnancy, the ease of being with someone with more similar social conditioning, and so on. Most important, the psychic cost of denying one's love for a particular person can be astronomical.

Internalized Biphobia

Biphobia does not come only from the outside. Internalized biphobia can be powerful, sometimes overpowering, and the experience of isolation, illegitimacy, shame, and confusion felt by many bisexuals can be disempowering, even disabling.

Even today, with modest improvements in this area, bisexuals have few role models. Due to bisexual invisibility and the paucity of bisexual role models or bisexual community, most bisexuals develop and maintain our bisexual identities in isolation.

Most bisexuals spend a majority of our time in the community that corresponds with the sex and sexual orientation of our romantic partner. As a result, we may experience a sense of discontinuity if we change partners and our partner is of a different sex, or if we shift back and forth between two differing communities over time. Other bisexuals have a strong social affiliation with either a heterosexual, lesbian, or gay community. This can result in another set of conflicts: if our partner is not of the "correct" sex, then we may feel guilt or shame for having "betrayed" our friends and community. Because of these potential difficulties, many people privately identify as bisexual but, to avoid conflict and preserve their ties to a treasured community, choose to identify publicly as lesbian, gay, or straight or to stay silent, allowing others to presume that they do, further contributing to bisexual invisibility.

Therefore, it is not surprising that some bisexuals find their bisexual desire more a burden than a gift. They may feel a pressure or a wish to choose between heterosexuality and homosexuality to make their lives easier and avoid internal and external conflict. Many desire the ease they imagine would come with having one clear, fixed, socially acceptable identity. The behavior of individual bi people, as members of a stigmatized group, is frequently seen as representative of all bisexuals. Thus, a bi-identified person may feel a sense of shame when any bisexual person behaves in such a way as to reinforce negative stereotypes of bisexual people. And we can feel an even more profound sense of shame when our own behavior happens to mirror one of the existing stereotypes of bisexuals (such as practicing polyamory, or leaving one relationship for another). Although some bisexual people do behave in ways that conform to negative stereotypes about bisexuals, it is actually the dynamics of prejudice that cause others to use such actions to generalize their stereotyping and prejudiced behavior to an entire group.

Ironically, bisexual individuals in monogamous relationships may also experience difficulties, feeling that their maintenance of a bisexual identity constitutes a double betrayal of both their community of primary identification (straight or gay) and of their partner. Alternatively, the bi person's partner may feel that a bi person's decision to continue to identify as bisexual, despite being in a monogamous relationship, somehow withholds full commitment to the relationship and holds out the possibility of other relationships. This overlooks the fact that one's identity is, in actuality, separate from particular choices made about relationship involvement or monogamy.

So, how do we make things better? Given so many obstacles, both internal and external, discussed above, how can a bisexual person come to a positive bisexual identity?

Understand the social dynamics of oppression and stereotyping. Get support and validation from others. Join a support group, subscribe to an email list, attend a conference, read books about bisexuality. Get a good bi-positive therapist, and find a friend (or two or twenty) to talk to.

Silence kills. I encourage bisexual people to come out as bisexual to the maximum extent that you can do so safely. Life in the closet takes an enormous toll on our emotional well-being. Bisexuals must remember that neither bisexuals nor gays and lesbians created heterosexism and that as bisexuals, we are its victims as well as potential beneficiaries. Although we must be aware that we, as bisexuals, sometimes have privileges that have been denied to gays, lesbians, and transgendered people of any orientation, this simply calls for us to make thoughtful decisions about how to live our lives. We did not create the inequities, and we must not feel guilty for who we are; we need only be responsible for what we do.

Bisexuals, along with lesbians, gay men, and supportive heterosexuals must open our hearts and minds to celebrate the true diversity among us. Our success lies in creating a space where the full spectrum of our relationships is respected and valued, including those that are unlike our own. We must remember that each person is unique and also that we have much in common. Labels can unite us, but they can also stifle us and constrict our thinking when we forget that they are merely tools. Human beings are complex, and labels will never be adequate to the task of representing us. It is impossible to reduce a lifetime of experience to a single word.

If biphobia and homophobia are not allowed to control us, we can move beyond our fears and learn to value our differences as well as our similarities.

Bibliography

Allport, Gordon, *The Nature of Prejudice.* Reading MA, etc.: Addison Wesley Publishing Co., 1954.

Lorde, Audre, *Sister Outsider.* Freedom, CA: The Crossing Press, 1984.

Rust, Paula, "The Politics of Sexual Identity: Sexual Attraction and Behavior Among Lesbian and Bisexual Women," in *Social Problems*, Vol. 39, No. 4. (Nov. 1992).

Thompson, Cooper and Zoloth, Barbara, "Homophobia," a pamphlet produced by the Campaign to End Homophobia (Cambridge MA, 1990).

Safer and Sexier

bi Cianna Stewart

So I've been asked to talk to you about safer sex. But really I'd rather just talk about sex because it's more fun to talk about enjoying good sex and how to keep having it. Really, safer sex is about sex. I know sometimes we forget that. Even more importantly, staying safe doesn't start when you're already having sex. But we'll get to that.

So about sex...

Do you like having sex?
What kind of sex do you like?
What do you mean by "sex"?
Do you know what will make you feel good during sex?
Do you like to talk during sex?
Do you like to talk before having sex?
Do you hate to talk about sex?
Do you only talk about sex when you're not having it?
Do you know how to ask for what you want?
Can you say something would feel better if...
Can you tell a sex partner that something they're doing
does not feel good?
What words do you use to describe your body?
What words do you use for different sexual/sensual acts?
What kind of sex makes you feel unsafe?
What are your boundaries?
What are your partner's boundaries?
Are you more willing to stop having sex or to try doing it with latex?

Some things to remember:

1) It's OK to have a hard time with safer sex. What is most important is to recognize that getting to be safe is a series of steps. If you've never tried safer sex, and you use a condom or glove or whatever for the first time, you're safer than you were before. Congratulations!

2) Don't dwell on the times that you weren't 100% safe. This world gives us plenty of reasons to feel bad about sex and about our bodies. We don't need to create new ones.

3) The "good old days" weren't really so good. Sexually transmitted diseases (STDs) have always been around and people have always needed to take some kind of precautions to protect themselves. So taking care of yourself should be nothing new.

4) Good sex is not a myth. And I've had some very good sex that was very

safe. And that's why I've been asked to talk about all this with you.

HIV

So there's this thing out there called HIV (the virus that's been linked to AIDS), and while it seems like it's everywhere, you can actually track its path and stop it before it gets to you. Really.

Who me?

HIV has no biases for or against a group of people. It does, however, have a particular fondness for bodily fluids that have a high level of white blood cells and for activities which transmit those fluids from one person to another. It therefore affects all people doing certain "unsafe activities," regardless of sexual identity, gender, age, race, class or regional location.

Yes, you.

What else is out there?

There are many other diseases and infections you could potentially contract or transmit through sex. These diseases and infections can almost all be treated, but they can cause problems ranging from sores to very painful infections. Syphilis, hepatitis A, B, and C, gonorrhea, and chlamydia can all be transmitted through sex. Genital herpes and genital warts are transmitted through contact with the herpes or warts. Safer sex will help protect you from all of these. Pubic lice can also be transmitted through sex, or any close physical contact, or sharing clothing.

Syphilis is caused by bacteria. In addition to causing sores on the genitals, anus, or mouth, it produces fever and can damage internal organs if left untreated. Antibiotics are very successful in treating syphilis if it's detected early. Hepatitis is a virus that causes inflammation of the liver. Vaccines are available for Hepatitis A and B. Gonorrhea and chlamydia are bacterial infections treatable with antibiotics. Herpes and warts are both viruses and thus cannot be

permanently cured, but symptoms can be eased through the treatment of outbreaks. Pubic lice, while easy to catch, are also easily treated with medicated lotions.

There are many bacteria and viruses out there that would love to make their home in your body. But this doesn't mean you should panic. It means that if you have strange symptoms, including sores on the genitals or mouth, strangely colored urine, or burning/unusual discharge from the genitals, then you should contact a doctor to see if you've contracted a disease or nfection through sexual contact. And remember, playing safe can help to ιrotect you from these problems.

Vhat about pregnancy?

For men and women having sex, pregnancy prevention can be very nportant. Remember that pregnancy prevention is not the same as safer sex. ʹhough the Pill or a diaphragm can usually prevent pregnancy, they can't ιrotect you from sexually transmitted diseases or infections.

If your partner or you do get pregnant without wanting to, you have everal options. While many people chose parenting or giving their child up for doption, some choose to abort the pregnancy. Abortions are usually performed ʹuring the first two trimesters of a pregnancy. Legal restrictions on abortion vary rom country to country and within the United States from state to state. Many tates in the USA restrict a young woman's access to abortion, often requiring a ʹoman under the age of 18 to obtain her parents' permission before obtaining n abortion. In some areas, certain abortion methods, like partial extraction, re restricted. Those who can contact a local or national reproductive health ιrovider and/or advocacy group, such as Planned Parenthood in the United ʹtates, can find out more specific information about abortion access in their rea. Be warned, though, that many places called "pregnancy crisis centers" are ιot reproductive health clinics. They are anti-abortion and encourage adoption nd parenting only.

"Bodily fluids"

HIV lives in white blood cells. The fluids in your body with a high oncentration of white blood cells are blood, semen, and vaginal fluids (i.e. um, discharge, ejaculate, etc.). HIV may also be transmitted through breast nilk. Menstrual blood contains regular blood, and could easily transmit HIV. ʹaliva, tears, and sweat have such low traces of white blood cells that you'd ιave to drink gallons to put yourself seriously at risk. Urine is sterile and does ιot transmit HIV. Feces, however, often have blood in them and are therefore onsidered unsafe.

"Unsafe activities"

A short (and incomplete) list of activities that are potentially unsafe when ngaged in without the use of a barrier:
- Sexual intercourse involving penetration by a penis
- Anal finger play or fisting
- Vaginal finger play or fisting
- Oral sex on a penis or vagina
- Sharing any part of a rig used for injecting drugs or hormones
- Cuttings, piercings, or whipping until blood is drawn
- Kissing while there are open sores on the mouth

Safer injecting

Injection drug and hormone use is responsible for an increasingly high percentage of new HIV infections. This is especially true in urban areas, and for women. While many people think of addicts when hearing about injection drugs, the number of people who use drugs recreationally at dance clubs and parties is growing, and many of them are sharing their works. Hormones and steroids are also injected, and therefore share the same risks as injection drugs.

The important thing to remember is that it's not important what is injected, simply that you are injecting something. Blood can stay in the needle, syringe, or any other part of the rig. Because of this, using someone else's rig (also called "sharing works") makes it possible to inject their blood along with everything else.

Bleach will kill HIV, but only if it stays in the rig for at least 30 seconds. Drawing up water and bleach alternatively at least 5 times will usually fill the time minimum. Most people don't take this much time when they're using bleach. Also, there's always a possibility that some bleach will stay in the rig and this hurts when it's injected.

The most effective way to stay safe if you inject drugs, hormones, steroids or anything else, is to own your own rig, and not to share needles, syringes, cottons, cookers, or water with anyone else. Having your own works means that you care about staying alive.

Safer Sex: what it means and doesn't mean

Safer sex means using barriers during sex to keep yourself and your partner(s) from exchanging bodily fluids which carry HIV. Using safer sex also protects you from other sexually transmitted diseases.

Safer sex does not mean asking your partners about who they've slept with and then deciding, based on that information alone, that it's okay to have unsafe sex. This ignores the fact that there are a number of ways to contract HIV, including sharing rigs while injecting drugs. This also does not ask what kinds of sex they had, whether safe or not, and does not at all address what partners their partners have had. This is not a safe method for many bisexual people, since both homophobia and biphobia on the part of our partners can affect how we answer and/or how they answer us. Beyond that, people may change their answer based on whether they think you'll still sleep with them if they answer honestly.

Safer sex does not mean simply being in a monogamous relationship. You may have been monogamous for all of two weeks. Or perhaps either you or your partner is a serial monogamist, who still has had many partners in one year.

Safer sex does mean educating yourself, planning enough to get the supplies, and keeping them close at hand. If you have to get out of bed, go into another room, or if you simply left the stuff at home, you're giving yourself one more excuse not to play safely. Keep some next to your bed, in the kitchen, out by the pool, in your jacket, in your car, at the office, wherever you have sex. (Lucky you – at the office?)

Safer Sex
Condoms
So available, so colorful, so user friendly. Condoms are usually unrolled over a hard penis before penetration. They can also be used to cover dildoes, vibrators, and other sex toys so that they're easier to clean and safer to share. You can also cut a condom into a flat sheet and use it to protect yourself when doing oral sex on a vagina.

Condoms have gotten a bad rap in some circles about breaking, but when a condom breaks it's usually because it was used incorrectly. Check the expiration date on the package. Keep condoms (and all latex stuff) away from heat (unless it's your body heat). Always be sure to use a lubricated condom, or use some lube with unlubed condoms. NEVER use a petroleum-based lube with latex (like Vaseline, baby oil, Penzoil, whatever your fetish)—it breaks down the latex and will cause it to tear.

Tips:
- Put a little lube in the end of the condom before unrolling it onto the penis. It makes the tip much more sensitive.
- Try different kinds of condoms. Some feel better than others and the shape is very personal.
- Put on two condoms, then part-way through, remove one. The increased sensation is fabulous.
- If you're sharing a toy (like a dildo or vibrator) put a couple of condoms over it first. Then before you trade it, take one off. It's much faster than putting on a fresh condom in the middle of playing.

Gloves
For all "digital play" (i.e. using your fingers in someone's vagina or anus) wear a latex glove, and use lots of lubricant. Gloves can be cut open by removing the fingers and thumb and cutting open one side to give you nice, large, stretchy piece of latex for oral sex on women or for rimming. I love gloves because they make everything smoother, silkier. They are a fashion statement, especially when

you coordinate the colored ones with your outfit. You can get boxes of gloves at beauty supply houses and medical supply stores.

Tips:

- If you're sensitive to the powder on gloves (or on latex), pre-rinse them in water, then let them dry. They'll be all ready to use when the occasion arises.
- If you'll be changing orifices mid-play (e.g. anus to vagina, one butt to another, etc.), put two gloves on at the beginning. Then when you want to switch, just take one off, and you're ready.
- Try lube on the inside of the glove. You'll feel more and the glove seems thinner.

Lubricant

For a lot of sex play, especially with latex, using a lubricant of some kind is highly recommended. Use a water-based one, because petroleum products break down latex. Lube makes everything wet and slippery. I can feel more. So can my partner(s). I can play longer. A lot longer. I have become a major lube fetishist. So can you.

Tips:

- Many lubes contain Nonoxynol-9, which does not protect against HIV and may also cause an allergic reaction. Women are especially sensitive to it. Check the ingredient list.
- Keep some water near wherever you have sex in a spray bottle or a squirt gun. If your lube begins to dry out, add water.
- For your travel pack, pick up lube samples from anywhere you buy lube. You can also often get some for free from health offices, AIDS outreach services, and from HIV testing sites.

Plastic Wrap

Plastic wrap is an excellent barrier for oral sex. Thin, clear, and tasteless, it allows you to feel and smell everything you want in sex. Also, it can be torn off in large sheets so you can cover everything that you need to. Be sure to use a name brand plastic wrap—they're usually stronger and more rigidly tested. And in case you've heard some warnings: It's o.k. to use microwavable wrap (unless your body heats up to over 150°F).

Tips:

- Take the roll out of the box before you start to play. The cutter on the side of the box is too easy to cut yourself on (especially when distracted).
- Wrap the sheet around each leg (not too tightly) to create a barrier that you don't have to hold in place.
- Drip some lube on your partner's skin before setting down the sheet. This will help hold the plastic in place and increase the sensation.

What if your protection fails?

If you are engaged in an activity with a particularly high risk for HIV infection and your protection fails—for example, if a condom breaks during anal or vaginal intercourse, or you use someone else's rig while injecting-then you can take high doses of anti—HIV medications for four to six weeks. This procedure is called Post Exposure Prophylaxis and must be started within 72 hours of the incident. PEP is not guaranteed, and it is no substitute for safer injecting or safer sex. Being safer is also simpler and potentially more fun.

Coming out to your Doctor

There are many other health concerns for all people, bi, gay, lesbian, straight, trans, or pansexual. But to get the care we all need to stay healthy, we need to be honest with our doctors. Many people are tempted to lie to their doctors about things like smoking or drug use, because they are embarrassed or worried about confidentiality, even though doctors are normally required to keep what we tell them confidential. For queer people of all kinds there is the added concern of homophobia, biphobia and transphobia. Coming out to your doctor can greatly improve the quality of your care, not only because it helps you be honest with her about your sexual activity in the past and the present, but also because honesty and comfortability with your healthcare provider(s) is important for the kind of positive relationship that leads to your improved health.

Coming out to healthcare providers is not for everyone. If you cannot come out, don't feel guilty. But do know that you have a right to quality care from a doctor who isn't prejudiced against you. There are services available to help you find a doctor who is queer-friendly. The best reference for a healthcare provider are your queer or queer-supportive friends. You can also try a GLBT hotline or HIV hotline.

If you do want to come out to your doctor, here are some tips: Assure confidentiality if you need to. If you aren't out to your community, it might make you feel better just to hear your doctor promise you that she will respect your right to confidentiality. Also, wait until you feel comfortable. Maybe you don't want to come out to your doctor on the first visit. Get to know her first if it will make you feel safer. You might never feel 100% comfortable coming out to your doctor, but that's okay, too. It's her job to look after your health, and by coming out you are helping her to do that job well.

That's all for now. Now go get turned on and have some excellent sex.

Finding Bisexuality in Fiction
Robyn Ochs

This section contains an annotated bibliography (or bi–bliography) of books with bisexual content: books about the subject of bisexuality and books with bi characters. Now it's very easy to tell if a non-fiction book is about bisexuality; it's usually called *Bisexual Lives*, or *Bisexual Politics*, or something like that. But it's a lot harder to tell if a work of fiction is a "bisexual book."

As in real life, it can be difficult to determine whether someone is "really" bisexual. How do you decide how to "read" someone? If a female character is with a man at the beginning of a book, falls in love with another woman, breaks up with the man and at the book's conclusion is deeply in love with the woman, is she "really" a bisexual, or is she "really" a lesbian? Is this story a bisexual or a lesbian coming out narrative? If she never labels herself as lesbian or bisexual, and if the author does not assign her a label, the reader will obviously be making a subjective interpretation, projecting her own assumptions and definitions onto the character.

It is important to keep in mind that the author's intent and the readers' interpretations are not always the same. This was demonstrated to me very clearly in the winter of 1996 as I was organizing a panel at the Out/Write conference here in Boston. I provided conference organizer Michael Bronski with a list of a dozen fiction writers whom I thought would be excellent choices for a panel on bi characters in fiction. Michael reported back to me that one woman whom he had called—several of whose novels appear on my list of books with bi characters—had wondered aloud to him why she was being asked to be on this particular panel. "I don't write about bisexuals," she said, "I write about straight women who become lesbians." Well, she certainly could have fooled me, and, to be quite honest, I felt disappointed, though of course I recognize the right of the author to understand her own creations as she chooses.

It would not be an understatement to say that we are starved for reflections of our lives, and as a result grab at whatever scraps we can find.

So, how can you recognize a bisexual? There is a presumption in Western cultures that all people are heterosexual, expanded somewhat in this century to the presumption that all people are either heterosexual or become homosexual. Bisexuality, for the most part, remains invisible—invisible, that is, except as a point of conflict or transition. In other words, an action or event must occur to make bisexuality visible to the viewer. Thus, with rare exceptions, the only bisexuals who are seen as bisexual are those who are known to be in relationships with more than one partner (of more than one sex), and bisexuals who are leaving a partner of one sex for a partner of a different sex. Bisexuals whose lives are celibate, monogamous, and/or without conflict or triangulation are rarely read as bisexual by the outside viewer, but rather are seen by others as either straight or gay. Hence, here is an inevitable association of bisexuality with non-monogamy, conflict and transition.

In our review of bisexuality in literature, certain general themes can be found.

One major theme is triangulation, usually accompanied by jealousy and the fracturing of one relationship for another. The bisexual person is usually located at the triangle's apex. Two examples are Anaïs Nin's *Henry and June,* which is about a triangulated relationship with between Henry, June and Anaïs, with June at the apex; and Earnest Hemmingway's *Garden of Eden,* with Catherine at the apex between Marita and David.

Then there's the "discovery novel," popular in lesbian literature of the 1970s, in which a previously heterosexual woman discovers her lesbianism by falling in love with a woman. Because at the end of the book she is happily paired with another woman, she is commonly read as a lesbian. But one might ask whether her previous relationships should be considered valid, as well as questioning the stability of her identity over time: should her current relationship end, what might this woman's future hold? Despite statistical probability, because we live in a "happily ever after" culture, we are not supposed to ask this latter question. Another common character found in discovery novels is the woman (sometimes the (ex)partner of the woman described above) who can't handle the societal stigma attached to a same-sex relationship and "goes back" to men (is she really a lesbian unwilling to admit it, or is she really bi, or really straight?).

Another place we can sometimes find bisexuality is in fantasy/science fiction/Utopian novels. Here, bisexuality is normal, a given, not stigmatized. By setting a story outside of the current reality, a great deal more leeway is allowed. A few examples are Starhawk's *The 5th Sacred Thing,* Samuel Delaney's *Dhalgren,* Marge Piercy's *Woman on the Edge of Time,* James Varley's *Titan, Wizard,* and *Demon* series, and Melissa Scott's *Burning Bright* and *Shadow Man.*

Historical novels are another place to locate the elusive bisexual. Here, safely far away from the present time, men (and almost all of the historical bisexuals I've been able to located are male) are bisexual—no big deal—though they re not called bisexual or gay. Examples: most of the historical novels by Mary Renault (about ancient Greece), and Lucia St. Clair Robson's *Tokaido Road* (set in 17th-century Japan).

And then there's what I call "1970s bisexuality" where bisexuality equals free love. These novels are usually written by men and, in contrast to historical novels, the bisexuals characters are almost always women who share their voluptuous bodies with both women and (primarily) with men. Authors Robert Heinlein, Tom Robbins, and John Irving would all be included under this heading.

Then there's adolescent bisexuality, sometimes written off as youthful teenage experimentation: Hanif Kureishi's, *The Buddha of Suburbia,* Felice Picano's, *Ambidextrous,* and Judy Blume's *Summer Sisters.*

There's the hedonistic bisexual who is often self-destructive and may leave a trail of broken lives (including his or her own), for example, Leonard Cohen's *Beautiful Losers*, Rupert Everett's *Hello, Darling, Are You Working?* and Carole Maso's *The American Woman in the Chinese Hat*.

Finally, there's what might be called lifespan bisexuality, stories that take place over many years, in which a character experiences a long and committed relationship with one person followed later in life by a relationship with someone of a different sex. Viewed from a long-term perspective, a bisexual life becomes visible. Julia Álvarez's *In the Name of Salomé*, May Sarton's *Mrs. Stevens Hears the Mermaids Singing* and Michael Cunningham's *The Hours* are excellent examples. Carol Anshaw provides a fascinating spin on this genre with her novel *Aquamarine*, which explores three possible outcomes to one person's life. In each, the protagonist ends up with a different life and life partner. In two of her futures, she is partnered with a man; in one she is partnered with a woman.

But few authors actually use the "b-word." Among the few who do are Emma Donohue, Larry Duplechan, E. Lynn Harris, Dan Kavanagh, M.E. Kerr, Starhawk and poets Michael Montgomery and Michelle Clinton.

In *Vice Versa: Bisexuality and the Eroticism of Everyday Life*, author Marjorie Garber says that we write our life histories backward, from the present, eliminating facts that do not fit our current stories. Someone who currently identifies as a gay man, therefore, might discount all past heterosexual experience, even if it felt meaningful and "real" at the time. And authors may do the same for their characters. Unlike those of us in the real world, the authors, of course, have this right: they can see into their characters' minds. The characters are, after all, their creations.

One thing I learned from my experience organizing the writers' panel is that in my hunger to find myself in fiction, I was focusing too hard. I can find aspects of myself not only in fictional characters that self-identify as bisexual, but also in the experiences of characters of various sexual orientations.

Labels are tools, which help us to describe ourselves to ourselves as well as to others. They are not fixed and unchanging essences. The reality is that each of us is unique. Labels, however useful, will never be fully adequate to the task of describing real people, and should not be confused with reality. In that sense, we may be able to find our own bisexual experiences in fiction, regardless of the self-identification of the character or the intent of the author.

Beginning on page 234 is a list of books that contain within their pages some degree of bisexual content.

221

Quotes of Note

Following is a collection of favorite quotes. Some are specifically about bisexuality, others are more general but can easily be applied to this subject. Enjoy!

SUSAN B. ANTHONY
"Cautious, careful people, always casting about to preserve their reputation and social standing, can never bring about a reform. Those who are really in earnest must be willing to be anything or nothing in the world's estimation, and publicly and privately, in season and out, avow their sympathies with despised and persecuted ideas and their advocates, and bear the consequences."

JOAN BAEZ
"I was not confused about what I was feeling, which seemed very clear to me, but rather about what to do about what I was feeling. What I wanted to do was lie down with her in a field of daisies and hold her and let her hold me, and then probably kiss. That was as far as my fantasies went. My confusion came mainly from what everybody else would think."
—*in* And a Voice to Sing With, *p. 77.*

JANE BARNES
"Next question's inevitable. What's the difference? he asks. I mean, how do you choose…and the question slides into a shrug. // I want to say, There's no choice. The answer appears on the tip of my tongue. Just like on his. Instead I say, Sometimes I want chocolate Häagen-Dazs. Sometimes Crema de Lechery Er, Leche. I only know when the scrawny kid with the nose ring at the counter has given me a taste on a teeny sppon and it's actually in my mouth. // Am I your teeny spoon? my date asks. // Yeah, I say, I'll take two scoops."

L. FRANK BAUM
"Of course, some people *do* go both ways."
—*The Scarecrow, Wizard of Oz (1939)*

KATE BORNSTEIN
"I think binary thinking is a tool to control folks by limiting their choices to only two. If I do that I control what you choose. I may even create a dilemma in which you feel you have no choice."

MARLON BRANDO
"Like a large number of men, I, too, have had homosexual experiences and I am not ashamed."

ROBERT BRAY

"When the wall of homophobia is just too damn high and the mountain of intolerance too wide, it's easier to just drop some of the weight, which usually means elderly gays, queer youth, drag queens, leather folks, sexual outlaws, bisexuals. I've always believed, to be honest with you, that there is no dress code for civil rights in this country."

WAYNE BRYANT

"Bisexuality is only a phase. But often as not, it's the phase between gay and death."

BILL BURLESON

"Organizing bisexuals is like starting an atheist church. If you wanted to go to church... you wouldn't be an atheist."

TERRIE L. BURLEY

"[I like being bisexual because] I can listen to any love song and not have to change the gender."

GRETA CHRISTINA

"And the truth of my experience is this: my sexuality is whole. I am not straight with men and lesbian with women; I am bisexual with both. Enjoying sex with both women and men is no more an inherently schizophrenic form of sexuality than enjoying both intercourse and oral sex."
—*in* Bisexual Politics

ANI DI FRANCO

"i speak without reservation from what i know and who i am. i do so with the understanding that all people should have the right to offer their voice to the chorus whether the result is harmony or dissonance. the worldsong is a colorless dirge without the differences that distinguish us, and it is that difference which should be celebrated not condemned. should any part of my music offend you, please do not close your ears to it. just take what you can use and go on."
—*interview in* Deneuve *Jan/Feb 1995*

"There's a lot of pressure on me to toe the line. Dykes say I waffle, but I can only be myself....I don't care so much about labels. To me, there's not a big line down the middle of the human race. I mean, how much more out can I be?"
—*interview in* Deneuve *Jan/Feb 1995.*

"their eyes are all asking
are you in or are you out
and I think, oh man,
what is this about
tonight you can't put me
up on any shelf

because I came here alone
and I'm going to leave by myself..."
—*from her song "In or Out"*

DR. SEUSS
"Be who you are and say what you feel, because those who mind don't matter and those who matter don't mind."

BARBARA EHRENREICH
"...either 'bisexuality' is a very common condition, or another artificial category concealing the overlaps. What heterosexuals really fear, is not that 'they'—an alien subgroup with perverse tastes in bedfellows—are getting an undue share of power and attention, but that 'they' might well be us."

PAUL EMMONS
"The consecration of Gene Robinson as bishop of the New Hampshire Diocese of the Episcopal Church is an affront to Christians everywhere. I am just thankful that the church's founder, Henry VIII, and his wife Catherine of Aragon, and his wife Anne Boleyn, and his wife Jane Seymour, and his wife Anne of Cleves, and his wife Katherine Howard, and his wife Catherine Parr are no longer here to suffer through this assault on traditional Christian marriage."

MELISSA ETHERIDGE
"The more the world understands their bisexuality the better we'll be. I'm attracted to souls. I can be attracted to both."

IBRAHIM ABDURRAHMAN FARAJAJÉ
"What is exciting is the possibility of giving birth to a different future, one in which there is truly unity-in-diversity, one in which we can all learn to live *with* and *in* the differences. My commitment is to bring the intelligence of the heart to its rightful place. I struggle to do this now, to create the future today."

RON C. FOX
"Theories of lesbian and gay development have typically regarded establishing a lesbian or gay identity as the end point of the coming out process. Bisexuality was thought to be a transitional experience and identification, whereas, in reality, it can be an endpoint, phase, or place of recurrent visitation."
—*in BiNet USA press packet*

LUCY FRIEDLAND
"Like homosexuality, bisexuality can be poison to the heterosexist power structure. Bisexuality, in its own way, makes everyone more difficult to control, to coerce. Bisexuality confounds the paradigm that pits straights against gays, and the so-called 'normal' people against the 'deviants.'"
—*in "Bi Pride & Gay Sensibility in* Bi Women *(V6, No3, June/July 1988)*

"Ever notice how so many bisexuals refuse to call themselves bisexual? Many people who lead bisexual lives would rather call themselves nothing at all before calling themselves bi. Now some people are simply anti-label. You ask them why they don't call themselves bisexual, and they tell you that labels are too limiting. That they don't want to exclude themselves from any groups of people. Other people aren't anti-label *per se*, they just don't like the "b" word. They say they can't relate to it, that they don't even know what it means. You even come across certain 'extreme' types, who definitely aren't squeamish about labels given that they adopt other stigmatized labels like sado-masochist, anarchist, pagan, or punk, but even THEY wouldn't call themselves bisexual....The BLAS's, the Bisexual Label Avoidance Syndrome, seems to affect a large segment of the bi population. Now I believe that everyone has the right to label or not to label themselves. We don't need a bunch of people becoming the Label Police. But the consequences of the BLAS—invisibility, discrimination, biphobia—are truly damaging. Until more of us start taking on the bisexual label, the growth of the bi community and the bi political movement will be stymied."
—*in* Bi Women *Oct-Nov, 1989.*

MARJORIE GARBER
"If bisexuality is in fact, as I suspect it to be, not just another sexual orientation but rather a sexuality that undoes sexual orientation as a category,... then the search for the meaning of the word 'bisexual' offers a different kind of lesson. Rather than naming an invisible, undernoticed minority now finding its place in the sun, 'bisexual' turns out to be, like bisexuals themselves, everywhere and nowhere. There is, in short, no 'really' about it. The question of whether someone was 'really' straight or 'really' gay misrecognizes the nature of sexuality, which is fluid, not fixed, a narrative that changes over time rather than a fixed identity, however complex. The erotic discovery of bisexuality is the fact that it reveals sexuality to be a process of growth, transformation, and surprise, not a stable and knowable state of being."
—*in* Vice Versa: Bisexuality and the Eroticism of Everyday Life

"On the open range, fences exist because there are no natural boundaries."
—*in* Vice Versa: Bisexuality and the Eroticism of Everyday Life

Ultimately, the questions of whether someone is 'really' straight or 'really' gay or even 'really' bisexual "misrecognizes the nature of sexuality, which is fluid not fixed, a narrative that changes over time rather than a fixed identity, however complex."
—*in* Vice Versa: Bisexuality and the Eroticism of Everyday Life

LEISHA HAILEY
"I want to represent bisexuals as well as I want the straight girls on the show to represent lesbians. I've really come to learn that bisexuality is a true, legitimate sexual orientation. It's not about crossing over from straight to gay, which is an idea that Alice has to argue a lot with her friends. They all want her to stay in their camp, but Alice is looking for love, and she literally doesn't care if it ends up being with a man or a woman. I think that's beautiful."
—*Leisha is a real-life lesbian who plays Alice, a bisexual character on Showtime's* The L Word.

SOPHIE B. HAWKINS
"I still maintain it's valid to live not calling yourself gay or straight and follow your heart as it expands."

CHARLES HAYNES
Geraldo: "Suppose when your son is 16 he comes to you and says 'Dad, I want to be a bisexual.' What do you tell him? Do you tell him it's ok?"

Charles Haynes: "I say, 'What is this 'want to be?' Are you or aren't you?'"
—on the *Geraldo* show

MARY HEATH
"Many of us experience choosing bisexual identity as a homecoming. It allows us to name feelings, experiences, and self understandings as part of a whole, rather than demanding that we attempt to understand ourselves or explain ourselves to others as sometimes one thing and sometimes another. In a sense, it is a choice in the direction of unification, exactly the opposite of being split."

ERICA JONG
"If you're lucky enough to love, who cares what decorative flesh your lover sports?"

LANI KA'AHUMANU
"Building community is about holding out possibilities and making sure some of them happen. It's like flirting."

"I am a free-range chicken // don't fence me in // I can cockadoodle doo your do // and lay with the best of your hens."
—in "That Naked Place"

"My light skin // My female lover // when I have one, // or for that matter, // My male lover // when I have one, // are tickets // to games // I don't want to play
—in "That Naked Place"

RUTH HUBBARD

"The use of the phrase 'sexual orientation' to describe only a person's having sex with members of their own gender or the other sex obscures the fact that many of us have other strong and consistent sexual orientations—toward certain hair colors, body shapes, racial types. It would be as logical to look for genes associated with these orientations as for 'homosexual genes.'"
— *"False Genetic Markers," in* The New York Times," 8/2/93.

PATRICIA IRELAND

"There are few people in this country who are as out as I am. I have a husband, and I have a woman companion. There is an obsession with trying to define women by their sexuality. People don't know how to deal with you if they can't define your sexuality. I'm just perverse enough to like that."

JUNE JORDAN

"I am black and I am female and I am a mother and I am a bisexual and I am a nationalist and I am an anti-nationalist. And I mean to be fully and freely all that I am!...I believe I have worked as hard as I could, and then harder than that, on behalf of equality and justice—for African-Americans, for the Palestinian people, and for people of color everywhere. And no, I do not believe it is blasphemous to compare oppressions of sexuality to oppressions of race and ethnicity: Freedom is indivisible or it is nothing at all."

"If you are free, you are not predictable and you are not controllable. To my mind, that is the keenly positive, politicizing significance of bisexual affirmation."

CORETTA SCOTT KING

"Freedom and justice cannot be parceled out in pieces to suit political convenience. Like Martin, I don't believe you can stand for freedom for one group and deny it to others."

ALFRED KINSEY

"There are not two discrete populations, heterosexual and homosexual... Only the human mind invents categories and tries to force fact into separated pigeon holes. The sooner we learn this...the sooner we shall reach a sound understanding of the realities of sex."

MICHAEL LANGLOIS

"I am bisexual.
I am not confused.
I am confusing.
I am sorry if you
are confused by that."

LYNN LAVNER
"The Bible contains 6 admonishments to homosexuals and 362 admonishments to heterosexuals. That doesn't mean that God doesn't love heterosexuals. It's just that they need more supervision."

JOHN LELAND
"This is the new bisexual movement in a nutshell: hard fought, hard thought, and distinctly individual."
—Newsweek *7/17/95*

TOM LIMONCELLI
"Cookies are both round and square; I like them both, I do not care."

AUDRE LORDE
"It was a while before we came to realize that our place was the very house of difference rather than the security of any one particular difference."
—*in* Zami *(Persephone Press, Watertown MA, 1982, p. 226)*

MARGARET MEAD
"I think rigid heterosexuality is a perversion of nature."

"Even a superficial look at other societies and some groups in our own society should be enough to convince us that a very large number of human beings—probably a majority—are bisexual in their potential capacity for love. Whether they will become exclusively heterosexual or exclusively homosexual for all their lives and in all circumstances or whether they will be able to enter into sexual and love relationships with members of both sexes is, in fact, a consequence of the way they have been brought up, of the particular beliefs and prejudices of the society they live in and, to some extent, of their own life history."
— *(1975) from* Redbook

"What is new is not bisexuality but rather the widening of our awareness and acceptance of human capacities for sexual love."
— *(1975) from* Redbook

"We shall not really succeed in discarding the straight jacket of our own cultural beliefs about sexual choice if we fail to come to terms with the well-documented, normal human capacity to love members of both sexes."

"Never doubt that a small group of thoughtful, committed citizens can change the world; indeed, it's the only thing that ever does."

DEE MOSCHBACKER

"We in the movement must learn to honor, embrace and defend our diverse selves. If we do this, we can win."
—*at Creating Change Conference, Los Angeles CA, 11/14/92.*

ROBIN MORGAN

"The very first consciousness-raising session I ever went to, for example, gave met he warning. We were talking about sexuality, and I described myself as a bisexual (this was even before the birth of the first Gay Liberation Front, and long before bisexual became a naughty or cop-out word—besides, it did seem an accurate way of describing my situation). Every woman in the room moved, almost imperceptibly, an inch or so away from me. Wow, I thought. It was not the last time I was to have such an articulate reaction."
—*1973 speech, quoted in We Are Everywhere, p. 425)*

JULIE MULLARD

"We were bisexual. We never thought of ourselves as ... lesbians. What we thought was: our feeling about sex was unique. We had no idea that there were people like us all over."
—Julie Mullard, Mary Renault's (1905-1983) life partner. Interview by Sweetman, tape 17, side B, December 4, 1991

"Julie [Mullard] repeatedly stressed their bisexuality—'We were both attracted to men and women'—while making clear that lesbian feelings were confined to and defined for them by their relationship—'once we met, neither of us ever looked at another woman.' For her part, Renault declared, 'I think a lot of people are intermediately sexed...it's like something shading from white to black, and all sorts of grays in the middle.' Julie would even insist that in her work Mary 'was always trying to say that people can be bisexual. To be bisexual is not necessarily a bad thing. It can be painful and difficult to live with and whatever, but it exists.' And in fact, their bisexuality presented difficulties that overshadowed the issue of lesbian desire or identity."
—*in Carolyn Zilboorg, The Masks of Mary Renault (Missouri, 2001), p. 271*

KATHY NAJIMY

"I have been a Gay and Lesbian rights activist since I was 18. I believe that we all have the potential to love any human being, and that genetics, upbringing, choice, social conditioning and environment play a major part in which way we sway. I am proud of the ability that I have to love both men and women and am very proud of the 6 year monogamous relationship I have with my soul mate, my husband. Just love who you wish and celebrate it the best you can. Love is a gift. Between anyone."

MILTON NASCIMIENTO
Any way of loving is worth it,
any way of loving is worth loving.
(Cualquier manera de amor vale la pena,
cualquier manera de amor vale amar.)

GEORGIA O'KEEFE
"I've been absolutely terrified every moment of my life and I've never let it keep me from doing a single thing I wanted to do."

ROBYN OCHS
"We are a homosexual community, but we are by no means homogeneous. ... May I live to see the day when we are secure and courageous enough to accept and celebrate one another and all of our similarities and differences. We have long been told by the 'straight' world that we are not acceptable, and many gay men and lesbians have long fought for the right to love whomever we choose, and to be accepted exactly as we are. Are we to deny others this basic human right?"
—*in* Outlook, *letter to the editor, Summer 1990.*

"Someone wrote on one of the email lists 'How many letters do we need to have'…My response: as many letters as it takes to ensure that everyone feels included. I'm willing to make the time."

"Some folks say that bisexuals are not oppressed because at least we are accepted by mainstream society when we are involved with members of the opposite sex. Agreed, society may like us when we show that piece of who we are. But conditional acceptance is not really acceptance at all. When we show our other side, our gay side, we suffer the same discrimination as other gay men and lesbians. We don't lose only half our children in custody battles. When homophobia hits, we don't get just half fired from our jobs (put on half time, perhaps?). We don't get just half gaybashed when we are out with our same-sex lovers ("Oh please, only hit me on my left side. You see, I'm bisexual!'). We, too, get discriminated against because we are gay."

MARGE PIERCY
"You could say love leaps burning / hot in me like the fires
of a star and it needs many / windows, many doors, or it eats
me to ash. Energy forces me / outward expanding like a universe
yet I can stand to leave / nothing, no one I have loved."
—*from "How I Weave Trouble"*

"In another life, dear sister, I too would bear six fat children. In another life, dear sister, I too would love another woman and raise one child together as if that it pushed from both our wombs. In another life, sister, I too would dwell solitary and splendid as a lighthouse on the rocks or be born to mate for life like the faithful goose. Praise all our choices. Praise any woman who chooses, and make safe her choice."

TOM ROBINSON
"I'm simply trying to live a both/and life in an either/or world."

"Why not join forces to embrace and celebrate that diversity - and blow away the notion that 'being bi' is some kind of timid, closety attempt to cling onto respectability. The hell with respectability...Let's all get together and make *a bigger splash.*"

GEORGE BERNARD SHAW
"Pardon him Theodotus: he is a barbarian, and thinks that the customs of his tribe and island are the laws of nature."
—*Julius Caesar in George Bernard Shaw's* Caesar and Cleopatra

PATTI SMITH
"As far as I'm concerned, being any gender is a drag."

STARHAWK
"Erotic energy holds the universe together. What is gravity but the desire of one body for another?"
—*Washington DC 4/24/93.*

ADLAI STEVENSON
"My definition of a free society is a society where it is safe to be unpopular."

EDNA ST. VINCENT MILLAY
"Oh, you mean I'm homosexual! Of course I am, and heterosexual too. But what's that got to do with my headache?"
—*in response to her doctor who hinted that her severe headache might be due to repressed lesbian impulses.*

ABIGAIL VAN BUREN
"You could move."
—*responding in her "Dear Abby" column to a reader who wrote about a gay couple moving in across the street and asked, "How can we improve the quality of the ...neighborhood?"*

GORE VIDAL
"Many human beings enjoy sexual relations with their own sex, many don't; many respond to both. The plurality is the fact of our nature and not worth fretting about."
—*from "The Birds and The Bees" in* The Nation *10/28/91*

MARY WATKINS
"It's a crime, it's an evil, dangerous thing
To stifle the gift of love and the joy it surely brings
Well, I'll love who I please, I'm gonna give the best of me
Walking tall, and blessed with the right to be."

ELIZABETH REBA WEISE
"[Some] claim that bisexuals are not discriminated against when we are perceived as straight. Well, lesbians & gays aren't discriminated against when they are perceived as straight, either."

E.B. WHITE
"There's no limit on how complicated things can get, on account of one thing always leading to another."

WALT WHITMAN
"Each of us is inevitable; each of us limitless; each of us with his or her right upon the earth."

Bisexual Stories:
An annotated bi-bliography

Robyn Ochs

All of the books listed below deal in some way with bisexual identity and/or behavior, though few of the narrators or characters in the books listed below use the word bisexual. Rather, each book has at least one character whose life history can be interpreted as bisexual. This list is by no means exhaustive; rather it is a place to begin. Your suggestions for books to be listed in future versions of this list are welcome. All books listed below are in English, except as noted. Many of these books can be ordered through the Bisexual Bookstore on the World Wide Web: http://www.biresource.org/bookstore/index.html.

BIOGRAPHIES/AUTOBIOGRAPHIES

Elizabeth J. Andrew, *Swinging on the Garden Gate: A Spiritual Memoir*. Skinner House Books, Unitarian Universalist Association, 2000. The author's account of her own spiritual journey and of coming to terms with her bisexual identity.

Reinaldo Arenas, *Before Night Falls*. Penguin, 1993. Chronicle of his life, from his birth in Cuba (1943), to his death in New York (1990). Arenas, a gay man, provides a fascinating—and disturbing—account of male (gay? bisexual?) behavior in Cuba.

Louis W. Banner, *Intertwined Lives: Margaret Mead, Ruth Benedict, and their Circle*. Knopf, 2003. Anthropologist **Margaret Mead** (1901-1978) was an advocate for bisexuality, and she and **Ruth Benedict** were both sexually and intellectually interwined.

James Broughton, *Coming Unbuttoned*. City Lights Books, 1993. Born in 1913, poet and independent filmmaker Broughton does not delve into the meaning of his bisexual identity, but he (and many others in his story) clearly identifies as such. Over the course of his life, Broughton had relationships with men and women.

John Cheever, *The Journals of John Cheever*. Knopf, 1990. Includes discussion of the writer's bisexuality and extramarital relationships.

Cyril Collard, *Savage Nights*. The Overlook Press, 1993 (originally *Les Nuits Fauves*). French writer, film director, actor and self-identified bisexual writes of his HIV diagnosis and subsequent relationships with a 17-year-old woman and two young men. Set in Paris, this disturbing and powerful story includes discussions of unprotected sex, anonymous s/m sex, and the author's view of how male and female partners differ.

Samuel R. Delany, *The Motion of Light in Water*. Arbor House, 1988. Fascinating autobiography of the African-American science fiction writer's teens and twenties in New York City, 1957-1965. While Delany currently identifies as gay, his history and his former identification are bisexual.

Erica Fischer, *Aimée and Jaguar: A Love Story, Berlin 1943*. (translated from the German) HarperCollins, 1995. In World War II Germany, **Elisabeth Wust**, a married Christian mother of four, falls in love with Felice Schragenheim, a Jew living underground. Though sexual orientation identity is never discussed, Elisabeth could be "read" as bisexual (though only she knows for sure). A true story, told by Wust 50 years after the fact.

Ruth Falk, Random House, 1975. *Women Loving: A Journey Toward Becoming An Independent Woman*. In–depth personal account of the author's process of coming to terms with and honoring her bisexuality.

Barbara Guest, *Herself Defined: The Poet H.D. and Her World*. Doubleday, 1984. Biography of American expatriate writer **H.D.** (1886-1961). Thorough and respectful representation of her significant romantic relationships, which included both women and men.

Meredith Maran, *What's It Like to Live Now*. Bantam Books, 1995. *Notes from an Incomplete Revolution: Real Life Since Feminism*. Bantam Books, 1997. Autobiographical writing by bi-identified mother of two sons in a long-term same–sex relationship. She's an ex-hippie of the 60s generation living in Oakland California, a dedicated activist struggling to figure out how to live ethically in today's world.

Anchee Min, *Red Azalea*. Berkeley Books, 1994. Fascinating autobiography of a woman growing up in Maoist China. The woman Min loves in her youth, and perhaps Min herself, are bisexual.

Anaïs Nin, *Henry and June*. Harcourt, Brace, Jovanovich, 1986. Nin's diary from 1931-1932, in which she recounts her relationships with her husband, Hugo, and with Henry and June Miller. Beautiful writing. Much discussion of her relationships and their meaning to her.

Kate Millett, *Flying.* Simon & Schuster, 1974. *Sita.* Simon & Schuster, 1976. Autobiographical novels by a self-identified bi and a leader of the modern women's movement.

Nigel Nicolson, *Portrait of a Marriage.* Weidenfeld & Nicolson, 1973. Biography of **Vita Sackville-West & Harold Nicolson** by their son. Born in the late 19th century, Vita was a self-identified bi woman of the British upper class in love with Violet Trefusis.

Carol Queen, *Real live nude girl: Chronicles of sex-positive culture.* Cleis Press, 1997. Collection of autobiographical essays by a leading bi-identified exponent and proponent of sexual diversity and sex-positivity.

Wallace P. Rusterholtz, *My not-so-gay life.* First Unitarian Society of Chicago, 1996. Rusterholtz, born in 1909, discusses his experiences as a bisexual man, his World War II service in Iran, memories of the Chicago Unitarian Church, and opinions on contemporary political and religious issues.

Hannah Tillich, *From Time to Time.* Stein and Day, 1974. Tillich (1896-1988) chronicles her childhood in Germany, including love affairs with other girls, her first marriage, her second—open and enduring—marriage to theologian Paul Tillich, their move during the rise of Naziism to the United States, and their subsequent life.

Blanche Weisen, *Eleanor Roosevelt* (2 volumes). Penguin, 1992. Includes substantial discussion of the intimate relationships of the bisexual American First Lady.

In German:
Irmela v.d. Lühe, *Erika Mann: Eine Biografie* Fisher, 1996. Biography of German writer and actress Erika Mann (1905-1969). Mann, born in München as Erika Julia Hedwig Mann, was the daughter of writer Thomas Mann and sister of gay writer Klaus Mann. Her second husband was gay British poet W.H. Auden.

GENERAL FICTION

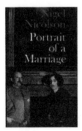

(This list is far from exhaustive.)

Swan Adamson, *My Three Husbands.* Strapless Kensington, 2003. Directionless 25-year-old protagonist has two gay dads, works in a porn store, and is about to marry her third husband, whose past—like hers—includes men as well as women. A fun read.

J. R. Ackerley, *We Think the World of You*. Poseidon Press, 1989. First published in 1960, this is a British novel about Frank, a middle-aged homosexual man and his obsession and longstanding relationship with Johnny, a young working-class married man. Johnny is arrested for theft, and subsequently convicted, and Frank's economic and emotional entanglement with Johnny, his family and his dog unfold. A beautifully written psychological novel.

Lisa Alther, *Five Minutes in Heaven*. Dutton, 1995. Three of the four main characters could all be classified more or less as Kinsey-5s, and the fourth is—who knows—but much as she'd like to be—not a Kinsey zero. *Bedrock*. Ivy Books, 1990. Two married women, best friends, and their love for each other. *Other Women*. Knopf, 1984. A woman with a bi history comes to terms, through therapy, with herself and her love for women. *Original Sins*. Signet, 1982. Story of five people growing up in Tennessee, including two with bisexual experiences. *Kinflicks*. Knopf, 1976. Woman with bi history struggles to understand herself and her relationship with her mother.

Julia Alvarez, *In the Name of Salomé*. Plume, 2000. Complex, historical novel set in the Americas (Dominican Republic, Cuba, USA). Salomé Camila, (1894-1973), attempts three relationships over the course of her life. Two, with men, are brief and ultimately unsuccessful. The important and most enduring one is with Marion, a woman who, in her later years marries a man. I would consider both Marion and Salomé Camila bisexual women, high-scorers on the Kinsey Scale.

Carol Anshaw, *Aquamarine*. Washington Square Press, 1992. Interesting and thought-provoking novel taking the life of a competitor in the 1968 Olympics and projecting 20 years into her future. Three different possible futures are presented, each based on the reverberations of choices made shortly after the Olympics. In each of her equally possible futures, she has married or remained single, loved women or men, become a parent or not, stayed in her Missouri hometown or moved to New York City. *Seven Moves*. Houghton Mifflin, 1996. A lesbian therapist's lover disappears. One of her best friends (a minor character) is a woman married to a man who is also seeing another woman.

Diane Ayres, *Other Girls*. Kensington Books, 2002. Elizabeth is at a women's college in the mid–1970s. She falls in love with a fellow student, but for quite some time is also attached to her heterosexual identity/image. Her friends see her as bisexual, though she herself does not say how/whether she identifies. Among all the book's characters (of all sexual orientations) there are complicated relationships, both serious and casual. Other themes: domestic violence, mental illness, being a survivor of incest and sexual abuse.

James Baldwin, *Another Country*. Vintage, 1992. From 1960, about race, sexuality & friendship between men. *Giovanni's Room*. Dell, 1988 (1956). Two male expatriates in France—one from the USA, one Italian—fall in love. One is engaged to be married to a woman. Beautifully written, lots of internal struggle and self-hatred. *Tell Me How Long The Train's Been Gone*. Dell, 1968. About an African American man who becomes an actor. Probably the most clearly bisexual of all of Baldwin's characters.

Ann Bannon, *Odd Girl Out*. Naiad, 1983 (originally 1957) and *Beebo Brinker*. Naiad, 1986—originally 1962. Two in a series of five novels published in the late 1950s and early 1960s, these are fascinating representations of gay and bisexual life in that time period. *Odd Girl Out* is the story of two young college women who have a relationship until one leaves the other for a man. *Beebo Brinker* is the story of a lesbian in New York's Village scene. Several characters in the book could be characterized as bisexual, but none are overly loveable.

Pat Barker, *The Eye in the Door*. Plume/Penguin, 1993. Set in England during World War I, psychological novel about Billy Prior, an intelligence agent who is bisexual, as is one other male character. *The Ghost Road*. More about Billy Prior. Both of these books are excellent reads.

Peggy Ullman Bell, *Psappha: A Novel of Sappho*. Upstart, 2000. Fictionalized account of the life of Sappho, Greek poet from the seventh century B.C. whose love for men and for women is documented.

Judy Blume, *Summer Sisters*. Dell, 1998. Beginning in 1977, the friendship and coming of age of two girls. Teenage same-sex experimentation, and later heterosexual relationships.

Blanche McCrary Boyd, *Terminal Velocity*. Knopf, 1997. It's 1970, and Ellen, a Southern-raised book editor, leaves her husband for a radical lesbian commune full of processing and drugs. Her story is, indisputably, a bisexual one. An interesting, if disturbing, look at a moment of United States history.

Christopher Bram, *Almost History*. Plume/Penguin, 1993. Fascinating historical novel about a gay American diplomat who spends much of his career in the Marcos-controlled Phillipines. Beginning in the 1950s and moving forward in time to just beyond the fall of the Marcos regime, many of the secondary male characters are bisexual in identity and/or behavior.

Joyce Bright, *Sunday's Child*. Naiad, 1988. A California feminist movement saga. Two women, Kate and Angie—both runners—fall in love and leave relationships to be with each other. One is—at the book's beginning—straight-identified and with a man, but she's not enough in love with him. The other is with a woman who is married to a man. Both could be called bisexual.

Rita Mae Brown, *Rubyfruit Jungle*. Daughters, Inc., 1973. Most of the characters behave bisexually. About sexuality & growing up poor. *Six of One*. Bantam Books, 1978. Set in a small southern town & spanning 1909-1980, the book has two bi women: the narrator and Ramelle. *Southern Discomfort*. Bantam Books, 1982. Set in Alabama in the early 20th century, two secondary characters—Grace and Payson—are bisexual. *Venus Envy*. Bantam Books, 1993. Set in present–day Virginia, about a woman's relationships with family and friends.

Sylvia Brownrigg, *Pages for You*. Picador USA, 2001. First–year college student falls in love with a female graduate student who is bisexual.

Truman Capote, *Answered Prayers*. Random House, 1987. Bi hustler makes his way through the upper crust of USA, and US ex-pat society. This unfinished novel apparently lost Capote most of his friends, as he does mention names, and even those whose names are not explicitly mentioned are at times thinly disguised.

Jackie Calhoun, *Lifestyles*. The Naiad Press, 1990. Can be read as a bisexual or lesbian coming out story. A woman who has been left by her husband of many years meets and falls in love with another woman.

Michael Chabon, *The Mysteries of Pittsburgh*. Morrow, 1988. Coming of age story. Recent graduate Art Bechstein, son of a gangster, struggles with his sexual orientation as he finds himself attracted to two people, one male, one female.

Susan Taylor Chehak, *Dancing on Glass*. Fawcett Crest, 1993. Man goes back to the town of his childhood to resurrect his family name. Falls in love with a woman whose family is historically interwoven with his, marries her, but then becomes obsessed with a teenaged boy. Kind of soap-operatic.

Leonard Cohen, *Beautiful Losers*. Vintage, 1966. Yes, *that* Leonard Cohen. The songwriter. Poetic, erotic and disturbing novel set in Montreal. Both of the male characters are bisexual.

Nicole Conn, *Claire of the Moon*. The Naiad Press, Inc., 1993. A (formerly), straight woman discovers love with a lesbian therapist (no, not hers) at a writers retreat.

T. Cooper, *Some of The Parts*. Akashic Books, 2002. Four interconnected people, three biologically related, trying to figure out what to do next: a young woman who has had boyfriends and girlfriends (though she never identifies herself); her mother; her HIV positive gay uncle; and his friend Isak, a gender-transgressor.

Alan Cumming, *Tommy's Tale*. ReganBooks, 2002. 29–year–old hedonistic self-identified *and* behaviorally bi guy in London. Drugs, sex, lack of direction, fear of commitment.

Michael Cunningham, *The Hours*. Picador, 1998. One day in the lives of three women: Virginia Woolf in 1923, Laura Brown in the 1950s, and Clarissa Vaughan in the 1990s, somehow intertwined, and poetically written. Both Clarissa and Richard, her former lover and lifelong friend, have loved a man and a woman. The "b"word is not used, but it is clear that the characters honor both of their lifetime loves. *A Home at the End of the World*. Picador, 1990. At least two of the three main characters could be characterized as bisexual.

Stacy D'Erasmo, *Tea*. Washington Square Press, 2000. Isabel, whose mother has taken her own life, is in a Philadelphia high school, looking for connection. She finds a community theater group whose charismatic leader is clearly described as bisexual and, considers this identity for herself (for a while or for good?). Not a major theme, but bisexuality is clearly and explicitly present.

Emma Donohue, *Stir Fry*. HarperCollins, 1994. In Dublin, a 17-year-old woman begins university and discovers her two new women roommates are a couple. One self-identifies as bi. *Hood*. Harper Collins, 1996. A lesbian in Ireland is partnered with a woman who has has a history with both men and women. Note: Emma Donohoe is a contributor to the *Bisexual Horizons* anthology.

Joan Drury, *Closed in Silence*. Spinsters, Inc., 1998. In this who-done-it, a group of college friends, lesbian feminist activists in the early 1970s, reunite on an island. Five of the women are still lesbian-identified, while the sixth is (after her seven-year relationship to one of the women at the reunion) married to a man. Written from the point of view of her ex-lover, we witness how she is seen by others. The word bisexual is not used, but by the end of the novel both her former and current relationships are given credit for mattering.

Larry Duplechan, *Eight Days A Week*. Alyson, 1985. Johnny Ray Rousseau, a 22-year-old African-American nightclub singer by night, legal secretary by day in pre-AIDS Los Angeles, meets and falls for a blond bisexual banker who is portrayed as somewhat of a jerk—not because he is bisexual, but because he is possessive. Sexually explicit, and lots of musical references.

Andrea Dworkin, *Mercy*. Four Walls, Eight Windows, 1990. Unsettling story. A girl grows up and is abused by one man after another. Narrator also has sexual relationships with women. Well-written, upsetting, graphic violence.

Adrienne Eisen, *Making Scenes*. Alt-X Press, 2002. 20-something woman obsessed with sex, food, literature and volleyball. She goes from boyfriend to boyfriend, afraid of being alone, and can't quite figure out how to (or whether she really wants to) get involved with a woman. Dysfunction reigns. Entertaining.

Brett Easton Ellis, *The Rules of Attraction*. Penguin, 1987. Depressing book about private college students who take lots of drugs, sleep with each other (while drunk or high), and never go to class. Most of the men sleep with lots of men and women; the women sleep with the men.

Rupert Everett, *Hello Darling, Are You Working?* Avon Books, 1992. The British narrator, Rhys, is a bisexual actor, drug addict and sometimes prostitute.

Harvey Fierstein, *Torch Song Trilogy*. Villard Books, 1983. (A play.) The protagonist's lover/ex-lover Ed is a self-identified bisexual. He is also closeted and would prefer to be straight, but he makes makes progress through the play. Some focus on Arnold's unwillingness to accept that Ed might actually be bisexual.

E.M. Forster, *Maurice*. W.W. Norton & Co., 1971. About a homosexual man in love with another homosexual man who "goes straight." Is he bisexual? Historically. Is he denying his homosexual feelings? Probably. Are his heterosexual feelings "real"? Probably. Listed here mainly because it was written in 1913-1914, it is beautifully written, and one of the few early gay-themed novels that end happily.

Alan Garganus, *Plays Well With Others*. Alfred A. Knopf, 1997. In the 1980s, a group of artistic friends in the New York City confronts the AIDS epidemic. One of the two best friends is described by the narrator as bisexual.

Paul Goodman, *Making Do*. Macmillan, 1963. Set in the very early 1960s, several of the male characters are bisexual, none of the women. Disturbing look at a specific time and place in history, replete with racism, misogyny and violence. Helps us understand the subsequent rise of feminism and lesbian separatism.

Stephanie Grant, *The Passion of Alice*. Houghton Mifflin, 1995. Set in Massachusetts in the mid 1980s. About a hospitalized anorexic woman. Maeve, a bulimic woman on the same ward, and a major character, is behaviorally bisexual, though there is no discussion of identity.

Carol Guess, *Seeing Dell.* Cleis Press, 1995. Dell, a taxi driver, has died suddenly, leaving behind two lovers, one male, one female. Set in a small town in the midwestern USA. It's refreshing to see a novel about working class people.

Diana Hammond, *The Impersonator.* Doubleday, 1992. About a sexually compelling man who lacks inner direction and gets through life by dissembling and by attaching himselves to various lovers, one of whom is a man. Two male characters could be called bisexual.

Joseph Hansen, *Job's Year.* Plume Fiction, 1983. About a primarily gay actor with other bi characters as well. *A Smile in His Lifetime.* Plume Fiction, 1981. A married man deals with his homosexuality.

E. Lynn Harris, *Invisible Life.* Doubleday, 1991. *Just As I Am.* Doubleday, 1994. A middle-class African–American man struggles to deal with his bisexuality and with coming out. Issues such as relationships, being in the closet, dis/honesty, HIV. *And This Too Shall Pass.* Doubleday, 1996. A pro football player comes to identify as gay. A few of the other male characters in the book could be identified as bisexual, especially Basil, the closeted and dishonest man who appears in Harris' earlier books. *Any Way the Wind Blows.* Doubleday 2001. Basil's story continues. More life "on the down low." *A Love of My Own.* Anchor Books, 2002 the story continues. Raymond decides that women are not in his future. Basil decides men (or at least one in particular) are. And Trent...well he's full of surprises, too.

Ernest Hemingway, *The Garden of Eden.* Collier Books, 1986 (written 1961). His last work, about a male/female couple and a woman who enters their relationship. Transgender issues, jealousy, bisexuality. Among Hemmingway's short stories is "The Sea Change," in which a woman tells her male beloved that she has fallen in love with a woman.

John Irving, *A Son of the Circus.* Ballantine, 1995. Set in Bombay and Toronto, a bizarre, sometimes brilliant and 682–page–long narrative full of transvestites, hjiras, homosexuals and even two bisexuals (one man and one woman, both unlikable white people from the USA).

Greg Johnson, *Pagan Babies.* Plume, 1993. Since their days together in Catholic school, Janice and Clifford's lives are intertwined. Janice is straight, and Clifford gay—well, except that he and Janice are boyfriend/girlfriend for years, with an active sexual relationship during some of that time. This novel is about growing up Catholic in the USA, about AIDS, friendship, expectations and disappointments.

James Kirkwood, *P.S. Your Cat is Dead.* Warner Books, 1972. An underemployed New York City actor/writer catches the (bi) burglar who is in the process of robbing him (not for the first time), and ties him up in his kitchen. The actor's recently deceased best friend and one other character, are also bisexual. Entertaining.

Edith Konecky, *A Place at the Table.* Ballantine Books, 1989. Middle–aged Rachel is "a perfectly ordinary woman who sometimes falls in love with other women."

Hanif Kureishi, *The Buddha of Suburbia.* Penguin Books, 1990. In suburban London, the story of the bi son of an Indian father and English mother.

D.H. Lawrence, *The Fox.* Bantam Books, 1923, 1951. In rural England, two women live together as a couple. Tensions arise when a man arrives and courts one of the women. No explicit bisexuality, but the two women are obviously—sexual or not—a couple.

Jane Lazarre, *The Powers of Charlotte.* The Crossing Press, 1987. A psychological novel about a woman from a Jewish Communist family. Bisexuality is not a central theme, but four characters have varying degrees of bisexual histories.

Rosamond Lehman, *Dusty Answer.* Harcourt, Brace, Janovich, 1927. A young wealthy English woman's search for love. Both the man and the woman with whom she falls in love are, ultimately, unattainable. Quite an amazing book, considering it was published in 1927. I'm surprised it isn't better known.

Jennifer Levin, *Water Dancer.* Penguin Books, 1994. A marathon swimmer, training for a race, stays with her trainer and his wife. This book is about motivation, relationships, swimming, and has a bisexual character.

Anna Livia, *Bruised Fruit.* Firebrand, 1999. Quirky novel involving a bisexual woman, an intersexed person, a lesbian and other assorted characters including a bisexual man. Patti, the bi woman, has a history of abuse that shapes and colors her current relationships and results in her murdering several of her male lovers when they do her wrong. But she and the lesbian end up together.

Erika Lopez, *Flaming Iguanas: An Illustrated All Girl Road Novel Thing.* Simon & Schuster, 1997. Two twenty-something Puerto Rican women from New Jersey take off across the USA on newly–acquired motorcycles. Tomato Rodriguez, the narrator, is trying to figure out whether she's bisexual. Unique and highly entertaining. *They Call Me Mad Dog! A Story for Bitter, Lonely People.* Simon & Schuster, 1998. Part novel, part comic book, strange and graphic continuation of the story of

Tomato Rodriguez, a self-identified San Francisco-based bisexual artist who makes dildos, hires a bisexual hit man to get revenge on her ex-lover, and is then arrested and jailed for her murder.

Daniel Magida, *The Rules of Seduction*. Houghton Mifflin, 1992. Jack Newland is a wealthy New York socialite who has had relationships with both men and with women, as have some of his male friends.

Jaye Maiman, *I Left My Heart*. Naiad, 1991. Adventures of Robin Miller, romance novel writer and detective. Among the characters is Patty, a former lesbian now married to a man, and Carl, a straight man turned on by lesbians/bi women. *Crazy for Loving*. Naiad, 1992. Is the murdered man, David Ross, bisexual? Robin thinks he might be, and that this information might provide clues to his death.

Dacia Maraini, *Women at War*. Italica Press, 1988. (originally published in Italian, as *Donna in guerra* in 1975. A working–class schoolteacher and her mechanic husband vacation in the Bay of Naples. Previously passive and unpolitical, Vannina meets various people and begins to develop a feminist and political consciousness. This book has female and male bisexual characters. *Letters to Marina* (originally published in Italian in 1981 as *Lettere a Marina*). The Crossing Press, 1988. A feminist woman talks about her past and current experiences in a series of letters to Marina, her ex-lover. She and some of her past and present lovers love both men and women. The author referred this book to me as one with bisexual characters, when I told her of this project.

Carole Maso, *The American Woman in the Chinese Hat*. Penguin Books, 1994. Shortly after the her brother's death from AIDS, a New York writer named Catherine leaves her female lover of twelve years and goes to the French Riviera, where she comes apart, having a number of affairs with men and women in the process.

Valerie Miner, *Movement*. The Crossing Press, 1982. A decade in the life of a journalist who is married to a draft resister in the 1960s and 1970s. She and one of her woman friends have bisexual experience/attractions. *All Good Women*, The Crossing Press, 1987. In San Francisco during World War II, four women from diverse backgrounds meet at secretarial school and subsequently

share a house. One, Teddy, comes out as a lesbian, and another whose (ex)boyfriend has gone overseas and left her pregnant falls in love with Teddy but several blissful months later decides to marry her ex-boyfriend for the sake of the child. It's the 1940s, and the lesbian, while heartbroken, believes it's in the best interest of the child, so keeps silent. Teddy ends up with her first love: a "real" lesbian.

Paul Monette, *Afterlife.* Avon Books, 1990. HIV+ men coping with the recent death of their loved ones. It's set in Los Angeles, so there's a lot of money, gyms, drugs and sex. Sean Pfeiffer, a very minor character, appears, from his collection of Polaroid photos, to be bisexual. Negative portrayal of bisexual identity, but a moving and beautifully-written account of the earlier years of the AIDS crisis.

Bárbara Mujica, *Frida.* Plume, 2002. A novel based on the life of Frida Kahlo, the Mexican painter who was lovers with Diego Rivera, Leon Trotsky, and other men and women. Written from the perspective of her sister Cristina.

Elias Miguel Munoz, *Crazy Love.* Arte Publico Press, 1988. About a boy growing up in one Cuban American family. Focus on family dynamics and expectations, and on his sexual experiences, both consensual (with women and men) and nonconsensual (with men), while growing up and as an adult.

Gloria Naylor, *Bailey's Cafe.* Vintage Contemporaries, 1993. A book about suffering & survival with Jesse Bell, a bi character.

Ben Neihart, *Burning Girl.* Perennial, 1999. A working class college student in Baltimore is enthralled by his wealthy friend and her brother. Secrets emerge, and he tries to figure out the truth and where his loyalties lie. All of the major characters appear to be bisexual.

Edna O'Brien, *The High Road.* Plume, 1988. An Irish woman, goes to an island in Spain, heartbroken by her male lover, and becomes attracted to a Spanish woman. Also *Casualties of Peace*, 1966 in *An Edna O'Brien Reader.* Warner Books, 1994. O'Brien is an Irish author whose books were banned in Ireland in the 1960s. From an Irish woman's perspective, she deals quite explicitly with life, sexuality and emotion.

Barbara Novak, *The Margaret-Ghost.* George Braziller, 2003. Follows the lives of a young present-day feminist scholar and the subject of her research, 19th century USA writer/feminist Margaret Fuller. Direct, unambiguous discussion of Fuller's bisexuality.

Jacquelyn Holt Park, *A Stone Gone Mad.* Random House, 1991. The story of a young lesbian attempting to come to terms with her sexuality. Two of the women in her life could be characterized as bisexual. An interesting portrayal of life in the mid-1900s.

Sparrow Patterson, *Synthetic Bi Products.* Akashic Books, 2002. A rudderless teenager in the American Midwest falls repeatedly into trouble with drugs and sex. She is most definitely bisexual, though apolitical. A disturbing novel, though a good read.

Felice Picano, *Late in the Season*. Gay Presses of New York, 1984. Gay-identified man in a long–term relationship with a man meets and gets involved with a college-aged woman. *Ambidextrous*. Gay Presses, 1985. A currently gay–identified man looks back on his bisexual childhood and adolescence in New York City.

Marge Piercy, *Summer People*. Fawcett Crest, 1989. Two women and a man in a triad relationship.

Robert Plunkett, *Love Junkie*. Harper, 1992. A wealthy suburban matron lacking meaning and purpose becomes attached to gay New York City of the early 1980s, and falls in (unrequited) love with Joel, a porn star, who is (quite) bisexually active. Joel's porn star girlfriend also expresses her desire to have sex with the protagonist. The word bisexual is not used. Humorous though disturbing look at a seriously dysfunctional social world.

Manuel Puig, *Kiss of the Spider Woman*. Vintage Books, 1980. Story of two men, a homosexual window dresser and a heterosexual revolutionary, imprisoned in the same cell in a Latin American prison. Situational bisexuality.

Jane Ransom, *Bye Bye*. New York University Press, 1997. Psychological satire of New York City and its art scene. A New York woman thrown out by her husband for nonconsensual infidelity changes her identity, disappearing and then reappearing as "Rosie," whose lovers include two women and one man.

Mary Renault, *The Persian Boy*. Vintage Books, 1972. A fictionalized version of the story of the Persian king Darius and Alexander the Great, through the eyes of the eunuch slave boy Bagoas. Darius and Alexander are portrayed as bisexual, with Alexander way up there on the Kinsey Scale, and Darius somewhere in the middle. *The Last of the Wine*. Vintage Books, 1975. Set in ancient Athens, some men are heterosexual, some homosexual and some bisexual. The male protagonist's male lover is bisexual.

Harold Robbins, *Dreams Die First*. Pocket, 1977. 1970s male fantasy. The protagonist, who builds up a porn and casino empire, is himself bisexual (though for him it's all male/female sex until page 372). He takes a lot of drugs and has several female lovers, most of whom get it on as well with other women. As I said, 1970s.

Tom Robbins, *Even Cowgirls Get the Blues*. Bantam Books, 1976. A straight man's perspective of female bisexuality.

Lucia St. Clair Robson, *The Tokaido Road*. Ballantine Books, 1991. Set in 17th-century Japan. Many of the male characters are behaviorally bisexual.

Jane Rule, *The Young in One Another's Arms*. Naiad Press, 1984. In a Vancouver commune, two women have relationships with each other and with men. Themes include triangulation and redefinition of "family." *This is Not for You*. Naiad, 1982. The narrator, a lesbian?/bisexual? woman, is in love with a female college classmate but despite reciprocated feeling refuses to allow a romantic or sexual relationship to develop. She later has a relationship with a woman who is married to a man.

François Sagan, *Painting in Blood*. (originally in French: *Un sang d'aquarelle*. Éditions Gallimard, 1987. Penguin, 1991). An "apolitical" Hollywood director moves in 1942 to occupied France to make films for the Nazis and gradually realizes of the horror of the Nazi regime. His male and female lovers, both past and present, are prominent. One of his male lovers could be characterized as bisexual.

Mayra Santos-Febres, *Sirena Selena*. Picador, 2000. In San Juan, a homeless 15-year-old is "adopted" by Martha, a drag performer, who takes the child to the Dominican Republic to make him/her a star. Martha, in one chapter, delivers a critical monologue to the "indecisos" (undecideds) in her audience who "don't believe in classification." (Mayra is a contributor to this anthology).

May Sarton, *Mrs. Stevens Hears the Mermaids Singing*. W.W. Norton and Company, 1965. A poet looks back over her long life and recalls past loves, male and female, trying to understand their relationship to the development of her poetry and her self. Sarton herself self-identified, at various times, as lesbian and bisexual.

Cathleen Schine, *Rameau's Niece*. Plume (Penguin), 1994. A present-day New York City author gets caught up in the manuscript she is reading and her sexual fantasies run rampant. Their subjects are both male and female. *She is Me*. Little, Brown & Co., 2003. Four generations of a family come together around family illness. Greta, who has been happily married to a man for 30 years, falls in love with a woman. Her daughter asks "You were happy?" "Very." "You're happy now?" "Yes."

Sarah Schulman, *People in Trouble*. E.P. Dutton, 1990. A main character, Kate, loves her husband and falls in love with a lesbian AIDS activist. Like all of Schulman's books, a fascinating if sometimes depressing look at New York City life.

Dani Shapiro, *Playing With Fire*. Doubleday, 1989. Two young women, one from a religious Jewish family, the other a Christian socialite. They meet in college, fall in love, then are pulled apart by a third party. Set in high society, a novel about family and boundaries.

Tom Spanbauer. *The Man Who Fell in Love With the Moon.* Atlantic Monthly Press, 1991. Several bi characters in this novel set in 19th-century Idaho.

Carole Spearin McCauley, *The Honesty Tree.* Frog in the Well Books, 1985. Two women in a relationship.

Starhawk, *Walking to Mercury.* Bantam, 1997. American writer and Wiccan priestess Maya Greenwood, approaching 40, goes on a pilgrimage to Nepal to lay her past to rest and figure out her future. She and her partner Johanna both identify as bisexual. This book contains discussions of identity!

Elizabeth Stark, *Shy Girl.* Seal, 1999. Two young women reunite in San Francisco, where one tries to make sense of their shared past, family secrets, and relationship to each other. Shy, the other character, can be easily read as bisexual.

Junichiro Tanizaki, *Quicksand.* Alfred A. Knopf, 1993 (originally 1947). In 1920s Japan, a married female art student falls in love with a woman. Both are bisexual. A story of obsession and betrayal.

Carla Tomaso, *The House of Real Love.* Plume, 1992. One of the narrator's lovers as well as the architect she is writing about have had relationships with both men and women. *Matricide.* Plume, 1994. One of the narrator's sidekicks is a woman just out of high school who self-identifies as bisexual.

Gore Vidal, *Myra Breckenridge.* Bantam, 1968. Scandalous when first published! Myra (née Myron) goes to Los Angeles, seeking her inheritance. She's outrageous, witty and insane. There are a number of references to bisexuality, with the topic even mentioned explicitly. Several characters have bisexual experiences. *The City and the Pillar.* Dutton, 1948. Coming out story of a young gay man. Contains several explicit, usually negative, mentions of bisexuality.

Alice Walker, *The Color Purple.* Harcourt Brace Janovich, 1982. Shug, a major character, is bisexual. *Possessing the Secret of Joy.* Pocket Books, 1992. Pierre, a self-declared bisexual, is a minor character who discusses, briefly, not only his own bisexuality, but his pansexual identity.

Jess Wells, *AfterShocks.* Third Side Press, 1992. In more or less today's San Francisco, *the* big earthquake has created havoc. Cherise, a secondary lesbian-identified character, has trouble committing to *any* relationship, and finds herself, after the quake, attracted to a man.

Edmund White, *The Beautiful Room is Empty.* Ballantine Books, 1988. The narrator's best female friend, Maria, self-identifies as bisexual. Also a minor male bisexual character. Autobiographical novel about growing up gay in New York in the 1950s and 1960s.

Stevie White, *Boy Cuddle.* Penguin, 1992. A bisexual boxer in a relationship with a male prostitute, who also becomes involved with a female prostitute. About life on the streets of South London. The front cover reads "Amoral. Bisexual. In love ...?"

Bett Williams, *Girl Walking Backward.* St. Martin's, 1998. Coming of age novel about a white teenage girl in Los Angeles. Pagans, Goths, drugs, self-help and self-injury surround her search for love. Not in love with her boyfriend, she is obsessed with other girls. Maybe bisexual, perhaps on the road to becoming a lesbian. Humorous, poignant, disturbing.

Jeanette Winterson, *The Passion.* Vintage International, 1987. Set in France and Italy during Napoleon's reign, one of the protagonists is a bisexual woman. *Written on the Body.* Vintage International (Random House), 1992. The name and gender of the narrator (who talks of past relationships with men and with women) is never stated. Fascinating and unsettling. *Gut Symmetries.* Knopf, 1997. Two physicists, a married man and a single woman, have an affair, then she meets and falls for his wife. Beautifully written story.

Shay Youngblood, *Soul Kiss.* Riverhead Books, 2000. African-American girl left at age seven by her addict mother with two "aunts" (actually a couple) grows up, searches for love, and develops her sexuality. Her experience is bisexual, though her identity may not be. Beautifully written. *Black Girl in Paris.* Riverhead Books, 2000. Young African-American woman travels to Paris in the footsteps of her hero, author James Baldwin. Her adventures include affairs with a male musician and a female thief.

Eda Zahl, *Fluffy Butch.* Mandarin Fiction, 1994. Quirky novel about a young woman living in Los Angeles who dates men and women.

FANTASY & SCIENCE FICTION

Wilhelmina Baird, *Crashcourse.* Ace, 1993. Two men and a woman, all have-nots in a future society, in a three-way relationship. Based on a brilliant concept, although the book's beginning is its strongest part.

Gael Baudino, *Gossamer Axe*. Penguin Books, 1990. Ancient Irish Pagan religion meets heavy metal. A harper born in the sixth century finds her way to present-day Denver, where she uses heavy metal music to rescue her true love from centuries of imprisonment. Both she and her love are bisexual. *Maze of Moonlight*. Penguin Books, 1993. Set in Europe during the Crusades and the last days of the Elves. A couple of the male characters are behaviorally bisexual.

Greg Bear, *Anvil of Stars*. Warner Books, 1992. A ship of children sent on a mission to locate and punish those who have destroyed Earth are not bound by the old rules. Neither monogamy nor heterosexuality is enforced, although both are presented as somewhat more satisfying and more mature.

Sybil Claiborne, *In the Garden of Dead Cars*. Cleis Press, 1993. In what was once New York, the AIDS virus has mutated to spread through casual contact, leaving survivors terrified of human, and especially sexual, contact. Teenager Emma meets one of her mother's friends who, in the old days, had male and female lovers. Emma herself comes very close to falling for a close female friend, and later gets involved with a male co-worker (the penalty for which could be death).

Samuel Delany, *Dhalgren*. Bantam Books, 1975. Disturbing story of a young drifter who enters the remains of a destroyed city. Set on Earth more or less in the present. The protagonist is bisexual, and a couple of the other characters have bisexual histories or experiences.

Diane Duane, *Door Into Fire*. Tom Doherty Associates, Inc., 1979. *Door Into Shadow*. Tom Doherty Associates, Inc., 1984. *Door into Sunset*. Tom Doherty Associates, Inc., 1992. Well-written fantasy series in which most people are bisexual, and homophobia is nonexistent.

Robert A. Heinlein, *Friday*. Ballantine Books, 1982. Set in a future society where casual sex, polyamory and sex between women are all considered acceptable. Interestingly, heterosexual relationships are still privileged, and almost all of the women and *none* of the men in the book are actively bisexual. Could this book have been written by a straight man? Yes, indeed!

Ellen Kushner, *Swordspoint*. Tor Books, 1987. A professional swordsman whose current relationship is with a man, and whose past love was a woman, is involved in the intrigues of the nobles, one of whom is a bisexual man.

Mercedes Lackey and Ellen Guon, *Summoned to Tourney*. Baen, 1992. A male elf is involved in a three way relationship with two humans (one male, one female). They are street musicians who ride magic steeds that look like motorcycles, struggling to save San Francisco from destruction.

Ursula LeGuin, *The Dispossessed*. Granada Publishing, 1975. Set far in the future on a moon far from earth, this philosophical social utopian novel involves a society in which there is no stigma attached to sexual orientation or sexual behavior. The protagonist, primarily heterosexually oriented, has homosexual experiences. *The Birthday of the World*. HarperCollins, 2002. This collection of short stories focusing on gender sent my head happily spinning! LeGuin imagines so many ways to shape family and to have relationships. Bisexuality is unremarkable on some of her worlds.

Shariann Lewitt, *Rebel Sutra*. Tor, 2000. On this world bisexuality is taken for granted, and people make commitments to small family groups called "circles."

Vonda N. McIntyre, *Starfarers*. Ace Books, 1989. On a research spaceship, a woman and two men in a romantic partnership are considered old-fashioned by some because theirs is a closed relationship.

Pat Murphy, *Nadya*. Tom Doherty, 1996. Chronicles the adventures of a young woman in the 1800s who becomes a wolf once a month. She travels from Missouri to the west coast, and in the course of her travels falls for a man, and then for a woman, and then for a different man.

Marge Piercy, *Woman on the Edge of Time*. Fawcett Cress, 1976. Sci-fi/fantasy novel about a Latina woman in a New York City mental hospital who time travels to a future utopian society in which bisexuality and homosexuality are completely accepted.

Anne Rice, *The Tale of the Body Thief*. Ballantine Books, 1992. Though I have heard it said that all of Rice's vampire stories contain bisexual content, this is the first of the several that I've read which does so explicitly. Narrator Lestat refers specifically and directly in this book to his sexual desire for men and for women. Another is a 1000+ page book, *The Witching Hour* (Ballantine, 1990) which has at least three human male bisexual characters. In this book, even the title character, who is not human, can be classified as bisexual.

J.F. Rivkin, *Silverglass*. Ace Fantasy, 1986; *Web of Wind*. 1987; *Witch of Rhostshyl*, 1989. Sci-fi/fantasy trilogy about two women, a mercenary and a noblewoman, both of whom happen to be bisexual.

Mary Rosenblum, *Chimera*. Del Ray/Ballantine Books, 1993. It's the future, and for many people life takes place as much in virtual reality as in the flesh world. At least one character in this book, a virtual reality artist, is clearly bisexual, though the "b-word" is not used.

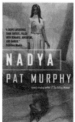

Melissa Scott, *Burning Bright.* Tor/Tom Doherty Associates, 1993. Hi-tech sci-fi based on concept of virtual reality games. One male character and (likely) the female protagonist are bi. *Shadow Man.* Tor/Tom Doherty Associates, 1995. In this future, it has finally been determined that there are five sexes, not two. One colony among all of the planets hasn't accepted this fact, with a resultant culture clash between indigenes and off-worlders. With five sexes, there are nine different sexual orientations, including bi, omni, demi and hemi.

Starhawk, *The Fifth Sacred Thing.* Bantam Books, 1993. Futuristic utopian novel with two competing cultures: one egalitarian in which bisexuality is taken for granted, and the other oppressive and authoritarian.

John Varley, *Steel Beach.* Putnam, 1992. After an invasion of Earth, humans have moved to the moon (and elsewhere). People—who can now live a very long time—are hetero-, homo-, or bisexually oriented, and also can (and sometimes do) change sexes surgically. The main character mostly is heterosexual, attracted to woman when he is a man, and to men when she is a woman. Other characters are differently oriented.

Margaret Weis and Tracy Hickman, *Rose of the Prophet,* Volumes I (1998), II (1998) and III (1999). Bantam Books. In this trilogy 20 Gods, each with different abilities and his or her own followers, rule the world but now they are at war. Mathew, an androgynous man, is in love with the other two central characters, a woman and her husband, though he never has a sexual relationship with either.

Walter Jon Williams, *Aristoi.* Tor Books, 1993. In the far future, all sexual orientations are accepted. Gabriel, the protagonist, the creator and leader of a number of worlds, has a number of concurrent relationships with men (including one whom he impregnates) and women.

Molleen Zanger, *The Year Seven.* Naiad, 1993. Almost all humans have died suddenly, except for a few survivors, almost all female. In one minor thread of the book the protagonist moves into the apartment of a dead woman, finds and reads her journals, and learns that she had self-identified as bisexual. From her journal: "How I long to be one or the other, either. Not straight but not truly gay either, does this make me merely cheerful? Strange that I am not happy about it."

MYSTERY

Antoinette Azolakov, *Skiptrace.* Banned Books, 1998. Butch dyke tries to trace old girlfriend. Lesbian-killer at large. Secondary character (the woman her ex left her for) likes men too, and chooses to marry one because she can't stand the heat of homophobia.

Joseph Hansen, *Backtrack*. Backcountry Publications, 1982. A primarily gay young man trying to find out who murdered his primarily gay father. *Steps Going Down*. Penguin, 1982. There are two bisexual men in this crime book, both utterly unlikeable—but then this book contains unlikeable characters of several sexual orientations.

Ellen Hart, *Stage Fright*. Seal Press, 1992. Jane Lawless, a lesbian restauranteur and part-time sleuth, takes on a theatrical mystery. A minor character, Dorrie, who is on the city council, comes out to her as bisexual (she even uses the word), and says "I hope I have another good relationship in my life, somewhere down the line, but it doesn't make much difference to me whether it's a man or a woman." *The Merchant of Venus*. St. Martin's Minotaur, 2002. The granddaughter of the murdered man (a famous Hollywood producer) self-identifies as bisexual and broadcasts her life on a webcam. There is also talk about the closeted gay and bisexual Hollywood stars of yesteryear. *A Killing Cure*. Seal Press, 1993. Protagonist's lover self-identifies as bisexual. Not a major part of the story, but clear nonetheless.

Dick Kavanagh (pseudonym of Julian Barnes), *Duffy*. Pantheon Books, 1980. *Fiddle City*, *Putting the Boot In*, and *Going to the Dogs* (all Penguin, 1987). Standard English detective fare, except that the protagonist, Duffy, is a bisexual ex-cop.

Carole Spearin McCauley. *Cold Steal*. The Women's Press, 1991. Mystery set in a cancer research lab. The protagonist and her former and current women lovers self-identify as bisexual. Lots of "oh, it's so hard to be bisexual cause no one will understand or like you" angst.

Claire McNab, *Fatal Reunion*. Naiad Press, 1989. Part of the Carol Ashton detective series and falling within the general subject heading of what I refer to as "lesbiana." Police detective Carol Ashton was left three years ago by a woman who was unwilling to leave her husband. Now the husband was dead, and the bisexual (at least in her behavior) ex-lover is accused of murder. Did she do it? *Death Understood*. Naiad, 2000. Lesbian thriller set in Australia. Secondary character, white supremacist Becky Hiddwing "was known to swing both ways. Not that she'd ever admitted to bisexuality, but enough discarded lovers had been indiscreet to ensure public knowledge of her healthy appetites." (p. 53)

Barbara Wilson, *Ambitious Women*. Seal Press, 1982. Three women in Seattle's progressive community are caught up in a Grand Jury investigation into terrorism. One is bisexual and more comfortable with casual relationships than monogamous ones. Another's identity goes from straight to lesbian. *Trouble in Transylvania*. Seal Press, 1993. One of the minor characters of this novel about foreign tourists set in Transylvania is a young Berkeley student who is referred to as bisexual and who self-

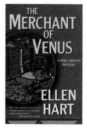

identifies as queer: "I personally identify as queer. It doesn't matter who I sleep with, I'm always queer."

Mary Wings, *She Came By The Book.* Berkeley Prime Crime Book, 1996. Set in San Francisco's gay community, this murder mystery includes a very minor bisexual plot twist. It's interesting nonetheless, if you're interested in a story that's not too far off from real–life community politics.

YOUNG ADULT

Garret Freymann-Weyr, *My Heartbeat.* Houghton Mifflin, 2002. Set in NYC and viewed through the eyes of a 14-year-old girl, two 17-year-old-boys struggle to understand desire, relationships and their potential futures. Their stories are bisexual, their future identities as yet unknown.

Brent Hartinger, *Geography Club.* HarperTempest, 2003. A group of high school students struggle to come out. The protagonist's best friend Min self-identifies as bisexual in delightful portrayal, as she is the most confident, ethical and unconflicted of the group.

M.E. Kerr, *Hello, I Lied.* Harper Collins, 1997. A teenage boy summering in an estate (where his mother is employed as cook for a retired rock star), has a boyfriend back in New York, is dealing with being gay, then falls in love with a French girl who is a guest of the rock star. Oops. Is he really gay? What will his friends think now?

David Levithan, *Boy Meets Boy.* Knopf, 2003. High school in a very progressive suburb of New York City. Protagonist is gay, and his circle includes Kyle, a boy who likes both boys and girls and is gradually coming to terms with his sexuality as well as with his crush on the protagonist.

Alex Sanchez, *Rainbow Boys.* Simon & Schuster, 2001. *Rainbow High.* Simon & Schuster, 2003. The continuing story of three high school seniors exploring issues of identity and coming out. One of the boys explores bisexual identity.

Jacqueline Woodson, *The House You Pass on the Way.* Laurel-Leaf Books, 1997. Staggerlee, a biracial teenager in the U.S. south, finds  herself in love with girls including her cousin Trout, who comes to spend the summer because, it turns out, Trout has her own history with a girl. After returning home, Trout meets a boy she likes and has to tell Stagerlee.

POETRY

Michelle Clinton, *Good Sense & The Faithless*. West End Press, 1994. About life, complexity, racism, being bisexual, politics and more.

M.S. Montgomery, *Telling the Beads*. Chestnut Hills Press, 1994. An explicit and emotionally gripping book of sonnets, a journey across the life of one bisexual man.

SHORT STORIES:

Becky Birtha, "Ice Castle," in *Go the Way Your Blood Beats: An Anthology of Fiction by African-American Writers*. Ed., Shawn Stewart Ruff. Henry Holt & Co., 1996, pp. 93-121.

Samuel Delaney, "Citre et Trans," in *Shade: An Anthology of Fiction by Gay Men of African Descent*, ed. Bruce Morrow and Charles H. Rowell. Avon: 1996, pp. 303-334.

Ursula LeGuin, "A Fisherman of the Inland Sea," in *A Fisherman of the Inland Sea*. Eos, 1995. Introduces the Planet of O, where all marriages consist of four people (2 men, 2 women).

Ruthann Robson, *Eye of a Hurricane*. Firebrand Books, 1989. Some of these short stories have bisexual characters.

Jane Rule, *Inland Passage*. Naiad Press, 1985. "His Nor Hers," "Puzzle," and possibly "Inland Passage" have bisexual characters.

Michelene Wandor, "Some of My Best Friends," in *Passion Fruit*. Ed. Jeanette Winterson. Pandora: 1986. pp. 143-156. In the UK in the mid-1980s, a lesbian and a gay man have a relationship, much to the dismay of their activist community.

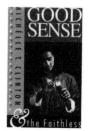

Nonfiction Books on Bisexuality

Ronald C. Fox

The following books are recommended non-fiction readings that focus on all aspects of bisexuality and that take an affirmative approach to bisexuality and bisexual issues. This list is by no means exhaustive. An extended and updated version including books, book chapters and journal articles can be found on the author's website by following a link from the Bisexual Resource Center's website: http://www.biresource.org.

Aggleton, P. (Ed.). (1996). *Bisexualities & AIDS: International perspectives.* London: Taylor & Francis. Collection of essays and reviews of the research literature on bisexual behavior among men in a number of modern cultures, including Australia, Brazil, Canada, China, Costa Rica, the Dominican Republic, France, India, Mexico, Papua New Guinea, Peru, the Philippines and the UK

Alexander, J., & Yescavage, K. (Eds.). (2004). *Bisexuality and transgenderism: InterSEXions of the others.* New York: Harrington Park Press. A ground-breaking collection of essays examining the inter-connectedness of bisexual and transgender issues. Also published as a special issue of the *Journal of Bisexuality* (Vol. 3, Issue 3/4).

Anderlini-D'Onofrio, S. (Ed.). (2003). *Women and bisexuality: A global perspective.* New York: Harrington Park Press. A collection of essays on bisexual women from an international perspective. Also published as a special issue of the *Journal of Bisexuality* (Vol. 3, Issue 1).

Anderlini-D'Onofrio, S. (Ed.). (2005). *Plural loves: Designs for bi and poly living.* New York: Harrington Park Press. A diverse collection of essays on bi and poly relationships. Also published as a special issue of the *Journal of Bisexuality* (Vol. 4, Issue 3/4).

Angelides, S. (2001). *A history of bisexuality.* Chicago University of Chicago Press. A critical review of how bisexuality has been understood in biology, genetics, psychoanalytic thinking and queer theory in relationship to heterosexuality and homosexuality.

Atkins, D. (Ed.). (2002). *Bisexual women in the twenty-first century.* New York: Harrington Park Press. A collection of essays and research on bisexual women, identity, sexuality, relationships and politics. Also published as a special issue of the *Journal of Bisexuality* (Vol. 2, Issue 2/3).

Beemyn, B., & Steinman, E. (Eds.). (2000). *Bisexuality in the lives of men: Facts and fictions.* New York: Harrington Park Press. A collection of essays and research on bisexual men and identity, community, HIV, biphobia and marriage. Also published as a special issue of the *Journal of Bisexuality* (Vol. 1, Issue 2/3).

Beemyn, B., & Steinman, E. (Eds.). (2002). *Bisexual men in culture and society.* New York: Harrington Park Press. A collection of post-modern essays on bisexual men and masculinity in the context of literature and the media. Also published as a special issue of the *Journal of Bisexuality* (Vol. 2, Issue 1).

Bi Academic Intervention (P. Davidson, J. Eadie, C. Hemmings, A. Kaloski, & M. Storr) (Eds.). (1997). *The bisexual imaginary: Representation, identity, and desire.* London: Cassell. Collection of essays on bisexuality in history, literature, film and cultural studies.

Bisexual Anthology Collective (L. Acharya, N. Chater, D. Falconer, S. Lewis, L. McLannan, & S. Nosov) (Eds.). (1995). *Plural desires: Writing bisexual women's realities.* Toronto: Sister Vision Press. An anthology of writings by a diverse group of women from Canada and the USA.

Bode, J. (1976). *View from another closet: Exploring bisexuality in women.* New York: Hawthorne. One of the first books on bisexuality, based on the author's interviews with bisexual women.

Bryant, W. (1997). *Bisexual characters in film: From Anaïs to Zee.* New York: Harrington Park Press. Descriptive compilation of films with bisexual characters.

Cantarella, E. (1992). *Bisexuality in the ancient world.* New Haven, CT: Yale University Press. Translated from the Italian. A scholarly examination of bisexuality in ancient classical Greece and Rome.

Deschamps, C. (2002). *Le miroir bisexuel: Une socio-anthropologie de l'invisible.* [The bisexual mirror: A social anthropology of the invisible]. Paris: Balland. An in-depth look at bisexuality in France today, based on the author's study of a Parisian support group for bisexual women and bisexual men.

Feldhorst, A. (1996). (Ed.). *Bisexualitäten.* [Bisexualities]. Berlin: Deutsche AIDS-Hilfe. Collection of essays on bisexual identity, relationships and communities in Germany.

Firestein, B. A. (Ed.). (1996). *Bisexuality: The psychology and politics of an invisible minority.* Thousand Oaks, CA: Sage. A collection of essays that provides the most comprehensive overview and review of bisexuality and psychology to date, with chapters by Ron Fox, Loraine Hutchins, Carol Queen, Maggie Rubenstein, Paula Rust, Robyn Ochs and others.

Fox, R. (Ed.). (2004). *Current research on bisexuality.* New York: Harrington Park Press. A collection of research and reviews of the bisexuality literature, with articles on bisexual identity, bisexuality and relationships, bisexuality and ethnicity, and attitudes toward bisexual people, as well as an extended reading list by the editor on bisexuality in the social sciences. Also published as a special issue of the *Journal of Bisexuality* (Vol. 4, Issue 1/2).

Fraser, M. (1999). *Identity without selfhood: Simone de Beauvoir and bisexuality.* New York: Cambridge University Press. The author examines how feminism, queer theory, and post-modern analysis have viewed Simone de Beauvoir and how the emphasis on deconstruction of Western approaches to sexuality present obstacles to acknowledging and validating bisexuality as a sexual orientation and identity.

Garber, M. (1995). *Vice versa: Bisexuality & the eroticism of everyday life.* New York: Simon & Schuster. If you are interested in an in-depth look at bisexuality in literature, popular culture or psychoanalysis, this book is for you.

Geissler, S.-A. (1993). *Doppelte Lust: Bisexualität heute—Erfahrungen und Bekenntnisse.* [Dual desire—Bisexuality today: Experiences and confessions]. Munich: Wilhelm Heyne. An exploration of bisexuality in Germany, based on author's interviews with bisexual women and bisexual men.

Geller, T. (Ed.). (1990). *Bisexuality: A reader & sourcebook.* Ojai, CA: Times Change Press. Collection of interviews & articles.

George, S. (1993). *Women & bisexuality.* London: Scarlet Press. An examination of bisexual identity and relationships, based on the author's survey study of 150 self-identified bisexual women in the United Kingdom.

Gooß, U. (1995). *Sexualwissenschaftliche Konzepte der Bisexualität von Männern* [The concept of bisexuality in scientific discourse about human sexuality]. Stuttgart: Ferdinand Enke. Scholarly examination by a German psychiatrist of the origins and development of the concept of bisexuality in the fields of psychology and sexology, including an overview of current theory and research.

Haeberle, E. J., & Gindorf, R. (Eds.). (1994). *Bisexualitäten: Ideologie und Praxis des Sexualkontes mit beiden Geschlectern.* [Bisexualities: Theory and practice of sexual relations with both sexes]. Stuttgart: Gustav Fischer Verlag. Also published in 1998 in English as: *Bisexualities: The ideology and practice of sexual contact with both men and women.* New York: Continuum. Collection of essays by participants in the 1990 International Berlin Conference for Sexology. Most chapters reflect the beginnings of the shift in scholarly thinking about bisexuality that has come about as a result of subsequent and more current research on bisexuality and bisexual identity.

Hall, D. E., & Pramaggiore, M. (Eds.). (1996). *RePresenting bisexualities: Subjects & cultures of fluid desire.* New York: NYU Press. Collection of essays on bisexuality in queer theory, literature, film, and cultural studies.

Hansson, H. (Ed.). (1990). *Bisexuele levens in Nederland.* [Bisexual lives in the Netherlands]. Amsterdam: Orlando. Portrait of bisexual identity and relationships, based on the author's interviews with bisexual women and men.

Hemmings, C. (2002). *Bisexual spaces: A geography of sexuality and gender.* New York: Routledge. The author of several articles and book chapters on bisexuality and queer theory applies a postmodern perspective to sexuality, gender, and bisexual identity by examining the geography and culture of Northampton, Massachusetts and San Francisco, California.

Honnens, B. (1996). *Wenn die andere ein Mann ist: Frauen als Partnerinnen bisexueller Männer.* [When the other person is a man: Women partners of bisexual men]. Frankfurt: Campus. Explores the experiences of women in marriages with bisexual men in Germany, based on the author's interviews.

Hüsers, F. & König, A. (1995). *Bisexualität.* [Bisexuality]. Stuttgart: Georg Thieme. A sociologist and a psychiatrist provide a comprehensive and affirmative picture of and guide to bisexuality in Germany.

Hutchins, L., & Ka'ahumanu, L. (Eds.). (1991). *Bi any other name: Bisexual people speak out.* Boston: Alyson. Diverse collection of 75 essays and autobiographical narratives by bi-identified people from the United States.

Klein, F. (1993). *The bisexual option (2nd ed.).* New York: Harrington Park Press. Second edition of the one of the first affirmative books on bisexuality, originally published in 1978 (Charlotte Wolff's 1979 book, listed below, is the other). The author is also the creator of the well-known Klein Sexual Orientation Grid (KSOG), a multi-dimensional approach to sexual orientation & sexual identity.

Klein, F., & Schwartz, T. (2001). *Bisexual and gay husbands, their stories, their words.* New York: Harrington Park Press. A collection of personal accounts, based on contributions to an online discussion group for gay and bisexual married men.

Klein, F., & Wolf, T. J. (Eds.). (1985). *Two lives to lead: Bisexuality in men and women.* New York: Harrington Park Press. The first published scholarly collection of reports on 1980s research on bisexuality. Originally a special issue of the prestigious *Journal of Homosexuality* (1985, Vol. 11, Issue 1/2).

Kohn, B., & Matusow, A. (1980). *Barry & Alice: Portrait of a bisexual marriage.* Englewood Cliffs, NJ: Prentice-Hall. An autobiographical account of the authors' marriage and the impact of coming to terms with their bisexuality on their relationship.

Kolodny, D. R. (Ed.). (2000). *Blessed bi spirit: Bisexual people of faith.* New York: Continuum. A wide-ranging anthology, with contributions by 31 bisexual people of faith speaking in a most affirmative way about the intersection of spirituality and sexuality in their lives.

Kuppens, A. (1995). *Biseksuele identiteiten: Tussen verlangen en praktijk.* [Bisexual identities: Between desire and behavior]. Nijmegen, Netherlands: Wetenschapswinkel. Theoretical overview and discussion of bisexual identities, based on interviews with bisexual women and bisexual men.

Mendès-Leité, R., Deschamps, C., & Proth, B.-M. (1996). *Bisexualité: Le dernièr tabou.* [Bisexuality: The last taboo]. Paris: Calmann Levy. Portrait of bisexual identity and behavior among bisexual men in France, based on the authors' interviews.

Off Pink Collective. (1988). *Bisexual lives.* London: Off Pink Publishing. Collection of personal narratives by bisexual women and bisexual men in the UK.

Orndorff, K. (Ed.). (1999). *Bi lives: Bisexual women tell their stories.* Tucson, AZ: See Sharp Press. A collection of very thoughtful interviews with a diverse group of 18 women, with a focus on how they became aware of and came to terms with their bisexuality.

Rose, S., Stevens, C., & The Off-Pink Collective (Eds.) (1996). *Bisexual horizons: Politics, histories, lives.* London: Lawrence & Wishart. Diverse collection of 54 essays and autobiographical narratives by bi-identified people, mostly from the UK.

Rust, P. C. (1995). *Bisexuality and the challenge to lesbian politics: Sex, loyalty & evolution*. New York: NYU Press. The author traces the origins of the controversy about bisexuality among lesbians to the 1970s lesbian feminist debates, out of which, she argues, developed an environment in which bisexuality inevitably became a challenge to lesbian politics. She also discusses likely directions for the sexual politics of the future.

Rust, P. C. R. (Ed.). (2000). *Bisexuality in the United States: A Social science reader*. New York: Columbia University Press. Comprehensive collection of classic journal articles and book chapters on bisexuality, including many whose original references are included in this list, as well as in-depth reviews of the literature by the editor preceding each of the books sections.

Storr, M. (Ed.). (1999). *Bisexuality: A critical reader*. London: Routledge. Psychological, sociological, activist, and post-modern/cultural criticism perspectives are all included in this edited volume of previously published articles, book chapters and book excerpts. Features material by Freud, Ellis, and Kinsey, as well as bi authors Fritz Klein, Amanda Udis-Kessler, Sue George, Jo Eadie, Amber Ault, Clare Hemmings and Ann Kaloski.

Tielman, R. A. P., Carballo, M., & Hendriks, A. C. (Eds.). (1991). *Bisexuality & HIV/AIDS: A global perspective*. Buffalo, NY: Prometheus. Collection of essays and reviews of research on bisexual identity and behavior among men in a number of modern cultures, including Australia, India, Indonesia, Latin America, Mexico, the Netherlands, New Zealand, Sub-Saharan Africa, Thailand, the UK and the USA.

Tucker, N., Highleyman, L., & Kaplan, R. (Eds.). (1995). *Bisexual politics: Theories, queeries, & visions*. New York: Harrington Park Press. Diverse collection of essays exploring the history, philosophies, visioning, and strategies of bisexual politics in the USA.

van Kerkhof, M. P. N. (1997). *Beter Biseks: Mythen over biseksualiteit ontrafeld.* [Better bisexuality: Myths about bisexuality revealed]. Amsterdam: Schorer Boeken. Examination of bisexual identity and relationships, based on interviews with bisexual women and bisexual men.

Weatherburn, P., Reid, D. S., Beardsell, S., Davies, P. M., Stephens, M., Broderick, P., Keogh, P., & Hickson, F. (1996). *Behaviourally bisexual men in the UK: Identifying needs for HIV prevention*. London: Sigma Research. Results of a government–sponsored survey study of sexual behavior and HIV/AIDS awareness.

Weinberg, M. S., Williams, T. J., & Pryor, D. W. (1994). *Dual attraction: Understanding bisexuality*. New York: Oxford University Press. Results of the authors' interview and survey research on bisexual identity and relationships in 1980s San Francisco. Includes personal narratives, the authors' views on how bisexual identity develops, comparison of bisexual, heterosexual and lesbian/gay patterns of sexual attractions and relationships, and a portrait of the impact of HIV/AIDS on the lives of individuals from their original interviews.

Weise, E. R. (Ed.). (1992). *Closer to home: Bisexuality & feminism*. Seattle: Seal Press. Collection of 23 essays by bisexual feminist women on bisexuality, feminism and their intersection.

Williams, M. J. K. (1999). *Sexual pathways: Adapting to dual attraction*. Westport, CT: Praeger. A study of bisexual identity and relationships, based on the author's interviews with 30 American bisexual women and men.

Wolff, C. (1979). *Bisexuality: A study*. London: Quarter Books. One of the first books on bisexuality written from an affirmative perspective (Fritz Klein's *Bisexual Option*, listed above, is the other), based on the author's survey research on bisexual women and men in the U.K.

In addition, the *Journal of Bisexuality*, published by Harrington Park Press, is an invaluable resource of articles on bisexuality and related topics.

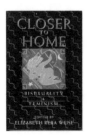

Organizations and Online Resources

Following is a listing of resources that is by no means intended to be comprehensive. Rather, the listings below are intended to be portals. Websites often link to other groups and resources, which link to other groups and resources.

INTERNATIONAL
International Gay & Lesbian Association. http://ilga.org/. Rue Marché-au-Charbon, 81, B 1000, Brussels, Belgium. Tel: +32-2-5022471; Email: ilga@ilga.org

International Gay & Lesbian Human Rights Commission. http://www.iglhrc.org/. 350 Fifth Av., 34th Floor New York, NY 10118 USA. Ph: 212-216-1814, Email: iglhrc@iglhrc.org

Human Rights Watch Lesbian & Gay Program. http://hrw.org/doc/?t=lgbt

Amnesty International Out Front. http://www.amnestyusa.org/outfront

REGIONAL
AFRICA
Behind the Mask. http://www.mask.org.za/. *A pan-African website for LGBT affairs.*

ASIA
Asian Pacific Rainbow Email List. *ap-rainbow@yahoogroups.com*

EUROPE
Euro-Bi Mailing List. http://bi.org/euro-bi/

Euro-BiNet. http://groups.yahoo.com/group/EURO-BINET/. *European Bisexual Network.*

BY COUNTRY
ARGENTINA
Links to various organizations. http://www.cha.org.ar/html/links/

AUSTRALIA
Australian Bisexual Network. http://members.optusnet.com.au/~ausbinet/

Bi Pride Australia. http://www.bi.org.au/bpa/

BARBADOS
Barbados Gays & Lesbians Against Discrimination. http://bglad2000.tripod.com/.

BELARUS
Gay Belarus. http://belgays.gay.ru